LLOYD D. NEWELL

HE SHALL *Fulfill* ALL OF HIS *Promises*

HOPE AND ENCOURAGEMENT FOR EVERY DAY OF THE YEAR

DESERET
BOOK

SALT LAKE CITY, UTAH

To my ancestors, who kept their promises

Library of Congress Cataloging-in-Publication Data
Newell, Lloyd D.
  He shall fulfill all of his promises : hope and encouragement for every day of the year / Lloyd D. Newell.
    p. cm.
  Includes bibliographical references.
  Summary: 365 quotations from general authorities and general officers of The Church of Jesus Christ of Latter-day Saints and the Bible, the Book of Mormon, the Doctrine and Covenants, and the Pearl of Great Price accompanied by insights and commentary.
  ISBN 978-1-60641-837-6 (hardbound : alk. paper)
  1. Devotional calendars—The Church of Jesus Christ of Latter-day Saints. 2. Quotations, American. 3. Bible—Quotations. 4. Book of Mormon—Quotations. 5. Doctrine and Covenants—Quotations. 6. Pearl of Great Price—Quotations. I. Title.
  BV4811.N495 2010
  242′.2—dc22   2010019446

Printed in the United States of America
Publishers Printing, Salt Lake City, UT

10 9 8 7 6 5 4 3 2 1

PREFACE

After the idea first came to write a daily devotional book on the Lord's promises to his children, I grew a little concerned about finding 365 promises. I was wrong. I soon found that this could easily be the first of many volumes on the Lord's promises. Almost every verse of scripture, almost every pronouncement given by prophets ancient and modern, contained a promise, either explicit or implicit. Perhaps the most fundamental promise, repeated countless times through all generations, is this: follow the Lord and keep his commandments, and you will be blessed. From this promise springs all the covenants and assurances of the Lord. The words of the Lord and his authorized servants—modern apostles, prophets, and other leaders—all testify that the promises of the Lord are great and that all his words shall be fulfilled (see 2 Nephi 10:21; Alma 37:17; Mormon 8:22).

I express thanks once again to the exceptional

people of Deseret Book Company: Jana Erickson for her steadfast support and encouragement; Suzanne Brady, Janna DeVore, and Derk Koldewyn for their editorial skills; Rachael Ward for her typesetting; and Heather Ward for her design work. Also, thanks to my able research assistant, Kendel Christensen. As always, I'm particularly grateful for my wife and four wonderful children who have cheered me on and been patient along the way. Most especially, I express abiding praise and thanks to God and his beloved Son, Jesus Christ, for the blessings of life and family, the inexhaustible gospel and infinite atonement, and his abundant and never-ending promises.

January

That which is of God is light; and he that receiveth light, and continueth in God, receiveth more light; and that light groweth brighter and brighter until the perfect day.

Doctrine & Covenants 50:24

Be of good cheer.
The future is as bright as your faith.

THOMAS S. MONSON
ENSIGN, MAY 2009, 92

New beginnings are invigorating. Just as a fresh blanket of snow changes the landscape into unmarked territory, calling out to little explorers with their sleds and snow boots, blank pages of a new calendar bring a sense of opportunity, possibility, and resolution. Whether beginning a new day or even a new year, something about starting over generates energy and commitment. We try a little harder, reach a little farther, and somehow do a little more. What may have seemed out of reach days before suddenly enters the realm of possibility. As we look back, we gain wisdom and understanding; and as we look forward, we garner the enthusiasm necessary for lasting faith and hope throughout the year. This year, strive to be of good cheer, remember those times that your testimony burned as fire and seek to stoke that flame in the days ahead.

*Every accountable child of God needs to set goals, short-
and long-range goals. A man who is pressing forward to
accomplish worthy goals can soon put despondency under his
feet, and once a goal is accomplished, others can be set up.*

EZRA TAFT BENSON
ENSIGN, NOVEMBER 1974, 67

President Ezra Taft Benson said: "Each week when we partake of the sacrament we commit ourselves to the goals of taking upon ourselves the name of Christ, of always remembering him and keeping his commandments. Of Jesus' preparation for his mission, the scripture states that he 'increased in wisdom and stature, and in favour with God and man' (Luke 2:52). This encompasses four main areas for goals: spiritual, mental, physical, and social. 'Therefore, what manner of men ought ye to be?' asked the Master, and he answered, 'Verily I say unto you, even as I am' (3 Nephi 27:27). Now there is a lifetime goal—to walk in his steps, to perfect ourselves in every virtue as he has done, to seek his face, and to work to make our calling and election sure" (*Ensign,* Nov. 1974, 67). Now is the time to seriously ponder what we most want in life, to look forward to the future, to set goals, and press forward to accomplish them.

*Keep your eyes on your dreams, however distant and far
away. Live to see the miracles of repentance and forgiveness,
of trust and divine love that will transform your life. . . .
That is a New Year's resolution I ask you to keep.*

JEFFREY R. HOLLAND
ENSIGN, JANUARY 2010, 27

Elder Jeffrey R. Holland exhorted us to do more than just forgive: "[D]o that which is sometimes harder than to forgive: forget. And when it comes to mind again, forget it again. You can remember just enough to avoid repeating the mistake, but then put the rest of it all on the dung heap Paul spoke of to the Philippians [Philippians 3:7–14]. Dismiss the destructive, and keep dismissing it until the beauty of the Atonement of Christ has revealed to you your bright future and the bright future of your family, your friends, and your neighbors. God doesn't care nearly as much about where you have been as He does about where you are and, with His help, where you are willing to go. . . . This is an important matter to consider at the start of a new year—and every day ought to be the start of a new year and a new life" (*Ensign*, Jan. 2010, 27).

Cling to the Church and live its principles and I . . .
promise you that your lives will be happy, that your
accomplishments will be significant, and that you will
have reason to get on your knees and thank the Lord.

GORDON B. HINCKLEY
CHURCH NEWS, 3 AUGUST 1996, 2

We are a blessed people. The Lord has given each of us so very much—our lives and unnumbered blessings, our wondrous world and the very air we breathe. He wants for us His life, His joy and happiness, His unending peace. He has given us a church wherein we can serve and associate with others on the pathway of discipleship. He has given us the principles of salvation and the necessary gospel ordinances for us to become worthy to inherit eternal life. What He asks of us is clear: be humble, be obedient, be faithful, be grateful. The Lord, who is perfectly loving and benevolent, is also demanding and non-indulgent. He understands perfectly what we must do to develop a heart like His. If we hold fast to the iron rod, adhere to the gospel, and strive with all our hearts to live its principles, we will "receive [our] reward, even peace in this world, and eternal life in the world to come" (D&C 59:23).

*If you understand the great plan of happiness
and follow it, what goes on in the world
will not determine your happiness.*

BOYD K. PACKER
ENSIGN, MAY 1994, 21

The great plan of salvation gives us a steady and re-liable foundation upon which to build our faith and testimony. In a world of uncertainty and fear, the Father's plan of happiness for His beloved children answers vital questions of why we are here, where we came from, and where we are going. With this awareness we have reasons to follow the Savior and keep the commandments, reasons to shun immoral-ity and become people of character, reasons to move forward with faith and keep trying, reasons to form a family and bring children into the world. Without this understanding, we are more likely to wander in confusion and insecurity, to question the purposes of mortality and remain agnostic as to our future pos-sibilities. We must tune out the clarion call of the world and keep our eyes and hearts riveted on the glorious gospel plan.

We don't have to be fast; we simply have to be
steady and move in the right direction, . . . one step
after another. . . . The only thing you need to worry
about is striving to be the best you can be.

JOSEPH B. WIRTHLIN
ENSIGN, NOVEMBER 2001, 26

We will never make a journey of a thousand miles by fretting about how long it will take or how hard it will be," said Elder Joseph B. Wirthlin. "We make the journey by taking each day step by step and then repeating it again and again until we reach our destination. The same principle applies to how you and I can climb to higher spirituality. . . . Our Heavenly Father loves each one of us and understands that this process of climbing higher takes preparation, time, and commitment. He understands that we will make mistakes at times, that we will stumble, that we will become discouraged and perhaps even wish to give up and say to ourselves it is not worth the struggle. We know it is worth the effort, for the prize, which is eternal life, is 'the greatest of all the gifts of God' [D&C 14:7]" (*Ensign,* Nov. 2001, 25–26).

JANUARY 7

The restored gospel of our Lord and Savior
Jesus Christ has the power to fill any emptiness,
heal any wound, and bridge any vale of sorrow.
It is the way of hope, faith, and trust in the Lord.

DIETER F. UCHTDORF
ENSIGN, MAY 2009, 78

As true believers, we center our attention and focus on the life and teachings of the Savior. "The gospel of Jesus Christ is taught in its fulness in The Church of Jesus Christ of Latter-day Saints," said President Dieter F. Uchtdorf. "This Church is led by a living prophet, authorized by the Lord Jesus Christ to provide direction and guidance to help us face the challenges of our day, as serious as they may be. I bear my solemn witness that Jesus the Christ lives. He is the Savior and Redeemer of the world. He is the promised Messiah. He lived a perfect life and atoned for our sins. He will ever be at our side. He will fight our battles. He is our hope; He is our salvation; He is the way" (*Ensign,* May 2009, 78). Our testimony and energy are devoted to emulating the life of the Master, knowing that in Him is life and salvation, strength and solace, direction and guidance.

*Have you wandered from the path of joy and now find
yourself where you do not want to be, with feelings
you do not want to have? . . . I invite you with all
the love of my heart to repent and come back.*

RICHARD G. SCOTT
ENSIGN, NOVEMBER 2000, 27

Over many years, Elder Richard G. Scott has
taught of a dear and precious friend that can lead us
to true peace and joy: "There is an essential aspect of
the plan of happiness of our Father in Heaven that is
often ignored even though it invariably yields peace
and joy. The Savior gave His life that it might be used
to bless every child of Father in Heaven. This subject is widely misunderstood and often feared. Some
feel that it is to be employed only by those in serious transgression, while the Lord intended that it be
consistently used by every one of His children. He
has repeatedly commanded His prophets and leaders
to proclaim it and to speak of little else [D&C 6:9].
I refer to the blessing of true, sincere, continuing repentance, the path to peace and joy. It is a conduit to
the reforming power of the Lord and, when understood and used, a dear and precious friend" (*Ensign*,
Nov. 2000, 25).

If our lives are centered in Christ, nothing can go permanently wrong. . . . if our lives are not centered on the Savior and his teachings, no other success can ever be permanently right.

HOWARD W. HUNTER
TEACHINGS OF HOWARD W. HUNTER, 1997, 40

We believe in Jesus Christ, our Rock and sure foundation, the Light and Life of the world; we are members of His restored latter-day church—the Church of Jesus Christ; we trust in His promise of salvation for those who obey Him and become His true disciples; we center our faith and hope in Him— the Savior of all mankind. With Jesus we can do all things (Philippians 4:13), and because of Him we can withstand the adversary's winds and storms and find peace and everlasting consolation (Helaman 5:12). We reiterate in proclamation and fervent belief the words of Nephi, "And we talk of Christ, we rejoice in Christ, we preach of Christ, we prophesy of Christ, and we write according to our prophecies, that our children may know to what source they may look for a remission of their sins" (2 Nephi 25:26). In all ways and all times, we firmly fix our eyes and hearts on Jesus Christ, the Redeemer of the world.

I, the Lord, am bound when ye do what I say;
but when ye do not what I say, ye have no promise.

DOCTRINE & COVENANTS 82:10

We know enough of the nature of God to know that He is perfect in His love, goodness, and compassion. He is our Father, our Father in Heaven. We, His children, can trust in His divine nature and eternal promises. As Paul wrote anciently, "In hope of eternal life, which God, that cannot lie, promised before the world began" (Titus 1:2). And in our dispensation, the Lord revealed to the Prophet Joseph, "I, the Lord, promise the faithful and cannot lie" (D&C 62:6). In these latter days, the Lord revealed that "when we obtain any blessing from God, it is by obedience to that law upon which it is predicated" (D&C 130:21). The Lord makes generous promises, and He certifies that He will not vary from these promises. What a blessing it is to know that we worship a loving Father, a perfect being, who makes promises to His children that are true and trustworthy.

*And after ye have obtained a hope in Christ
ye shall obtain riches, if ye seek them; and ye will seek
them for the intent to do good—to clothe the naked,
and to feed the hungry, and to liberate the captive,
and administer relief to the sick and the afflicted.*

JACOB 2:19

After the death of Nephi, Jacob spoke to the people of Nephi according to the responsibility which he was under "to God, to magnify [his] office with soberness" (Jacob 2:2). Modern inspired leaders likewise speak to us. Speaking of Jacob 2:18–19, President Henry B. Eyring said, "My experience has been that the promise in Jacob is true. When I have sought the kingdom first, I have been directed to seek other things later. And whatever intensity and singleness of heart I brought to my service to God has been extended into whatever else I have been led to seek. Seek seems to be the key word. That is a far cry from 'put in your time.' If you invest your time with faith and great energy, the promise by the Lord in Jacob is sure. The fact that God promises our motives will be changed and shaped to better ends as a reward should also direct the way you invest your time" ("Child of Promise," 127).

*As we draw closer to Him, we learn to love Him and
our Eternal Father, and we find ourselves showing
our love for them by keeping their commandments—
which helps us to become more like them.*

M. RUSSELL BALLARD
OUR SEARCH FOR HAPPINESS, 15

The faith and courage found in sincere obedience opens windows of heavenly inspiration and peace. The knowledge that we are moral agents striving to freely obey allows us to feel more powerfully the Spirit of the Lord and develop more fully the attributes of godliness. Humble obedience produces more love for God and for the Savior, which in turn generates a greater desire to keep their commandments and become more like them. This potent cycle produces within us a quiet but powerful explosion of faith and humility and love and light. As the Lord revealed, "That which is of God is light; and he that receiveth light, and continueth in God, receiveth more light; and that light groweth brighter and brighter until the perfect day" (D&C 50:24).

Then spake Jesus again unto them, saying, I am the light of the world: he that followeth me shall not walk in darkness, but shall have the light of life.

JOHN 8:12

Our sun is suspended in space, at the center of the solar system, approximately 93 million miles from Earth. Yet energy from the sun supports almost all life on our planet via photosynthesis and drives its climate and weather. In essence, the sun lights and warms our life. Our planet could not exist without the sun; yet many of us think little about it. So it is with the light of the gospel, and the Light of the World. Without the Son of God we are left with no hope, no redemption, no resurrection. We need the sun; and we especially need the Son. As Alma told his son Shiblon, "There is no other way or means whereby man can be saved, only in and through Christ. Behold, he is the life and the light of the world. Behold, he is the word of truth and righteousness" (Alma 38:9). Let us walk in the warm light of the Lord.

*Each one of us has been given the power to change
his or her life. As part of the Lord's great plan of
happiness, we have individual agency to make decisions.
We can decide to do better and to be better.*

JAMES E. FAUST
ENSIGN, NOVEMBER 2007, 122

God has provided a way out of "the gall of bitterness and bonds of iniquity" (Mosiah 27:29). If we humbly turn our hearts to the Lord and believe on His name, we can change and be made new creatures (Mosiah 27:25–26). Christ, who works from the inside out, will give us the power to change our habits and our lives, the power to resist bad thoughts and feelings, the power to be more kind and less selfish. We can be taken from "the darkest abyss" to "behold the marvelous light of God" (Mosiah 27:29). President James E. Faust said, "Each new day that dawns can be a new day for us to begin to change. We can change our environment. We can change our lives by substituting new habits for old. We can mold our character and future by purer thoughts and nobler actions" (*Ensign,* Nov. 2007, 124). Each day is a fresh start, a new beginning to make the decision to do and to be better.

Moment by moment, breath by breath, our lives are granted to us and are renewed. So it is with spiritual light. It must be renewed in us on a regular basis. We must generate it day by day, thought by thought, and with daily righteous action.

ROBERT D. HALES
ENSIGN, MAY 2002, 71

As a boy, Elder Robert D. Hales connected a small generator to his bicycle tire to produce a beam of light so he could see his way home at night: "But I had to pedal to make it work! I learned quickly that if I stopped pedaling my bicycle, the light would go out. I also learned that when I was 'anxiously engaged' [D&C 58:27] in pedaling, the light would become brighter and the darkness in front of me would be dispelled. The generation of spiritual light comes from daily spiritual pedaling. It comes from praying, studying the scriptures, fasting, and serving. . . . Sometimes people ask, . . . 'Why do I have to live the Word of Wisdom, pay tithing? Why can't I have one foot in Babylon?' May I tell you why? Because spiritual pedaling takes both feet! Unless you are fully engaged in living the gospel . . . you cannot generate enough spiritual light to push back the darkness" (*Ensign,* May 2002, 71).

What has our Savior done for us? He has given
us His Atonement, His gospel, and His Church,
a sacred combination that gives us the assurance of
immortality and the opportunity for eternal life.

DALLIN H. OAKS
ENSIGN, MAY 2002, 35

In the Church we have what we call our "triple combination," which consists of three of our standard works. But there is also a transcendent combination, a sacred combination, which is testified to in each of the standard works: the Atonement of Jesus Christ, the gospel of Jesus Christ, and the restored Church of Jesus Christ. The Savior has given us this sacred combination which gives us the promise of immortality and the potential for eternal life. Without this sacred combination we are left without hope of resurrection and redemption, left without eternal principles and saving truth, left without a road map and formal structure to guide and assist us along life's challenging pathway. Jesus Christ has given us everything we need for peace and happiness here and eternal life hereafter: His perfect life, law, and love.

We will prove them herewith, to see if they will do all things whatsoever the Lord their God shall command them; And they who keep their first estate shall be added upon; . . . and they who keep their second estate shall have glory added upon their heads for ever and ever.

ABRAHAM 3:25–26

All of us here on earth kept our first estate and therefore were born into mortality. We keep our second estate as we are obedient during mortal life. Elder Richard G. Scott said that the purpose for being on earth "is to prove yourself obedient to the commandments of the Lord and thereby grow in understanding, capacity, and every worthy trait. It is to receive every required ordinance and to make and keep every needed covenant. It is to form and nourish a family. This experience includes having periods of trial and happiness, with the objective of returning triumphantly, having met well the challenges and opportunities of mortal life to receive the glorious blessings promised for such obedience. So that the period of mortal testing and growth would yield its greatest benefit, you were taught and prepared for the circumstances you would personally encounter in mortality" (*Ensign,* Nov. 2005, 78).

*Implant in the hearts of your youth principles that will . . .
make them honorable, highminded, intelligent, virtuous, modest,
pure men and women, full of integrity and truth . . . that they
with you may have an inheritance in the kingdom of God.*

JOHN TAYLOR
JOHN TAYLOR, 63

No greater task or blessed opportunity exists than to parent children in the paths of righteousness. No other mission or prospect is so fraught with the potential for joy and celebration, pitfalls and perils. Parents have a sacred duty to "teach their children to . . . walk uprightly before the Lord" (D&C 68:28), and then those children teach their children—and the parenting chain continues. John Taylor said, "we ought to teach our children meekness and humility, integrity, virtue and the fear of God, that they may teach those principles to their children" (*John Taylor*, 63). If we strive to rear them in love and righteousness, setting an example of authentic gospel living, we will be blessed. Of course, there are no parenting guarantees—good parents have children who struggle, and bad parents have children who are faithful, but we can trust the Lord's promise that He will bless and magnify our sincere efforts.

Once you have felt your Savior's love for you, even the smallest part, you will feel secure, and a love for Him and for your Heavenly Father will grow within you. In your heart you will want to do what these holy beings ask of you.

D. TODD CHRISTOFFERSON
ENSIGN, MAY 2004, 12

To feel the Savior's love and to develop humility we must pray to be filled with the love of Christ. This love is given to those who are true followers of Jesus Christ, who ask for it with all the energy of their heart (Moroni 7:47–48). This love is the fruit of the tree of life (I Nephi 11:21–23), and tasting it is an essential part of conversion. Feeling the Savior's love changes our attitudes and actions—it initiates in us a mighty change of heart: we want to be more obedient, more humble and teachable, more loving and forgiving and patient with others and with ourselves, more desirous to serve and build the kingdom of God.

*It is imperative that we recognize that whatever
has happened to us has happened to others.
They have coped and so must we. We are not
alone. Heavenly Father's help is near.*

THOMAS S. MONSON
ENSIGN, NOVEMBER 1992, 69

We're all in this life together. We have our share—
sometimes it seems like an unfair share—of trials,
disappointments, pain, and heartache large and small.
But God will not leave us comfortless or alone (John
14:18); He has not left us without promised blessings and heavenly sustenance. We can communicate
with our Father in Heaven through the passport to
peace and consolation: prayer. President Thomas S.
Monson said, "To any who from anguish of heart and
sadness of soul have silently asked, 'Heavenly Father,
are you really there? . . . Do you hear and answer every . . . prayer?' (*Children's Songbook*, no. 12), I bear to
you my witness that He is there. He does hear and
answer every prayer. His Son, the Christ, burst the
bands of our earthly prisons. Heaven's blessings await
you" (*Ensign*, Nov. 1992, 70).

The devil has no power over us only as we permit him;
the moment we revolt at anything which comes
from God, the devil takes power. . . . The devil could
not compel mankind to do evil; all was voluntary.

JOSEPH SMITH
JOSEPH SMITH, 214

Heavenly Father will not compel us to be righteous; and the devil cannot force us to do evil. Just as we cannot truthfully say, "The devil made me do it," we also cannot say, "The Lord made me do it." We are free to choose to whom we will turn our hearts. Within us is an inner zone of volition, choice, and agency. But always, the Spirit of the Lord will prompt us to do good, whisper encouragement and inspiration, and strengthen us in our desires to choose righteousness. Paul taught that the Lord will ever be with us: "There hath no temptation taken you but such as is common to man: but God is faithful, who will not suffer you to be tempted above that ye are able; but will with the temptation also make a way to escape, that ye may be able to bear it" (1 Corinthians 10:13). The Lord will strengthen us in our temptations and buoy us up in our trials.

The Lord compensates the faithful for every loss.
That which is taken away from those who love the
Lord will be added unto them in His own way.

JOSEPH B. WIRTHLIN
ENSIGN, NOVEMBER 2008, 28

We can have perfect trust and faith in the Lord's plan and promises. His word is sure; His utterance secure. At times we may get frustrated or impatient; we may question trials and timetables. But the Lord is ever patient with us, ever kind and forgiving, ever watchful of our sincere desires and worthy efforts. If we are faithful and endure to the end, we will be given heaven's greatest gifts and blessings (D&C 14:7); our wrongs will be made right, our heartache healed, our losses compensated. Speaking of the Lord's promised recompense to the faithful, Elder Joseph B. Wirthlin said: "While it may not come at the time we desire, the faithful will know that every tear today will eventually be returned a hundredfold with tears of rejoicing and gratitude" (*Ensign,* Nov. 2008, 28).

*Our eyes and ears may be deceived
by the cunning and machination of man; but
the Holy Ghost never deceives anybody.*

WILFORD WOODRUFF
WILFORD WOODRUFF, 48

At times we are surrounded by the craftiness of evil people whose desire is to deceive us and destroy the work of the Lord. We need the Holy Ghost to withstand these wicked designs. Speaking of the Spirit of the Lord, President Wilford Woodruff said: "Every man who receives that Spirit has a comforter within—a leader to dictate and guide him. This Spirit reveals, day by day, to every man who has faith, those things which are for his benefit. . . . It is this inspiration of God to his children in every age of the world that is one of the necessary gifts to sustain man and enable him to walk by faith, and to go forth and obey all the dictations and commandments and revelations which God has given to His children to guide and direct them in life. Every man should get the Spirit of God, and then follow its dictates" (*Wilford Woodruff,* 51).

*For the Lamb which is in the midst
of the throne shall feed them, and shall lead
them unto living fountains of waters: and God
shall wipe away all tears from their eyes.*

REVELATION 7:17

The apostle John prophesied of a time when the saints of God would have their robes washed and would become white in the Atonement of Jesus Christ (Revelation 7:14). Then as now, the saints of God are redeemed and nourished by the living water and bread of life that is Christ (John 4:10–14; 6:35, 48). Those who exercise faith and come unto the Savior, partake of the fruits of the Atonement, receive ordinances, and keep the commandments, are promised to dwell with Christ during the Millennium and in the eternal kingdom to come. They are also promised that all their tears shall be wiped away, they will be comforted, healed, and find peace. This is not a promise to those of the meridian yesteryear—it is for each of us today. Only Christ, in a lasting and comprehensive way, can heal our broken hearts, wipe all tears away, right all wrongs, and soothe all sorrows.

*Self-reliance means using all of our blessings from Heavenly
Father to care for ourselves and our families. . . . Each of
us has a responsibility to try to avoid problems before they
happen and to learn to overcome challenges when they occur.*

JULIE B. BECK
ENSIGN, JANUARY 2010, 9

The Lord has promised us that we need not fear if we
are prepared (D&C 38:30). Preparation comes of diligence and effort, of sacrifice and service, of work and
education—which all lead to becoming self-reliant.
Self-reliance is essential to our spiritual and temporal
well-being; it is absolutely vital to our peace and happiness here and hereafter. Speaking of self-reliance,
Julie B. Beck, Relief Society general president,
said, "How do we become self-reliant? We become
self-reliant through obtaining sufficient knowledge,
education, and literacy; by managing money and resources wisely, being spiritually strong, preparing for
emergencies and eventualities; and by having physical
health and social and emotional well-being" (*Ensign,*
Jan. 2010, 9). As agents, we will be held accountable
for how we magnify our stewardships, responsibilities,
and blessings in caring for our families and ourselves.
Let us be anxiously engaged in becoming self-reliant.

Music has power to provide spiritual nourishment. It has healing power. It has the power to facilitate worship, allowing us to contemplate the Atonement and the Restoration of the gospel. . . . to express prayerful thoughts and bear testimony of sacred truths.

RUSSELL M. NELSON
ENSIGN, DECEMBER 2009, 16

Worthy music comes with a powerful promise—it has the power to help us become more humble, prayerful, obedient, and grateful. Inspiring music can promote harmony and love in the family; it can exert a continuing influence for good in our lives. "Do not degrade yourself with the numbing shabbiness and irreverence of music that is not worthy of you," said Elder Russell M. Nelson. "Delete the rubbish from your minds and your MP3 players. Protect your personal standards! Be selective! Be wise! Do not allow unworthy, raucous music to enter your life. It is *not* harmless. It can weaken your defense and allow unworthy thoughts into your mind and pave the way to unworthy acts. Please remember: 'That which doth not edify is not of God, and is darkness. That which is of God is light' (D&C 50:23–24). Fill your minds with worthy sights and sounds. Cultivate your precious gift of the Holy Ghost" (*Ensign*, Dec. 2009, 17).

For those who are truly repentant
but seem unable to feel relief: continue keeping the
commandments. I promise you, relief will come in the
timetable of the Lord. Healing also requires time.

NEIL L. ANDERSEN
ENSIGN, NOVEMBER 2009, 42

Whether our wounds are gaping or slight, whether our heartaches are large or small, we are all broken, all less than perfectly whole, all sinners who have fallen short, all in need of the Master Healer, the Master Forgiver. Elder Neil L. Andersen said, "For most, repentance is more a journey than a one-time event. It is not easy. To change is difficult. It requires running into the wind, swimming upstream. Jesus said, 'If any man will come after me, let him deny himself, and take up his cross and follow me' [Matthew 16:24]. Repentance is turning away from some things, such as dishonesty, pride, anger, and impure thoughts, and turning toward other things, such as kindness, unselfishness, patience, and spirituality. It is 're-turning' toward God" (*Ensign,* Nov. 2009, 41). Real change usually takes time. Healing is very often a gradual process of growth and recovery. Often not until years later do we see the healing that took place over time and in miraculous ways.

JANUARY 28

We should go to work with a united faith
like the heart of one man; and whatever we do should
be performed in the name of the Lord, and we will
then be blessed and prospered in all we do.

BRIGHAM YOUNG
BRIGHAM YOUNG, 353

True disciples of the Lord strive to be united—of one heart and one mind. Brigham Young said, "If we were one, we should then prove to heaven, to God our Father, to Jesus Christ our Elder Brother, to the angels, to the good upon the earth, and to all mankind that we are the disciples of the Lord Jesus Christ. If we are not one, we are not in the true sense of the word the disciples of the Lord Jesus" (see D&C 38:27; *Brigham Young,* 355). To be a disciple of Jesus Christ is to follow Him, to strive to become like Him, to develop within us His heart. In opposition to the hardness and harshness of the world, that disciple-heart would be soft: filled with love, compassion, long-suffering, forgiveness, and gentleness and would unite with others striving for a similar heart. For we truly become one—in our families, wards, and stakes—as we become disciples of Jesus Christ.

30

Don't be critical of people.
Find their virtues—they have some—
and build on those. You will be
very happy if you do.

GORDON B. HINCKLEY
TEACHINGS OF GORDON B. HINCKLEY, 412

One surefire way to be happy is to take off the judicial robes we so often wear and look for the good in people. We may have to search a bit, but goodness is found in virtually all people. We can find goodness if we look for it; and that goodness will continue to grow and blossom as we build upon it. Sometimes it's hard not to be critical, to focus on strengths instead of weaknesses, virtues instead of vices; but our hearts will begin to change as we sincerely strive to look for the good and not be critical. Being critical is a habit for some—a habit, like any other addiction, that is hard to break. Being critical can momentarily make us feel better or superior to others; it can help us to ignore or rationalize our own shortcomings. But it is not the Lord's way; it leads to enmity, envy, and strife. As followers of the Master, we are to build, bless, and strengthen one another.

*He shall bring salvation to all those who shall believe on
his name; this being the intent of this last sacrifice,
to bring about the bowels of mercy, which overpowereth
justice, and bringeth about means unto men that
they may have faith unto repentance.*

ALMA 34:15

Amulek taught: "And thus mercy can satisfy the
demands of justice, and encircles them in the arms
of safety, while he that exercises no faith unto repentance is exposed to the whole law of the demands of
justice; therefore only unto him that has faith unto
repentance is brought about the great and eternal
plan of redemption" (Alma 34:16). We are encircled
in the arms of safety as we exercise faith unto repentance and as we rely upon the merits and mercy of the
Savior. To be safe in the gospel sense means that we
are not deceived by false notions and false prophets;
we are fully and humbly aware that salvation, peace,
and true joy come only in and through the Savior. To
be safe means that we lock our hearts to immorality
and dishonesty, we bolt the doors of our soul to vanity and deception, we guard our thoughts and intents,
our actions and attitudes. True shelter is found in the
arms of Jesus (Mormon 5:11).

*If you, the youth of the Church, will have the courage to keep
your covenants and follow the counsel of your parents and
Church leaders, you will . . . be prepared for your responsibilities
in your homes, in the Church, and in your communities.*

M. Russell Ballard,
Ensign, May 1993, 8

Our youth carry the future on their shoulders. Elder M. Russell Ballard gave them specific counsel on how to stay strong in a wicked world: "Now, my dear young friends, I encourage you to take time each week to be by yourself, away from television and the crowd. Have your scriptures with you and as you read, ponder, and pray, take an honest look at your life. Evaluate where you stand with the promises you have made with Heavenly Father. If you have a problem, talk it over with the Lord in earnest and humble prayer. Counsel with your parents; they will help you. Your bishop and your Young Men and Young Women adult leaders will help. They love you and want you to be at peace with yourself so you can partake of the sacrament worthily each week. When all is said and done, however, only you know if you are living true to your covenants made with God" (*Ensign,* May 1993, 8).

FEBRUARY

My word shall not pass away,
but shall all be fulfilled, whether by mine own
voice or by the voice of my servants,
it is the same.

DOCTRINE & COVENANTS 1:38

*And, if you keep my commandments
and endure to the end you shall have eternal life,
which gift is the greatest of all the gifts of God.*

DOCTRINE & COVENANTS 14:7

The greatest gift we could receive is a prophet's reward (Matthew 10:41), even eternal life in the kingdom of God. Eternal life is the quality of life that our
Heavenly Father and Savior enjoy; it is to have their
everlasting joy and eternal felicity; it is to live forever
as families in the presence of God (see D&C 132:19–
20, 24, 55). Elder L. Tom Perry said, "I believe that if
we could create in our minds a clear and true picture
of eternal life, we would start behaving differently.
We would not need to be prodded to do the many
things involved with enduring to the end, like doing
our home teaching or visiting teaching, attending our
meetings, going to the temple, living moral lives, saying our prayers, or reading the scriptures. We would
want to do all these things and more because we realize they will prepare us to go somewhere we yearn to
go" (*Ensign,* May 2008, 44).

*By seriously trying to apply the Golden Rule that the Savior
gave to us, we will find greater joy, success, satisfaction,
and friendship as we go through life, and we will enjoy the
love of others and the Spirit of our Father in heaven.*

N. ELDON TANNER
ENSIGN, OCTOBER 1972, 2

The clarion call of the Master is to live as He lived,
love as He loved, become even as He is. The Golden
Rule, as taught by the Savior in the Sermon on the
Mount (Matthew 7:12), keeps us on the pathway
to true discipleship and authentic moral living. But
it is not enough to have the Golden Rule committed to memory; we must commit it to life. It is not
enough to proclaim the slogan *What Would Jesus Do;* we
must strive to become like the Savior. President N.
Eldon Tanner taught us an application of the Savior's
Golden Rule: "If we will always look for the best in
others, in our friends, in our neighbors, in our wife,
in our husband, in our children, they will turn out to
be the most wonderful people in the world. On the
other hand, if we are looking for their weaknesses and
faults and enlarge upon them, these same people may
become even despicable" (*Ensign,* Oct. 1972, 2).

One of the most vital things we can do is to express our testimonies through service, which will, in turn, produce spiritual growth, greater commitment, and a greater capacity to keep the commandments. . . . We cannot have spirituality without service!

SPENCER W. KIMBALL
ENSIGN, DECEMBER 1974, 5

Those who have taken upon themselves Christ's name through baptism have covenanted to serve others, to mourn with those that mourn and comfort those in need (Mosiah 18:8–9). President Spencer W. Kimball said, "When we are engaged in the service of our fellowmen, not only do our deeds assist them, but we put our own problems in a fresher perspective. When we concern ourselves more with others, there is less time to be concerned with ourselves. In the midst of the miracle of serving, there is the promise of Jesus, that by losing ourselves, we find ourselves. (See Matt. 10:39.) Not only do we 'find' ourselves in terms of acknowledging guidance in our lives, but the more we serve our fellowmen in appropriate ways, the more substance there is to our souls. We become more significant individuals as we serve others" (*Ensign,* Dec. 1974, 2).

*Where there is appreciation, there is courtesy, there is concern
for the rights and property of others. Without appreciation,
there is arrogance and evil. Where there is gratitude, there is
humility, as opposed to pride. How magnificently we are blessed!*

GORDON B. HINCKLEY
TEACHINGS OF GORDON B. HINCKLEY, 247

President Gordon B. Hinckley said, "Our society is afflicted by a spirit of thoughtless arrogance unbecoming those who have been so magnificently blessed. How grateful we should be for the bounties we enjoy. Absence of gratitude is the mark of the narrow, uneducated mind. It bespeaks a lack of knowledge and the ignorance of self-sufficiency. It expresses itself in ugly egotism and frequently in wanton mischief" (*Teachings of Gordon B. Hinckley,* 247). We, of all peoples, should have hearts that burn with the fervor of humble thanksgiving. Indeed, it is an unspeakable grace to have the assurance that God is in His heaven, Christ the Lord is leading His people, and that peace here and hereafter are within reach. Gratitude is a godly attribute; it lifts the soul; it focuses and refocuses the mind and heart upon primary causes; it yokes us to the Savior. Gratitude is the substance out of which celestial living, in this world and in the world to come, is made.

*Stay with it. We don't acquire eternal life in a sprint—
this is a race of endurance. We have to apply and
reapply the divine gospel principles. Day after day
we need to make them part of our normal life.*

DIETER F. UCHTDORF
ENSIGN, MAY 2009, 76

Too often we approach the gospel like a farmer who places a seed in the ground in the morning and expects corn on the cob by the afternoon," said President Dieter F. Uchtdorf. "When Alma compared the word of God to a seed, he explained that the seed grows into a fruit-bearing tree gradually, as a result of our 'faith, and [our] diligence, and patience, and long-suffering' [Alma 32:43]. . . . From the very moment we set foot upon the pathway of discipleship, seen and unseen blessings from God begin to attend us. But we cannot receive the fulness of those blessings if we 'neglect the tree, and take no thought for its nourishment' [Alma 32:38]. Knowing that the seed is good is not enough. We must 'nourish it with great care, that it may get root' [Alma 32:37]. Only then can we partake of the fruit that is 'sweet above all that is sweet' [Alma 32:42]" (*Ensign,* May 2009, 76).

Go to where you know the light of truth shines—to a worthy friend, a loving bishop or stake president, an understanding parent. Please come back. We love you. We need you. Follow the path to peace and joy through complete repentance.

RICHARD G. SCOTT
ENSIGN, NOVEMBER 2000, 27

Sin and sorrow will attend us during our mortal journey, but repentance and forgiveness keep us on the path of peace and joy. As we call upon the Lord in humble repentance, we will find "the peace of God, which passeth all understanding" (Philippians 4:7). Elder Richard G. Scott outlined the vital steps of repentance as recognition, sorrow, abandonment, confession, restitution where possible, and diligence in keeping the commandments of God and obeying the plan of happiness, including continuing repentance as needed. Repentance is centered in Jesus Christ and His Atonement, which "has efficacy because He willingly paid the full price through His redeeming sacrifice, motivated by a perfect love of His Father and of each of us" (*Ensign,* Nov. 2000, 26). The Savior will help us to obtain forgiveness. He is our Redeemer, our Advocate, our Lord, our Friend. His love for us is perfect, complete, and unending.

Spirit sons and daughters knew and worshiped God as their Eternal Father and accepted His plan by which His children could obtain a physical body and gain earthly experience to progress toward . . . his or her divine destiny as an heir of eternal life.

"THE FAMILY: A PROCLAMATION TO THE WORLD"
ENSIGN, NOVEMBER 1995, 102

Each of us is blessed with a sacred stewardship: the privilege of gaining both a body and earthly experience. Obtaining a physical body is central to the process of progressing toward our divine destiny. The Prophet Joseph Smith said, "We came to this earth that we might have a body and present it pure before God in the celestial kingdom. The great principle of happiness consists in having a body. The devil has no body, and herein is his punishment. He is pleased when he can obtain the tabernacle of man, and when cast out by the Savior he asked to go into the herd of swine, showing that he would prefer a swine's body to having none. All beings who have bodies have power over those who have not" (*Joseph Smith,* 211). We are here to gain experience as we care for this temple-body (1 Corinthians 6:19), to safeguard that which we bring into our minds and souls, to live worthy of the promise of eternal life.

For behold, the righteous shall not perish;
for the time surely must come that all they
who fight against Zion shall be cut off.

1 NEPHI 22:19

The power of the Lord will so terrify all Zion's enemies that they will fear to fight her. In the period before the return of the Lord, there will be no peace or security anywhere—or with anyone—outside of Zion. Zion will be the only refuge of safety on earth. For the righteous Saints, Zion will be glorious and peaceful: "a land of peace, a city of refuge, a place of safety for the saints of the Most High God; . . . the wicked will not come unto it, and it shall be called Zion. . . . It shall be the only people that shall not be at war one with another. And it shall be said among the wicked: Let us not go up to battle against Zion, for the inhabitants of Zion are terrible; wherefore we cannot stand" (D&C 45:66–70). We can have confidence in the Lord's promise that those who fight against Zion will fail.

Some put their highest trust in a friend or another family member, perhaps because they feel that person is more righteous or more wise than they. But that is not the Lord's way. He told us to put our faith and our trust in the Lord Jesus Christ.

DALLIN H. OAKS,
ENSIGN, MAY 1994, 99

Jesus taught the Nephites that they must pray always to the Father in his name, adding: "And whatsoever ye shall ask the Father in my name, which is right, believing that ye shall receive, behold it shall be given unto you" (3 Nephi 18:20). Elder Dallin H. Oaks said, "Faith, no matter how strong it is, cannot produce a result contrary to the will of him whose power it is. The exercise of faith in the Lord Jesus Christ is always subject to the order of heaven, to the goodness and will and wisdom and timing of the Lord. That is why we cannot have true faith in the Lord without also having complete trust in the Lord's will and in the Lord's timing" (*Ensign,* May 1994, 100). Faith and trust go together: we must trust the Lord in order to have faith in Him, and we exercise faith as we trust Him. When we exercise faith to trust Him enough we will be content to accept His will.

We should remember that bearing a heartfelt testimony is only a beginning. We need to bear testimony, we need to mean it, and most importantly we need consistently to live it. We need to both declare and live our testimonies.

DAVID A. BEDNAR
ENSIGN, NOVEMBER 2009, 19

We are blessed with daily opportunities to live and share our testimonies of gospel truth. Elder David A. Bednar said, "Brethren and sisters, when was the last time you bore testimony to your eternal companion? Parents, when was the last time you declared your witness to your children about the things you know to be true? And children, when was the last time you shared your testimony with your parents and family? Each of us already knows we should bear testimony to the people we love the most. But what we know is not always reflected in what we do. We may feel unsure, awkward, or even perhaps a bit embarrassed" (*Ensign,* Nov. 2009, 19). Perhaps now would be a good time to put aside any awkwardness and bear a brief, heartfelt testimony to someone you love. If you're alone, listen to and ponder your testimony in your heart, and you can express your gratitude and belief to Heavenly Father in prayer.

Save for the exception of the very few who defect to perdition, there is no habit, no addiction, no rebellion, no transgression, no apostasy, no crime exempted from the promise of complete forgiveness. That is the promise of the atonement of Christ.

BOYD K. PACKER
ENSIGN, NOVEMBER 1995, 20

President Boyd K. Packer has spoken for many decades about the brilliant morning of forgiveness: "The gospel teaches us that relief from torment and guilt can be earned through repentance. . . . there is no habit, no addiction, no rebellion, no transgression, no offense exempted from the promise of complete forgiveness. . . . How all can be repaired, we do not know. It may not all be accomplished in this life. We know from visions and visitations that the servants of the Lord continue the work of redemption beyond the veil [see D&C 138]. This knowledge should be as comforting to the innocent as it is to the guilty. . . . That great morning of forgiveness may not come at once. Do not give up if at first you fail. Often the most difficult part of repentance is to forgive yourself. Discouragement is part of that test. Do not give up. That brilliant morning will come" (*Ensign*, Nov. 1995, 19–20).

*God bless all who endeavor to be their brother's keeper.
... Have you noticed that such individuals have a
brighter smile? ... One cannot participate in helping
others without experiencing a rich blessing himself.*

THOMAS S. MONSON
ENSIGN, JUNE 1998, 39

One of the most remarkable blessings of life, and one of the greatest paradoxes, is that when we lose ourselves in the service of others, we truly find our best selves (Mark 8:35). Those who seek to ameliorate suffering, who strive with all their hearts to bless and lift another, will find greater happiness and peace. King Benjamin taught this timeless truth to the people of his day: "I tell you these things that ye may learn wisdom; that ye may learn that when ye are in the service of your fellow beings ye are only in the service of your God" (Mosiah 2:17). As disciples of the Master, we are not to sequester ourselves in seclusion from the world; the world needs our light, our love, our good news and good cheer. We are sanctified and blessed as we forget ourselves and turn outward to others in love and service.

My word shall not pass away,
but shall all be fulfilled, whether by mine own voice
or by the voice of my servants, it is the same.

DOCTRINE & COVENANTS 1:38

The Lord works through authorized representatives, apostles and prophets who have the keys of the priesthood and are known to the Church (1 Thessalonians 5:12). When these apostles and prophets speak in the name of the Lord, it is as though God himself has spoken. The commandments, promises, blessings, and admonitions of God are just as valid and binding upon us when voiced by His authorized servants as when voiced by God himself. The Lord's authorized representatives are His agents, surrogates, teachers, and spokesmen; however, unlike the Lord, who is perfect in every way, these servants are themselves imperfect and striving to overcome the world—like each of us. Nevertheless, they have been called by inspiration and magnified in their callings by the Lord. How blessed we are to have apostles and prophets on the earth, "holy men of God [who speak] as they [are] moved by the Holy Ghost" (2 Peter 1:21).

Trying to find love without helping and sacrificing for others is like trying to live without eating—it is against the laws of nature and cannot succeed. We cannot fake love. It must become part of us.

JOHN H. GROBERG
ENSIGN, NOVEMBER 2004, 9

Love changes everything. Love for God and for others changes our outlook, our prayers, our thoughts and desires. "When filled with God's love, we can do and see and understand things that we could not otherwise do or see or understand," said Elder John H. Groberg. "Filled with His love, we can endure pain, quell fear, forgive freely, avoid contention, renew strength, and bless and help others in ways surprising even to us" (*Ensign,* Nov. 2004, 11). That's why love is the guide to our walk and talk and is at the heart of what it means to be a disciple of Christ. We can fast and pray for the gift of charity. We can study the life and teachings of the Master and seek the Spirit in our lives, which will fill us with love. We can humble ourselves, strive to forgive, and soften our hearts by feasting upon the words of scripture. Love is a gift of God that will come to those who sincerely seek it.

*Obviously, the personal burdens of life vary from person
to person, but every one of us has them. Furthermore,
each trial in life is tailored to the individual's capacities
and needs as known by a loving Father in Heaven.*

HOWARD W. HUNTER
ENSIGN, NOVEMBER 1990, 18

Sometimes it is altogether human to wonder why we have to endure hardship and difficulty, why we must suffer heartache and pain. We wish, in a sense, to "return to Eden" where there is constant beauty and ease, no suffering, no sorrow. But we never really know deep joy unless we have known heartache; we can never really value peace unless we have known distress and turmoil. It is opposition, burden, trial, and trouble that allow us to experience the profound joy and peace that passes understanding or utterance (Philippians 4:7). We can take comfort in the fact that our trials are tailor-made by a loving God for our ultimate growth and happiness. He knows what we need and must experience in order to develop his attributes and heart. He will give us the courage and strength to press forward to Zion.

*In a gospel-sharing home we do not just pray for the health, safety,
and success of our missionaries throughout the world. We also
pray for our own missionary experiences and opportunities and
to be prepared to act on those impressions as they come our way.*

M. RUSSELL BALLARD
ENSIGN, MAY 2006, 86

We are a missionary-loving, missionary-sending,
and missionary-praying church that takes seriously
the commission to take the gospel to all the world
(Matthew 28:19). How often do we pray for the missionaries in our family, ward, and across the world, but
forget to pray for our own missionary opportunities?
Perhaps we expect the full-time missionaries to take
care of it. Perhaps we prefer to keep our mouths closed,
somewhat embarrassed or reluctant to seem different
or peculiar. Because "every member is a missionary," we
too have a sacred charge to share the gospel with others. When the fire of the covenant burns in our hearts,
we want others to see its light and feel its warmth. The
way we live sends a clear message to others. The way we
interact with others presents opportunities to befriend
and convey a message of gospel good news and reassuring hope. Opportunities to share the gospel will surely
come to those who pray, prepare, and dare.

*We who have been ordained to the priesthood of God can make
a difference. When we qualify for the help of the Lord, we
can build boys, we can mend men, we can accomplish miracles
in His holy service. Our opportunities are without limit.*

THOMAS S. MONSON
ENSIGN, MAY 2008, 65

Priesthood power is the power to act in the name
of God to accomplish His purposes, bless others, and
strengthen its beneficiaries—both those who exercise
its powers and receive its blessings and ordinances.
Worthy priesthood holders can make a difference, in
their own lives and in the lives of others, as they serve
and bless others.

Priesthood equals love: love of God, love of the
gospel, love for our fellowman, love for the holy honor
and sacred opportunity to act in the name of God to
bless mankind.

*We have the agency to make choices, but ultimately
we will be accountable for each choice we make. We may
deceive others, but there is One we will never deceive.*

JAMES E. FAUST
ENSIGN, NOVEMBER 1996, 42

An old saying, often attributed to Abraham
Lincoln, goes: "You can fool all the people some of
the time, and some of the people all the time, but
you cannot fool all the people all the time." Indeed,
we may even deceive ourselves some of the time.
But there is One who is never deceived; One who
knows the full truth; One to whom we are accountable for every choice we make. Jacob in the Book of
Mormon taught, "The keeper of the gate is the Holy
One of Israel; and he employeth no servant there; and
there is none other way save it be by the gate; for he
cannot be deceived, for the Lord God is his name"
(2 Nephi 9:41). The knowledge of an all-knowing,
ever-understanding Lord should inspire us to live
truthfully and with a sense of peace and security, not
fear and dread. The Lord knows all things about us,
yet "his hand is stretched out still" (2 Nephi 20:4).

The Lord is merciful unto all who will, in the sincerity of their hearts, call upon his holy name. . . . The gate of heaven is open unto all, even to those who will believe on the name of Jesus Christ, who is the Son of God.

HELAMAN 3:27–28

The gospel of Jesus Christ is not an exclusive club with restricted membership. The gospel gate is wide open for all who humble themselves, exercise faith in the Lord, repent, and accept the ordinances of salvation. In a similar way, the Church is not a cloistered monastery for perfect people. The Church is a place where imperfect people are striving to become more like Jesus, a place where we serve and fellowship with brothers and sisters in the faith who, like us, are struggling to overcome the world. The Church is the organized and formal structure, the scaffolding for the gospel; the gospel is the essence of our teachings and belief in the Lord, the great plan of happiness, scripture, latter-day prophets and modern revelation, and the restored truths made known by the Prophet Joseph Smith. These two—the gospel and the Church—are available to all who sincerely choose the Lord.

Isn't it marvelous . . . that God, who knows everything, still spends time listening to our prayers? Compared to that cosmic fact, what does the world really have to offer us? . . . one fleeting moment of adulation, or an approving glance from a phantom Caesar?

NEAL A. MAXWELL
ENSIGN, NOVEMBER 2000, 37

In a way incomprehensible to us, our loving Father in Heaven hears our prayers and cares about each of His children. Though we may not understand all things, we know enough of our Father's heart to respond as did Nephi to the question from the Spirit of the Lord: "I know that he loveth his children; nevertheless, I do not know the meaning of all things" (1 Nephi 11:17). Fully understanding is not necessary to fully believing. We live so much of our day-to-day life on faith; we enjoy so much that life has to offer without fully understanding, without even thinking much about it. How does electricity work? What keeps the earth suspended in the cosmos? Why are people so different? For some, these are questions with easy answers; for others, imponderables. The light of Christ whispers reassurance during dark moments. The Holy Ghost gently reaffirms that although we don't know everything, we know enough to trust the Lord and keep believing.

Fear thou not; for I am with thee: be not dismayed;
for I am thy God: I will strengthen thee;
yea, I will help thee; yea, I will uphold thee
with the right hand of my righteousness.

ISAIAH 41:10

The scriptures and the words of latter-day prophets are filled with counsel to "fear not" and "be of good cheer" and "rejoice." For example, "Wherefore, be of good cheer, and do not fear, for I the Lord am with you, and will stand by you" (D&C 68:6). And from the Book of Mormon, "Lift up your heads, and rejoice, and put your trust in God" (Mosiah 7:19). Scores of references appear in the standard works exhorting us to "be strong and of a good courage" (Deuteronomy 31:6) and to "rejoice in the Lord" (Philippians 3:1).

People of faith are people of hope, optimism, and courage. Followers of the Lord keep their eyes on the prize of eternal life, despite all the setbacks, trials, and vicissitudes of life. Even in these days of fear and uncertainty, we can strive to trust the Lord and His promises, fear not, be of good cheer, and rejoice.

*Wherefore, redemption cometh in and through
the Holy Messiah; for he is full of grace and truth.
Behold, he offereth himself a sacrifice for sin, to
answer the ends of the law, unto all those who
have a broken heart and a contrite spirit.*

2 NEPHI 2:6–7

Life is not fair. From our limited and very mortal perspective, we see good people suffer and bad people prosper. Yet some of the happiest people are those who endure more than their share of injustices. How is this possible? Perhaps it's because they stop competing with those around them; they simply do their best with what they have. They look forward instead of backward. They understand that "why me?" questions can't really be answered here and now, so they discard them. They've felt deeply of life's sorrows, so they actively look for and cultivate the joys. And somewhere deep in their hearts, they know they can trust in a loving God who is perfectly merciful and ultimately fair. All the disparities of life, all the heartache and unfairness, can be made right through the redemptive grace of our Savior. Incomprehensible to us, the Atonement of Jesus Christ makes right that which is wrong, heals that which is broken, soothes that which is distressed.

Apostasy . . . is a gradual growth in which darkness
through sin crowds out the spirit of light from the soul.
When a man who was once enlightened loses the Spirit of
truth, the darkness which takes its place is overwhelming.

JOSEPH FIELDING SMITH
CHURCH HISTORY AND MODERN REVELATION, 2:125

Apostasy means to leave the straight and narrow path that leads to eternal life, separate oneself from the household of faith, reject gospel light and truth, and wander in darkness. Most often it happens gradually, insidiously creeping into our thoughts and actions and driving out the Spirit. Once we embrace gospel truth, we are no longer on neutral ground: We have joined ourselves with light. If we later turn against what we once knew to be true, darkness will enter to fill its place: "And thus we can plainly discern, that after a people have been once enlightened by the Spirit of God, and have had great knowledge of things pertaining to righteousness, and then have fallen away into sin and transgression, they become more hardened, and thus their state becomes worse than though they had never known these things" (Alma 24:30). We must stay in tune with the Spirit, resist the tugs and pulls of the world, and steadfastly hold on to the iron rod.

Let us teach our children to treat others with friendship, respect, love, and admiration. That will yield a far better result than will an attitude of egotism and arrogance.

GORDON B. HINCKLEY
ENSIGN, MAY 2000, 87

President Gordon B. Hinckley said, "Let us as Latter-day Saints reach out to others not of our faith. Let us never act in a spirit of arrogance or with a holier-than-thou attitude. Rather, may we show love and respect and helpfulness toward them. We are greatly misunderstood, and I fear that much of it is of our own making. We can be more tolerant, more neighborly, more friendly, more of an example than we have been in the past. . . . Let us study the ways of the Lord, reading His life and teachings in the sacred scripture He has given us. Let us take a little time to meditate, to think of what we can do to improve our lives and to become better examples of what a Latter-day Saint should be" (*Ensign,* May 2000, 87). True disciples of the Lord strive to emulate His life as they reach out to others in love, kindness, and humility.

But as oft as they repented and sought forgiveness,
with real intent, they were forgiven.

MORONI 6:8

Repentance and forgiveness are lifelong processes, not one-time events. All along the life course we stumble and sin, we repent and repair, we ask for forgiveness and we forgive others. That is the gospel gate through which we enter at baptism and the pathway we walk all throughout mortality. The Lord taught Alma the eternal principles of repentance and forgiveness, "Yea, and as often as my people repent will I forgive them their trespasses against me. And ye shall also forgive one another your trespasses; for verily I say unto you, he that forgiveth not his neighbor's trespasses when he says that he repents, the same hath brought himself under condemnation. Now, I say unto you, Go; and whosoever will not repent of his sins the same shall not be numbered among my people" (Mosiah 26:30–32). If we repent and forgive with real intent we will come to know the transcendent joy of the Lord's amazing grace.

Instead of dwelling on your troubles, focus instead on creating something remarkable, something of eternal significance. Nurture a testimony, strengthen a relationship, write a family history, go to the temple, serve.

MARY ELLEN SMOOT
ENSIGN, MAY 2000, 65

Mary Ellen Smoot, former general president of the Relief Society, suggested four principles upon which to create a meaningful life: "First, go where the Spirit directs. Be still and listen. Your Heavenly Father will guide you as you draw near to Him. Immerse yourself in the holy word of the prophets, both ancient and modern, and the Spirit will speak to you. Be patient, ask in faith, and you will receive guidance in your creative efforts. Second, don't be paralyzed from fear of making mistakes. Thrust your hands into the clay of your lives and begin. . . . Of course you will make mistakes. Everyone does. Learn from them and move forward. Third, support others along the way. . . . We all have varied interests, abilities, and skills. We are each at different levels physically, spiritually, and emotionally. Finally, rejoice. Creation isn't drudgery. Creation flows from love. When we do what we love, we rejoice along the way" (*Ensign,* May 2000, 65).

*All saints who . . . keep and do these sayings, walking
in obedience to the commandments, shall receive health
in their navel and marrow to their bones; And shall
find wisdom and great treasures of knowledge.*

DOCTRINE & COVENANTS 89:18–19

The revelation called the Word of Wisdom (D&C 89) was given to the Prophet Joseph Smith in Kirtland, Ohio, on this date in 1833. It is a "principle with promise" (D&C 89:3) that will shield and protect us in these latter days. The revelation contains *proscriptions* that prohibit wine, strong drink, tobacco, and hot drinks (which were defined early as tea and coffee); *prescriptions* that direct the frequent use of herbs (including vegetables), fruits, and grains and the limited use of meat; and *promises* that Saints who obey these precepts will receive health, strength, wisdom, knowledge, and safety. If we follow the Word of Wisdom, we receive the Passover promise of ancient Israel that the destroying angel will pass us by, and we will be blessed with both physical and spiritual strength. We'll go forward in the confidence of the Lord, knowing that we have followed His law, kept his commandments, and been abundantly blessed.

Come now, and let us reason together, saith the Lord:
though your sins be as scarlet, they shall be as white as snow;
though they be red like crimson, they shall be as wool.

ISAIAH 1:18–19

The second article of faith makes clear that "men will be punished for their own sins, and not for Adam's transgression." Yet, how can we hope to be saved from the sin and heartache of this fallen world? The Atonement of Jesus Christ redeems mankind from Adam's fall and causes all to be accountable for their own lives. The divine Son of God, Jesus Christ, was the only one capable of making a perfect atonement for mankind. His selfless sacrifice for each of us in Gethsemane and Golgotha offered an unconditional gift for all mankind. All shall rise from the dead with immortal bodies, because of Jesus' Atonement (1 Corinthians 15: 22). The Atonement is *conditional,* however, so far as our individual sins are concerned, and it touches each of us to the degree we have faith in Jesus Christ, repent of our sins, and obey the gospel. The Atonement of Jesus Christ gives us the promise of resurrection, of forgiveness, of hope and healing.

MARCH

Keep all the commandments and covenants by which ye are bound; and I will cause the heavens to shake for your good, and Satan shall tremble and Zion shall rejoice upon the hills and flourish.

<small>DOCTRINE & COVENANTS 35:24</small>

Thou shalt love the Lord thy God with all thy heart,
with all thy might, mind, and strength; and in the name
of Jesus Christ thou shalt serve him. . . . Inasmuch
as ye do this, the fulness of the earth is yours.

DOCTRINE & COVENANTS 59: 5, 16

Doctrine & Covenants section fifty-nine was revealed to the Prophet Joseph Smith in Jackson
County, Missouri, on a Sunday—August 7, 1831. It
outlines what is expected of the Saints in Zion, including their enlightened observance of the Sabbath
day. In verses 5–16 we are commanded to love the
Lord and our neighbor, to not steal, commit adultery,
or kill. We are exhorted to be grateful, to offer to the
Lord a broken heart and contrite spirit. We are given
the Sabbath as a day of rejoicing and prayer, a day set
apart to strengthen us in our resolve to keep unspotted from the world. As we do these things with cheerful hearts and countenances, with thanksgiving and
humility, the Sabbath can be a day to help us forsake
worldliness and center our hearts on the Lord, His
blessings and abundance, and the real purpose for our
existence.

*The conquering of adversity produces
strength of character, forges self-confidence,
engenders self-respect, and assures
success in righteous endeavor.*

RICHARD G. SCOTT
ENSIGN, NOVEMBER 1981, 11

Adversity in one form or another comes to each of us. We wonder how we can cope, and we question our ability to endure and overcome. But good can come from heartache; strength can result from adversity. For Joseph of Egypt in ancient times, a famine became a blessing. It reunited Joseph with his family. Truly, it takes faith and courage to see life's challenges as blessings, especially when they can be so difficult—and so unexpected. Adversities can become turning points: opportunities to learn, to love more deeply, to develop greater kindness and patience, to forgive and cast aside old grudges or resentments. We can be blessed with wisdom when we understand, in very personal ways, that on the other side of suffering is a depth of feeling, a perspective on life and love, which we might not otherwise have known. Indeed, Shakespeare said it well, "Sweet are the uses of adversity" (*As You Like It,* 2.1.12).

Avoid the temptation of being cliquish at school or at church.
All of us can refrain from finding fault or alienating anyone.
. . . Guard against spreading rumors or saying unkind things
or allowing anything to occur that may hurt another.

M. RUSSELL BALLARD
ENSIGN, NOVEMBER 1997, 39

We as members of Christ's new covenant are to be "witnesses of God at all times and in all things, and in all places" (Mosiah 18:9). This is a lifelong covenant, a solemn commitment, a humble pledge that we will strive to become true disciples of the Master in thought, word, and deed. We are to be people of love and compassion, people of friendliness and goodwill, people of honor and integrity. The Savior's message is for all peoples: He reaches out in charity and kindness—to saint and sinner; He includes all who will open their hearts to the truth; He wants every soul to hear the good news of the gospel, repent, come unto Him and be saved. As disciples, we seek to model His life and live His teachings: become people of loyalty and benevolence, watch out for others and include them in our circle of friends, never ridicule or exclude another, and be an example of the believers (1 Timothy 4:12).

When heaven's promises sometimes seem afar off,
I pray that each of us will embrace these exceeding great
and precious promises and never let go. And just as
God remembered Rachel, God will remember you.

SPENCER J. CONDIE
ENSIGN, NOVEMBER 2007, 18

Elder Spencer J. Condie has outlined some of the great and precious promises of the Lord, including "forgiveness of our sins when we 'confess them and forsake them' (D&C 58:43; see also D&C 1:32). Opening the windows of heaven is a promise claimed by those who pay a faithful tithe (see Malachi 3:10), and finding 'great treasures of knowledge' accrues to those who observe the Word of Wisdom (D&C 89:19). Becoming unspotted from the world is a promise to those who keep the Sabbath holy (see D&C 59:9; Exodus 31:13). Divine guidance and inspiration are promised to those who 'feast upon the words of Christ' (2 Nephi 32:3) and who 'liken all scriptures' unto themselves (1 Nephi 19:23). The Lord also promised that 'whatsoever ye shall ask the Father in my name, which is right, believing that ye shall receive, behold it shall be given unto you' (3 Nephi 18:20)" (*Ensign,* Nov. 2007, 16). Indeed, great are the promises of the Lord.

We can lift ourselves . . . when we refuse to remain in the realm of negative thought and cultivate within our hearts an attitude of gratitude. If ingratitude be numbered among the serious sins, then gratitude takes its place among the noblest of virtues.

THOMAS S. MONSON
ENSIGN, MAY 1992, 54

Among the sins mentioned in scripture, ingratitude seems to draw some of the sternest condemnation (D&C 59:21; 2 Timothy 3:2). Ungratefulness reflects a dark plague in the heart—arrogance, forgetfulness, thoughtlessness, or indifference to both Him and the things that matter most. Gratitude is integral to other virtues, doctrines, and righteous acts; it is central to the development of authentic spirituality, true humility, and genuine happiness. As gratitude in the heart grows so do testimony and faith, so do humility and meekness, so do a disposition to do no evil and a desire to do the Lord's will. Indeed, an attitude of gratitude for God and the gospel, for family, friends, and freedom, for those who have blessed our lives, and for life itself, changes both our heart and our world.

*Just as expressing gratitude more often in our prayers
enlarges the conduit for revelation, so praying for
others with all of the energy of our souls increases our
capacity to hear and to heed the voice of the Lord.*

DAVID A. BEDNAR
ENSIGN, NOVEMBER 2008, 43

If prayer is, as we sing, the "soul's sincere desire, uttered or unexpressed" (*Hymns*, 145), what could be more worthy than praying for others with all the energy of our souls? Enos found that because of his faith and trust in Christ, and through mighty prayer and pondering, he received a remission of his sins and its accompanying unspeakable joy. But he didn't stop there. He also felt a desire for his brethren the Nephites and for their enemies, the Lamanites. He prayed for them with all diligence. It can be assumed that in his day-long prayer he offered more than petitions and requests. For this righteous and valiant soul, much time must have been spent in expressing gratitude and praise for the Lord, His mercy and kindness. Indeed, Enos is a noteworthy example of the power of prayer: "the motion of a hidden fire that trembles in the breast" (*Hymns*, 145).

*You will be blessed if you refrain
from setting your own wisdom or desires
ahead of the commandments of your Creator
and the warnings of His servants.*

DALLIN H. OAKS
ENSIGN, MAY 2002, 35

Elder Dallin H. Oaks is grateful for the warnings of the scriptures and Church leaders on things to avoid: "By following that counsel I have been able to avoid pitfalls that might otherwise have trapped and enslaved me. Alcohol, tobacco, drugs, pornography, and gambling are but a few examples of dangerous substances and addictive practices we have been warned to avoid. . . . The scriptures tell us to take upon us the 'whole armor' of God that we 'may be able to withstand the evil day.' They promise that the 'breastplate of righteousness' and 'the shield of faith' will 'quench all the fiery darts of the wicked' (D&C 27:15–17). I urge you to obey those teachings and lay claim on those blessings. They include the personal spiritual conversion— the 'mighty change . . . in our hearts' (Mosiah 5:2)— that helps us become what our Heavenly Father desires us to become" (*Ensign,* May 2002, 33). We are blessed as we follow the inspired counsel of our leaders.

[Lucifer], with the angels who followed him, will trouble the work of the Lord and destroy it if he can. But we will stay on course. . . . Whatever tests lie ahead, and they will be many, we must remain faithful and true.

BOYD K. PACKER
ENSIGN, NOVEMBER 2008, 91

In these perilous times and always, the Lord prepares a safe course to follow. Indeed, we will be protected through "obedience to the laws and ordinances of the Gospel" (Articles of Faith 1:3). President Boyd K. Packer taught, "We are guided by the same revelations and led by a prophet. When the Prophet Joseph Smith died, another took his place. The order of succession continues today. Six months ago at general conference, Thomas S. Monson was sustained as the 16th President of the Church, just five months before his 81st birthday. He succeeded President Gordon B. Hinckley. . . . The senior leaders of the Church will virtually always be seasoned by decades of preparation. President Monson is ideally suited for the challenges of our day. He is sustained by two counselors and the Quorum of the Twelve Apostles—all prophets, seers, and revelators" (*Ensign*, Nov. 2008, 91). We have no need to fear: The course is set, and God is at the helm.

How mighty a thing is prayer.
Of that I can testify and to that you can testify.
How tragic the loss for any family that fails to take
advantage of this precious and simple practice.

GORDON B. HINCKLEY
ENSIGN, SEPTEMBER 1996, 8

Something wonderful and powerful begins to happen to individuals and families when they pray. It's not immediate, and it's seldom dramatic; but it's real, and it takes place over time and with sincere effort and consistency. Prayer provides a window into the interior of a home. Where there is humility and devotion, there is prayer; where there is testimony and gratitude, there is prayer. Prayer can change hearts and homes, and is the passport to love, peace, and joy in families. Prayer creates an atmosphere of spirituality and a climate of righteousness in the home which family members can carry with them wherever they go, however life unfolds. The faith and strength of families are lessened if they fail to take advantage of the precious and simple practice of prayer. How great a blessing is prayer!

If there is any hope for the future of nations, that hope resides in the family. Our children are our wealth; our children are our strength; our children are indeed our future!

RUSSELL M. NELSON
CHURCH NEWS, AUGUST 15, 2009, 4

Elder Russell M. Nelson said: "Nothing, absolutely nothing, can provide the joy and growth that come from happy children who make a family circle. . . . Spiritually, we need children as much as they need us. They are our spiritual wealth. Children teach us the joy of building goodness that will outlive our own. They teach us the joy of loving someone more than self. . . . Future happiness and even the future of nations is linked to children. Families with children need to be re-enthroned as the fundamental unit of society. We simply must value children more than we do! Without a new generation to replace the old, there is no wealth; without families, there is no future" (*Church News,* August 15, 2009). The promise of our future as a church and as a nation depends on children—the desire to bring children into the world, and the effort to rear them in love and righteousness (D&C 93:40).

*Though you sometimes may not be able to see the way,
know that your Father in Heaven will never forsake His
righteous followers. He will not leave you comfortless. He
will be at your side, yes, guiding you every step of the way.*

JOSEPH B. WIRTHLIN
ENSIGN, NOVEMBER 2001, 27

The words of the psalmist inspire: "I will lift up mine eyes unto the hills, from whence cometh my help" (Psalm 121:1). The principle taught is familiar to experienced hikers. They know to keep their eyes fixed on a landmark in the distance: a tree, a rock, a hill. Then, even if their path takes them in directions they did not expect, as long as they keep that landmark in sight, they eventually reach their destination. Likewise, during our journey of life we can do our best to fix our eyes upon everlasting things. Elder Joseph B. Wirthlin said, "All too soon, our time is finished. . . . Let us walk in the right direction, taking one step after another. That is easy enough. We don't have to be perfect today. We don't have to be better than someone else. All we have to do is to be the very best we can" (*Ensign,* Nov. 2001, 27).

Help in maintaining the proper perspective in these permissive times can come to you from many sources. One valuable resource is your patriarchal blessing. Read it frequently. Study it carefully. Be guided by its cautions. Live to merit its promises.

THOMAS S. MONSON
ENSIGN, MAY 2009, 125

Every worthy member of the Church, having sufficient maturity to understand the nature and the importance of such blessings, is able to receive a patriarchal blessing by an ordained patriarch. That sacred blessing, given by the power of the Spirit, declares your lineage in the house of Israel and contains personal counsel and promises from the Lord that can provide guidance, comfort, and protection throughout your life. One should read a patriarchal blessing with an eternal perspective—its promises may extend into the eternities. If we are true and faithful, all blessings and promises will be fulfilled in the Lord's due time—either here or hereafter. A patriarchal blessing should be read frequently, humbly, and prayerfully. It can become as a personal Liahona to guide and inspire our efforts; it can provide a revelatory framework upon which to design our future. How blessed we are to have such sacred and personal blessings available to us!

The Lord has told us plainly that only those who are valiant in the testimony of Jesus will inherit celestial glory. It is the valiant who keep their testimonies aglow, and this they do by constant activity in the Church and continuous study of the gospel.

MARK E. PETERSEN
ENSIGN, DECEMBER 1974, 11

We keep our testimonies bright by staying strong in the Church and keeping the Sabbath holy. Elder Mark E. Petersen said to parents: "We are as saviors on Mount Zion. We must seek after the lost sheep. We must teach them and instruct them and rekindle in their hearts a thirst for the knowledge of God. . . . In a very real sense you are shepherds of the flock, and Sunday worship is one of your great responsibilities. The Lord says the thing that will be of most worth to us will be to bring souls unto him. This is our divinely given assignment. Is there a better way to do this than through family togetherness, where the family is truly a family in the home, where the gospel is lived in the home, and where the entire family will come together to the ward on Sunday and there worship the Lord their God? Sunday worship is everybody's responsibility" (*Ensign,* Dec. 1974, 11).

*If, as individual people, as families, communities, and
nations, we could, like Peter, fix our eyes on Jesus, we too
might walk triumphantly over the swelling waves of disbelief
and remain unterrified amid the rising winds of doubt.*

HOWARD W. HUNTER
THAT WE MIGHT HAVE JOY, 1994, 19–20

When we look to God, we live (Alma 37:47).
When we acknowledge God's goodness and mercy,
rejoice in the gift of the Holy Ghost, and strive with
all our hearts to be true to the gospel, we put away
the natural man and become a new creature in Christ
(2 Corinthians 5:17; Mosiah 3:19; 27:25–26). But why
are we commanded to render thanks? (D&C 59:7,
21). Why does God insist that we express gratitude?
Simply stated, it is to enable us to see things as they
really are. We cannot redeem ourselves from a fallen
world. We cannot forgive our own sins or work our
way into exaltation hereafter, any more than we can
create ourselves. We require a spiritual transforma-
tion of the heart and a divine enabling power to accomplish what would otherwise be the impossible.
We are utterly dependent on the mercy and grace of
the Father and the Son. Therefore, we fix our eyes
and hearts upon them in gratitude and devotion.

While many thousands of others truly mourn for the loss of their kindred, yet they rejoice and exult in the hope, and even know, according to the promises of the Lord, that they are raised to dwell at the right hand of God, in a state of never-ending happiness.

ALMA 28:12

The Lord said, "Thou shalt live together in love, insomuch that thou shalt weep for the loss of them that die" (D&C 42:45). It is natural to miss those who have passed on, but we can trust the Lord's promise that we will meet again after a season, and joyous will be our reunion. The Prophet Joseph said, "The expectation of seeing my friends in the morning of the resurrection cheers my soul. . . . It is like their taking a long journey, and on their return we meet them with increased joy" (*Teachings of the Prophet Joseph Smith*, 296). Those who die in the Lord are eternally knit together in love and joy and righteousness: "Thus we see the great reason of sorrow, and also of rejoicing—sorrow because of death . . . , and joy because of the light of Christ unto life" (Alma 28:14).

*If you have repented from serious transgression and
mistakenly believe that you will always be a second-class
citizen in the kingdom of God, learn that is not true.*

RICHARD G. SCOTT
ENSIGN, NOVEMBER 2000, 26

We have the promise of complete forgiveness
through sincere repentance. Elder Richard G. Scott
counseled, "Find encouragement in the lives of Alma
the Younger and the sons of Mosiah. They were tragi-
cally wicked. Yet their full repentance and service
qualified them to be considered as noble as righteous
Captain Moroni. To you who have sincerely repented
yet continue to feel the burden of guilt, realize that to
continue to suffer for sins when there has been proper
repentance and forgiveness of the Lord is prompted
by the master of deceit. Lucifer will encourage you to
continue to relive the details of past mistakes, knowing
that such thoughts can hamper your progress. Thus he
attempts to tie strings to the mind and body so that he
can manipulate you like a puppet to discourage personal achievement. I testify that Jesus Christ paid the
price and will satisfy the demands of justice for all who
are obedient to His teachings" (*Ensign,* Nov. 2000, 26).

*Real charity is not something you give away; it is
something that you acquire and make a part of yourself.
And when the virtue of charity becomes implanted
in your heart, you are never the same again.*

MARVIN J. ASHTON
ENSIGN, MAY 1992, 18–19

Elder Marvin J. Ashton said: "Perhaps the greatest charity comes when we are kind to each other, when we don't judge or categorize someone else, when we simply give each other the benefit of the doubt or remain quiet. Charity is accepting someone's differences, weaknesses, and shortcomings; having patience with someone who has let us down; or resisting the impulse to become offended when someone doesn't handle something the way we might have hoped. Charity is refusing to take advantage of another's weakness and being willing to forgive someone who has hurt us. Charity is expecting the best of each other. None of us need one more person bashing or pointing out where we have failed or fallen short. Most of us are already well aware of the areas in which we are weak. What each of us does need is [people] who believe in us, and who believe we're trying to do the best we can, in spite of our weaknesses" (*Ensign,* May 1992, 19).

*Kind looks, kind actions, kind words, and a lovely,
holy deportment towards them will bind our children
to us with bands that cannot be easily broken; while
abuse and unkindness will drive them from us.*

BRIGHAM YOUNG
BRIGHAM YOUNG, 166

Kind words and gentleness during times of dis-agreement show respect for the relationship—as does controlling one's emotions. Of course, developing parental self-control is easier said than done. As Brigham Young noted, "I have seen more parents who were unable to control themselves than I ever saw who were unable to control their children" (*Brigham Young*, 338). With heavenly help, we can learn to respond to frustrations with patience. It helps to remember that parenting is a fluid, dynamic process. It can take time to see the results of our efforts. What works today may not work next year or even tomorrow. And no parent handles every situation perfectly. When we fall short, it is important to apologize and try to do better. After all, parents are growing and learning too. With the Lord's help, parents can provide appropriate love, limits, and latitude that will enable their children to reach their full potential as sons and daughters of God.

I believe that in his justice and mercy [God] will give us the maximum reward for our acts, give us all that he can give, and in the reverse, I believe that he will impose upon us the minimum penalty which it is possible for him to impose.

J. REUBEN CLARK JR.
CONFERENCE REPORT, OCTOBER 1953, 84

We believe and have hope in the divine gift of mercy, of which Alma said, "God himself atoneth for the sins of the world, to bring about the plan of mercy, to appease the demands of justice, that God might be a perfect, just God, and a merciful God also" (Alma 42:15). President J. Reuben Clark Jr. said, "I believe that the Lord will help us. I believe if we go to him, he will give us wisdom, if we are living righteously. I believe he will answer our prayers. I believe that our Heavenly Father wants to save every one of his children. I do not think he intends to shut any of us off because of some slight transgression, some slight failure to observe some rule or regulation. There are the great elementals that we must observe, but he is not going to be captious about the lesser things" (Conference Report, 3 Oct. 1953, 84). How blessed we are to worship a merciful God!

When He says to the poor in spirit,
"Come unto me," He means He knows the way out
and He knows the way up. He knows it because He has
walked it. He knows the way because He is the way.

JEFFREY R. HOLLAND
ENSIGN, MAY 2006, 71

Reliance upon the merciful nature of God is at the very center of the gospel Christ taught," said Elder Jeffrey R. Holland. "I testify that the Savior's Atonement lifts from us not only the burden of our sins but also the burden of our disappointments and sorrows, our heartaches and our despair [Alma 7:11–12]. From the beginning, trust in such help was to give us both a reason and a way to improve, an incentive to lay down our burdens and take up our salvation. There can and will be plenty of difficulties in life. Nevertheless, the soul that comes unto Christ, who knows His voice and strives to do as He did, finds a strength, as the hymn says, 'beyond [his] own ["Lord, I Would Follow Thee," *Hymns,* no. 220].' The Savior reminds us that He has 'graven [us] upon the palms of [His] hands' [1 Nephi 21:16]" (*Ensign,* May 2006, 70–71).

*I, the Lord, am merciful and gracious
unto those who fear me, and delight to honor
those who serve me in righteousness and in truth
unto the end. Great shall be their reward
and eternal shall be their glory.*

DOCTRINE & COVENANTS 76:5–6

We are to worship and serve the Lord in sincerity and truth (Joshua 24:14). There is no salvation in sincerity devoid of righteousness and truth, just as there is no salvation in the worship of false gods or false doctrines. God is not honored or served by falsehood, however well intended it may be. A straight and narrow path leads to His presence, not a wide and deviating one. There is one faith, one Lord, one source of everlasting life, as Christ declared: "I am the way, the truth, and the life: no man cometh unto the Father, but by me" (John 14:6; see also 2 Nephi 25:20, Ephesians 4:4–6). The Lord honors those who worship Him in humility and sincerity; the Lord is merciful and gracious to those who serve Him in righteousness and truth. How great will be our eternal reward and glory if we love and follow the Lord with heartfelt devotion.

*The Prophet Joseph Smith declared . . . that the eternal
sealings of faithful parents and the divine promises made
to them for valiant service in the Cause of Truth, would
save not only themselves, but likewise their posterity.*

ORSON F. WHITNEY
CONFERENCE REPORT, APRIL 1929, 110

Elder Orson F. Whitney said: "Though some of the
sheep may wander, the eye of the Shepherd is upon
them, and sooner or later they will feel the tentacles
of Divine Providence reaching out after them and
drawing them back to the fold. Either in this life or
the life to come, they will return. They will have to
pay their debt to justice; they will suffer for their sins;
and may tread a thorny path; but if it leads them at
last, like the penitent Prodigal, to a loving and forgiving father's heart and home, the painful experience
will not have been in vain. Pray for your careless and
disobedient children; hold on to them with your faith.
Hope on, trust on, till you see the salvation of God"
(Conference Report, Apr. 1929, 110). Faithful but
brokenhearted parents of prodigal sons and daughters
can trust the Lord's promises: the Good Shepherd is
watching over them, and covenants will bind them
everlastingly.

*Tithing is a law of God
and the payment of tithes brings
peace and joy to the
Latter-day Saint who does it.*

HEBER J. GRANT
HEBER J. GRANT, 125

We are promised blessings of peace, prosperity, and contentment if we pay an honest tithe. That doesn't mean we won't suffer heartache and disappointment, nor does it mean we'll become wealthy. It does mean that the Lord will watch over us and bless and protect us. "There is a satisfaction that comes into the heart of the man who is absolutely honest with the Lord, in contributing of his means to the building up of the Church of Christ, and into the heart of every true, full tithe payer" said President Heber J. Grant. "Each and every blessing that you and I enjoy comes from God. We are under obligations to Him for the very breath of life, and He gives us everything that we have. He asks us to show our appreciation and acknowledge to Him His goodness, by returning to the Church for its benefit and for the spreading of the gospel at home and abroad, one-tenth of that which we receive" (*Heber J. Grant,* 125–26).

*Keep all the commandments and covenants by
which ye are bound; and I will cause the heavens to
shake for your good, and Satan shall tremble and
Zion shall rejoice upon the hills and flourish.*

DOCTRINE & COVENANTS 35:24

The Lord has told those who are His disciples to
"lift up your hearts and be glad, your redemption
draweth nigh. Fear not, little flock, the kingdom is
yours until I come" (D&C 35:26–27). We have no
need to fear if we hold tight to the iron rod, keep the
commandments and our covenants, and follow the
Lord in righteousness. Heaven surely pours out blessings upon the faithful—blessings of peace, comfort,
and sweet assurance. And although Satan seeks to
disrupt the gospel plan and our own happiness and
salvation, his influence is as nothing when compared
with the Lord. Even when dark clouds threaten, we
can have confidence that those on the Lord's side are
on the winning team.

*I hope that each of us will long remember . . . what we
have felt. May it become an anchor in our lives, a guide by
which to live, a training time where we learned to shape our
actions toward others and our attitudes toward ourselves.*

GORDON B. HINCKLEY
ENSIGN, MAY 2000, 87

General conference was first held in the magnificent Conference Center in April 2000, where, in his closing remarks, President Gordon B. Hinckley said, "There is something wonderfully significant about all of this. It is a time of new beginnings. . . . I hope that each one of us will be a better husband or wife, kinder to one another, more thoughtful, more restrained in criticism, and more generous with compliments. I hope that as fathers and mothers we will strive more fully to rear our children 'in the nurture and admonition of the Lord' (Eph. 6:4), treating them with respect and love, giving encouragement at every opportunity and subduing our critical remarks. I hope that as sons and daughters we will be more respectful than we have been, that we will look to our parents with the knowledge that they love us, and that we will try to be more obedient in following their counsel" (*Ensign,* May 2000, 87).

*Consider . . . the blessed and happy state of those that keep
the commandments of God. For behold, they are blessed
in all things, both temporal and spiritual; and if they hold
out faithful to the end they are received into heaven.*

MOSIAH 2:41

In all times and in all places, those who keep the
Lord's commandments are blessed with the fulness
of heaven and earth (D&C 59:16–21). Unnumbered
blessings, both temporal and spiritual, come to those
who grasp the iron rod and follow the Lord's path of
righteousness. For example, we can claim the spiritually liberating promise of fasting, which will "loose the
bands of wickedness," undo our "heavy burdens," and
"break every yoke" (Isaiah 58:6). Those who keep the
Sabbath holy are promised they will become unspotted
from the world (D&C 59:9). Darkness will disperse,
the gates of hell shall not prevail, and heaven will shake
for the good of those who follow the prophets (D&C
21:4–6). And those who are sealed in holy temples and
who faithfully keep their covenants will receive God's
glory, which "shall be a fulness and a continuation of
the seeds forever and ever" (D&C 132:19). Blessed and
happy are those who keep the commandments.

That great morning of forgiveness may not come at once. Do not give up if at first you fail. Often the most difficult part of repentance is to forgive yourself. Discouragement is part of that test. Do not give up. That brilliant morning will come.

BOYD K. PACKER
ENSIGN, NOVEMBER 1995, 20

Relief from guilt and sin is available to those who access the powers of the Atonement. We can be healed and made whole if we are willing to humble ourselves, come unto the Lord with full purpose of heart, and confess our sins in sincere repentance. As we are forgiven and as we forgive ourselves, we wish to offer mercy and forgiveness to others. President Boyd K. Packer said, "The Lord provides ways to pay our debts to Him. In one sense we ourselves may participate in an atonement. When we are willing to restore to others that which we have not taken, or heal wounds that we did not inflict, or pay a debt that we did not incur, we are emulating His part in the Atonement" (*Ensign,* Nov. 1995, 20). We become Saviors on Mount Zion as we ourselves are forgiven and then we extend forgiveness to others.

*The priesthood, by definition, is God's authority given to man
to do the things that He would do if He were here. That means
we are not only His witnesses, we are His representatives.
Standing for truth and right is not solely a Sunday thing.*

M. RUSSELL BALLARD
ENSIGN, NOVEMBER 1997, 38

To the brethren of the Church, Elder M. Russell Ballard said: "Those who deliberately choose to violate God's commandments or ignore the standards of the Church, even when promising themselves and others that someday they will be strong enough to repent, are stepping onto a dangerously slippery slope upon which many have lost their spiritual footing. . . . These are difficult times in which we are living. In some respects, it is perhaps the most challenging age of all time. We want you young men to know that we are aware of that. But we are also aware that God has reserved some of His strongest spirit children for these perilous days. While God's laws and standards of right and wrong are under attack at every turn, we are a great army of priesthood holders who are prepared to make a valiant stand for truth and right. Brethren, let us stand, shoulder to shoulder, as bearers of the priesthood of God and as followers of Christ" (*Ensign,* Nov. 1997, 40).

To receive the Lord's comfort, we must exercise faith.
The questions Why me? Why our family? Why now?
are usually unanswerable questions. These questions
detract from our spirituality and can destroy our faith.

ROBERT D. HALES
ENSIGN, NOVEMBER 1998, 15

Who among us has not been buffeted by the challenges and trials of life? Often in the midst of heartache we think that others must surely live a worry-free life, that all is well with everyone but us. We may wonder what we've done to deserve it, what we could have done differently, what the past has wrought and the future will bring. Elder Robert D. Hales said: "I have come to understand how useless it is to dwell on the *whys, what ifs,* and *if onlys* for which there likely will be given no answers in mortality. . . . We need to spend our time and energy building our faith by turning to the Lord and asking for strength to overcome the pains and trials of this world and to endure to the end for greater understanding" (*Ensign,* Nov. 1998, 14–15). Faith and hope nurture wide-angle eternal vision and Spirit-enhanced depth perception to help us understand both the promises and purposes of life.

*Death, divorce, and indeed lack of opportunity to marry
have in many instances made it necessary for a woman to
stand alone. In reality, she need not stand alone, for a loving
Heavenly Father will be by her side to give direction to her life.*

THOMAS S. MONSON
ENSIGN, NOVEMBER 1997, 96

If we are single, it's easy to feel that somehow God is punishing us or forgetting us, that somehow life has passed us by. And while each of us carries responsibility for our life, no one controls all their circumstances and consequences. What we can control is our response to them. We can accept our present state and move forward with making the best life possible. We can become anxiously engaged in good causes, including our own development; we can get involved and serve others, thereby creating a sense of well-being and belonging; we can actively participate in the three dimensions of the mission of the Church: preaching the gospel, perfecting the Saints, and redeeming the dead. Above all, we can trust that a loving God neither slumbers nor sleeps as he watches over each one of his precious children (Psalm 121:3–4).

As you tend to lost sheep, as you nurture the
seedlings of faith in others, you will find yourself saying,
"Is it already the end of the day?" rather than
"Will this day ever end?"

MARY ELLEN SMOOT
ENSIGN, NOVEMBER 1997, 13

Pioneer women did not have time to wallow in discouragement. They were too busy working their way toward Zion," said Mary Ellen Smoot, former general president of the Relief Society. "I thank my Father in Heaven for all the pioneers of the past and present who have put aside the things of the world. As we emulate their simple faith and virtues, we will find peace" (*Ensign,* Nov. 1997, 13). Pioneers are not a thing of the past, they are living and breathing now in our day. Pioneers are found serving and blessing others, building and strengthening wards and communities, developing within them strong faith and deep commitments. Pioneers are those who daily strive to put aside the things of the world and choose the better part in their actions and attitudes (D&C 25:10).

APRIL

*Be faithful and diligent in keeping the
commandments of God, and I will
encircle thee in the arms of my love.*

DOCTRINE & COVENANTS 6:20

We need not become paralyzed with fear of Satan's power.
He can have no power over us unless we permit it.
He is really a coward, and if we stand firm, he will retreat.

JAMES E. FAUST
ENSIGN, SEPTEMBER 1995, 6

Satan is bound by the power of God, our personal righteousness, and our determination not to listen or give heed to him, to resist and reject him with heart, mind, and soul. The apostle James counseled: "Submit yourselves . . . to God. Resist the devil, and he will flee from you" (James 4:7). The apostle Paul said, "God is faithful, who will not suffer you to be tempted above that ye are able; but will with the temptation also make a way to escape, that ye may be able to bear it" (1 Corinthians 10:13). We can trust God's promise that we will be strengthened if we are built upon "the rock of our Redeemer, who is Christ, the Son of God , . . . that when the devil shall send forth his mighty winds, yea, his shafts in the whirlwind , . . . it shall have no power over you to drag you down to the gulf of misery and endless wo" (Helaman 5:12).

Wo unto the rich, who are rich as to the things of the
world. For because they are rich they despise the poor,
and they persecute the meek, and their hearts are upon
their treasures; wherefore, their treasure is their god. And
behold, their treasure shall perish with them also.

2 NEPHI 9:30

The love of money, not money itself, is the root
of all evil (1 Timothy 6:10). Indeed, it is impossible
for those who trust in their riches to enter into the
kingdom of heaven (JST, Mark 10:26). Those who
have hearts centered on money and worldly prosperity worship a false and deceitful god; they despise the
poor, they persecute and look down upon the meek,
and they will surely perish along with their riches.
The Lord taught in his Sermon on the Mount: "Lay
not up for yourselves treasures upon earth, where
moth and rust doth corrupt, and where thieves break
through and steal: but lay up for yourselves treasures
in heaven, where neither moth nor rust doth corrupt,
and where thieves do not break through nor steal: for
where your treasure is, there will your heart be also"
(Matthew 6:19–21). Our hearts must be centered on
the Lord and His gospel.

*Each one of us is commanded to both repent
and to call upon God continually throughout life.
That pattern allows each day to be an unspoiled page
in the book of life, a new, fresh opportunity.*

RICHARD G. SCOTT
ENSIGN, NOVEMBER 2000, 25

Repentance is a continual process in life. An angel commanded Adam to "repent and call upon God in the name of the Son forevermore" (Moses 5:8). The Prophet Joseph prayed at the dedication of the Kirtland Temple: "And when thy people transgress, any of them, they may speedily repent and return unto thee, and find favor in thy sight, and be restored to the blessings which thou hast ordained to be poured out upon those who shall reverence thee in thy house" (D&C 109:21; see also JST, 1 John 3:9). The Lord understands that we will continue to stumble and be less than perfect throughout life. Saints of God daily and continually seek forgiveness, repent for sins of omission and commission, and ask the Lord for help and strength in overcoming the temptations of life. As we repent, we begin each day anew and feel the enabling power and cleansing purity of the Atonement in our lives.

*As [God's] children there is no attribute we ascribe to
Him that we do not possess, though they may be dormant
or in embryo. The mission of the Gospel is to develop
these powers and make us like our Heavenly Parent.*

GEORGE Q. CANNON
GOSPEL TRUTH, 1974, 3

Each of us has always existed in some form, so it
is more accurate to refer to our pre-earth life as pre-
mortality, not preexistence. The Lord revealed, "Man
was also in the beginning with God. Intelligence, or
the light of truth, was not created or made, neither indeed can be" (D&C 93:29). We are the spirit children
of heavenly parents, thereby inheriting the seeds of
godhood, and we were taught and nurtured by these
parents in the heavens. As such, we have something
of divinity, of godliness, within us. A veil of forgetfulness has been drawn over our minds, but with the
help of scriptures and words of the prophets, prayer,
personal revelation, and patriarchal blessings, we
gradually come to an awareness and understanding of
our true nature, potential, and destiny. Grasping this
reality, we can exercise the faith to move forward and
overcome the obstacles standing in our way of fulfill-
ing our foreordained destiny.

Resist evil, and there is no danger; God, men, and angels will not condemn those that resist everything that is evil, and devils cannot; as well might the devil seek to dethrone Jehovah, as overthrow an innocent soul that resists everything which is evil.

JOSEPH SMITH
JOSEPH SMITH, 214

To face the trials and temptations ahead, we must turn to the Lord, resist evil, and be fully engaged in the gospel. Casual standards and intermittent obedience do not prepare or strengthen our soul for the challenges and enticements ahead. The world is too appealing to the half-hearted who have one foot in Zion and the other in Babylon. What is needed is intentional gospel living and complete trust in and devotion to the Lord. The faithful need not worry; the consecrated need not fret. The Lord will bless and strengthen us as we strive to resist evil. Yes, we will still have our sorrows and difficulties, but we will be fortified as we reject the devil and that which is evil and turn our hearts, minds, and souls to the Lord.

We have basic cornerstones on which this great latter-day
church has been established by the Lord and built, "fitly framed
together" [Eph. 2: 21]. They are absolutely fundamental to
this work, the very foundation, anchors on which it stands.

GORDON B. HINCKLEY
ENSIGN, NOVEMBER 1984, 51

President Gordon B. Hinckley spoke of the unshakable cornerstones that anchor the Church, as well as our individual testimonies: "(1) the reality and the divinity of the Lord Jesus Christ as the Son of God; (2) the sublime vision given the Prophet Joseph Smith of the Father and the Son, ushering in the dispensation of the fulness of times; (3) the Book of Mormon as the word of God speaking in declaration of the divinity of the Savior; and (4) the priesthood of God divinely conferred to be exercised in righteousness for the blessing of our Father's children. Each of these cornerstones is related to the other, each connected by a foundation of Apostles and prophets, all tied to the chief cornerstone, Jesus Christ. On this has been established his Church. . . . It is the conservator of eternal truth and the teacher of the divine will. It is the true and living Church of the Master" (*Ensign*, Nov. 1984, 53).

*Search your own experience. You have already
received revelations, and you can receive more revelations because
communication from God to men and women is a reality.*

DALLIN H. OAKS
NEW ERA, SEPTEMBER 2004, 4–5

The Lord sheds light, whispers truth, and extends comfort to those who strive for righteousness and seek His guidance. Very often we neglect to see the hand of God in our lives—the constant promptings, the regular direction, the ever-present influence of the Lord's spirit in our daily walk and talk. Consider, with an eye of faith, your own experience: look for the Lord's guiding hand past and present, ponder the sweet assurance and provident direction you have received. The Lord will not leave His faithful saints without comfort or guidance, without promptings and revelations. The humble and meek who have entered a covenant with Christ are entitled to the grand privilege of the manifestations of the Spirit in their lives.

Your personal virtue will not only enable you to have the constant companionship of the Holy Ghost, but it will also enable you to make the decisions that will help you be worthy to enter the temple and there make and keep sacred covenants.

ELAINE S. DALTON
ENSIGN, MAY 2009, 122

Sister Elaine Dalton, general president of the Young Women, is also the mother of five sons and one daughter. Like all parents, she has learned from her children some great secrets: "Tonight my sons have given me permission to reveal one of those secrets to you. It is this: virtuous young men are attracted to virtuous young women. Before young men go on their missions, if you asked them the number one quality they were looking for in a young woman, they might mention a quality that is based on worldly standards, like looks. But after two years in the mission field, these same young men return home, and they have changed—their focus has changed—and the number one quality they are looking for in an eternal companion changed without your even knowing it! A virtuous returned missionary is attracted to a virtuous young woman—one who has a testimony of Jesus Christ and is committed to a life of purity" (*Ensign,* May 2009, 120).

And now, because of their steadfastness when they do believe
in that thing which they do believe, for because of their firmness
when they are once enlightened, behold, the Lord shall bless
them and prolong their days, notwithstanding their iniquity.

HELAMAN 15:10

The power of the word of God changes lives. As we come to the knowledge of truth we will want to enter and keep all our sacred covenants, we will be led to desire righteousness and become changed by the power of faith and repentance. Those who remain firm and steadfast in the faith experience a change of heart—a humble and meek heart that continues to learn, grow, soften, and change all across the life course. Faith and repentance are actions, not merely attitudes; they require sincere desire and conviction as well as diligent effort and energy. In a synergistic, ever-expanding way, faith and repentance lead to a change of heart, and a sincere change of heart increases our desire to continue to exercise faith and repent.

*We are God's spirit children. Therefore, we have a
vast capacity for love—it is part of our spiritual
heritage. What and how we love not only defines us
as individuals; it also defines us as a church.*

DIETER F. UCHTDORF
ENSIGN, NOVEMBER 2009, 22

Love is the essence of what it means to be a follower
of Jesus Christ. "Because love is the great commandment, it ought to be at the *center* of all and everything
we do in our own family, in our Church callings, and
in our livelihood," said President Dieter F. Uchtdorf.
"Love is the healing balm that repairs rifts in personal and family relationships. It is the bond that
unites families, communities, and nations. Love is the
power that initiates friendship, tolerance, civility, and
respect. It is the source that overcomes divisiveness
and hate. . . . Love should be our walk and our talk"
(*Ensign,* Nov. 2009, 21). Love gives meaning to life. It
keeps us going when we feel like giving up; it can get
us up in the morning and settle us into sweet dreams
when we sleep. Our efforts to nurture love would fail
were it not for infusions of divine love along the way.
Ultimately, all love comes from God.

There is no promise of safety and no promise of security except for those who love the Lord and who are seeking to do all that he commands.

BRUCE R. MCCONKIE
ENSIGN, MAY 1979, 93

No true or long-term safety or security exists outside of the Lord. We can surround ourselves with possessions, we can busy ourselves with busyness, we can seek the company of the agnostic and apathetic, and we can refuse to see and live truthfully in the hope that all will be right in the end. But only those who love the Lord and seek righteousness will have peace and safekeeping in the refuge of Zion. The Lord revealed, "Vengeance cometh speedily upon the ungodly as the whirlwind; and who shall escape it? . . . Zion shall escape if she observe to do all things whatsoever I have commanded her" (D&C 97:22, 25). Zion will always be a place of peace, a sanctuary from the storms of wickedness that rage around us in the world.

APRIL 12

Let us strive for peace and harmony in the home.
If we cannot keep quarreling, bickering, and selfishness out of our
home, how can we even hope to banish these evils from society?

DAVID O. MCKAY
GOSPEL IDEALS, 169

To hope for a measure of peace and happiness in the world, we must first strive for peace and happiness in our hearts and homes. We've all heard "home is where the heart is," "there's no place like home," and "home sweet home"—simple sayings that ring with truth and bear repeating. The hallmark of a happy home is not its size or location, but what goes on *inside* its walls. Small homes can be filled to overflowing with joy and contentment, and homes on "the other side of the tracks" can be grounded in goodness and decency. No matter the landscape, the path to home is always paved with love and kindness. And no matter how far we travel, we always come back—even if only in our memories—to such happy homes. Our homes, though sometimes noisy and chaotic, can be a refuge of serenity and a haven of safety from the wickedness and worries of the world.

Why are you here on planet earth? One of the most important reasons is to receive a mortal body. Another is to be tested . . . to determine what you will do with life's challenging opportunities. Those opportunities require you to make choices.

RUSSELL M. NELSON
ENSIGN, NOVEMBER 1990, 74

We are here to gain experience, to learn and grow and be tested in this school of mortality. We have been given soul freedom, the ability to choose and act for ourselves. When we use our agency to make righteous choices, we move along the pathway toward eternal life and more fully develop the attributes of godliness. But we are not left alone here to figure things out by ourselves. Elder Russell M. Nelson said, "Agency is a divine gift to you. You are free to choose what you will be and what you will do. And you are not without help. Counsel with your parents is a privilege at any age. Prayer provides communication with your Heavenly Father and invites the promptings of personal revelation. And in certain circumstances, consultation with professional advisers and with your local leaders in the Church may be highly advisable, especially when very difficult decisions must be made" (*Ensign,* Nov. 1990, 74).

There is a power in the [Book of Mormon]
which will begin to flow into your lives the moment
you begin a serious study of the book.

EZRA TAFT BENSON
ENSIGN, JANUARY 1992, 7

President Ezra Taft Benson outlined some of the promises available to those who undertake a sincere study of the Book of Mormon: "You will find greater power to resist temptation. You will find the power to avoid deception. You will find the power to stay on the strait and narrow path. The scriptures are called 'the words of life' (D&C 84:85), and nowhere is that more true than it is of the Book of Mormon. When you begin to hunger and thirst after those words, you will find life in greater and greater abundance. I implore you with all my heart that you consider with great solemnity the importance of the Book of Mormon to you personally and to the Church collectively. Let us not remain under condemnation, with its scourge and judgment, by treating lightly this great and marvelous gift the Lord has given to us. (See D&C 84:54–58.) Rather, let us win the promises associated with treasuring it up in our hearts" (*Ensign,* Jan. 1992, 7).

Patient endurance permits us to cling to our faith in the Lord and our faith in His timing when we are being tossed about by the surf of circumstance. Even when a seeming undertow grasps us, somehow, in the tumbling, we are being carried forward.

NEAL A. MAXWELL
ENSIGN, MAY 1990, 34

Without patient and meek endurance we will learn less, see less, feel less, and hear less," said Elder Neal A. Maxwell. "We who are egocentric and impatient shut down so much of our receiving capacity. . . . How could there be refining fires without enduring some heat? Or greater patience without enduring some instructive waiting? Or more empathy without bearing one another's burdens—not only that others' burdens may be lightened, but that we may be enlightened through greater empathy? How can there be later magnification without enduring some present deprivation? The enlarging of the soul requires not only some remodeling, but some excavating. Hypocrisy, guile, and other imbedded traits do not go gladly or easily, but if we "endure it well" (D&C 121:8), we will not grow testy while being tested. . . . We find that sorrow can actually enlarge the mind and heart in order to 'give place,' expanded space for later joy" (*Ensign*, May 1990, 34).

When we keep the commandments, we are clean;
and when we are clean in our thoughts, our words, and our
actions, we can hear the whisperings of the Holy Ghost.

ARDETH G. KAPP
ENSIGN, NOVEMBER 1990, 94

Every right choice builds within us greater spirituality and strengthens our desire to stay strong in the faith. Ardeth Kapp, former general president of the Young Women said, "Standards of the Church have been given to us to protect us and to help us grow spiritually. When the pioneers ended a day's journey, each night they checked their wagons for any needed repairs. They united in prayer for continued guidance and protection and took a reading of both distance and direction to see how far they had traveled and make sure they were on the right trail. We would do well to follow the same pattern today. A good measurement to ask concerning every important decision is whether or not this decision will move you toward or away from making and keeping sacred covenants and preparing for the ordinances of the temple" (*Ensign,* Nov. 1990, 95). Step by step, little by little, we can choose to move closer and closer to God and His kingdom.

*Security is not born of inexhaustible
wealth but of unquenchable faith.*

SPENCER W. KIMBALL
TEACHINGS OF SPENCER W. KIMBALL, 72–73

In these troubling times and disquieting days, we wonder in what we can trust, in whom we can rely. Celebrities come and go and so often disappoint; those with power, prestige, and prominence so often let us down. If we depend on the world and its wealth, if we count on fame and fortune, we will be forever disappointed and always dissatisfied. Peace and security and contentment are to be found in righteous living, in inside-out congruence and integrity, in honoring covenants and commitments, in exercising faith in the Lord Jesus Christ, and in trusting Heavenly Father's plan of happiness. Faith that burns like a fire unquenchable is born of humbly relying on the merits and mercy of the Savior, sincerely striving to do His will, and gratefully acknowledging the countless blessings and bounties of life that surround us. Faith is the great principle of power and action that gives us a sense of protection and safety in an evil and darkening world.

*That every man may act in doctrine and principle
pertaining to futurity, according to the moral agency
which I have given unto him, that every man may be
accountable for his own sins in the day of judgment.*

DOCTRINE & COVENANTS 101:78

To be accountable signifies that we can be counted
on in the discharge of our stewardship responsibilities. It also means that as stewards we are answer-
able and responsible for our actions (D&C 104:12–
13; 42:32). We are accountable for how we use our
God-given blessing of agency. Elder Quentin L. Cook
said, "We try to do what is right because we love and
want to please our Father in Heaven, not because
someone is forcing us to obey. The War in Heaven
was fought after Satan said that he would force everyone to obey his ideas. That was rejected. As a result,
we have our moral agency and the freedom to choose
our course in this life. But we also are accountable for
that agency. The Lord has said we will be 'accountable
for [our] own sins in the day of judgment'" [D&C
101:78]" (*Ensign,* Nov. 2009, 91). The principles of
agency, accountability, and stewardship are insepa-
rable; they are central to our doctrine.

For all who continue to have faith in the Lord Jesus Christ, who, regardless of circumstances, continue to be positive and obedient, . . . the times that follow will be the best of times.

H. DAVID BURTON
CHURCH NEWS, DECEMBER 5, 2009, 5

We live in a time of uncertainty and fear, a time when hearts are weary and souls are being tested like never before. It's not easy to stay positive and hopeful in an ever-darkening, ever-declining world filled with alluring temptations and rampant wickedness. There is good news to be found; there is a way to make these "the best of times." We need to keep our eyes and our hearts centered on the Savior of the world, on the sweet peace and steady reassurance the gospel can bring to our lives. Bishop H. David Burton said, "We need to 'remember, remember' during times that test our souls to enjoy and keep focused on our Father in Heaven's plan for eternal happiness, while at the same time carefully navigating through the best of times" (*Church News,* Dec. 5, 2009, 5). With faith in the Lord and in the plan we can safely chart our course to eternal life.

The object of prayer is not to change the will of God,
but to secure for ourselves and for others blessings
that God is already willing to grant, but that are
made conditional on our asking for them.

LDS BIBLE DICTIONARY, 753

In the LDS Bible Dictionary, we learn: "As soon as we learn the true relationship in which we stand toward God (namely, God is our Father, and we are his children), then at once prayer becomes natural and instinctive on our part (Matt. 7:7–11). Many of the so-called difficulties about prayer arise from forgetting this relationship. Prayer is the act by which the will of the Father and the will of the child are brought into correspondence with each other" (752–53). We build a relationship and receive blessings as we make efforts to communicate with our Father through prayer. If, however, we disconnect the blessing from the required effort, the needed work, we may feel not only entitled but also ultimately ungrateful for the blessings we receive. God wants us to put forth effort, to exert ourselves in some meaningful way to receive blessings and signify our desire to build a relationship with him.

*It is contrary to the law of God for the heavens
to be opened and messengers to come to do anything
for man that man can do for himself.*

JOSEPH FIELDING SMITH
DOCTRINES OF SALVATION, 1:196

It has been said that we should work as if everything
depended upon us and pray as if everything depended
upon God. Our own worthy efforts coupled with our
Heavenly Father's ready assistance will work miracles.
A student cannot expect help from the Lord on an
exam unless the price has been paid to study; and we
cannot expect heaven's help if we are not willing to
do our part. When we prepare and work, when we
pay the price to learn and achieve, when we recognize
that our efforts are minuscule compared to the merits
and mercy of the Lord and His redeeming grace, we
come to understand more fully the great plan of happiness. We also come to understand that there is so
much we simply cannot do for ourselves: we cannot
save ourselves; we cannot work our way into the highest heaven. We are to come to the Lord with all our
heart and work out our salvation with fear and trembling (Mormon 9:27; Philippians 2:12).

*If we are to put civility back into civilization,
the process must begin in the home with parents, while
children are very young. It will not happen otherwise.*

GORDON B. HINCKLEY
ENSIGN, SEPTEMBER 1996, 7

To realize the promise of peace in the heart and happiness in the home we must do all we can to live the gospel, to be people of honesty and integrity, "to do justly, and to love mercy, and to walk humbly with thy God" (Micah 6:8). Those who are untruthful, who steal, cheat, and lie, are living a duplicitous life well below their celestial potential and eternal purposes. For some, mendacity is a habit that must be broken, an addiction that must be stopped with sincere repentance and humility. Honesty, integrity, and civility change families and nations—but it all begins at home, with parents who love their children enough to do the hard work of righteous parenting. Parents are charged with the divine commission to bring up their children in light and truth (D&C 93:40); they are held accountable for how they live and teach truth.

*And see that all these things are done in wisdom
and order; for it is not requisite that a man
should run faster than he has strength.*

Mosiah 4:27

Mormonism has no ascetics, no hermits, no monasteries. We do not strive to so distance ourselves from the world that we become fanatic, overzealous, hyperobedient, and truer than true. So how can we stay steadfast and immovable and still keep balance and perspective in this time of such great temptation, wickedness, and uncertainty? We are to focus on the Lawgiver, and not solely the law: follow the Lord in humility and faith, keep ourselves in the mainstream of the Church, sustain the living apostles and prophets, reach out in charity and kindness to all peoples, and love God with our whole might, mind, and strength. As we are true to our covenants and strive to remain unspotted from the world, our desires become less self-centered and our sacrifices become easier. When we forget our own selfish concerns and dedicate ourselves to good causes, we will find both an inner power and a sweet assurance that are born of the Spirit.

*Testimony isn't something that you have today and you keep
always. . . . The testimony that we recapture day by day is
the thing that saves us from the pitfalls of the adversary.*

HAROLD B. LEE
HAROLD B. LEE, 43

We live in perilous, tumultuous, and worrisome
times. We question, as did Pilate two millennia ago,
"What is truth?" (John 18:38), and what are the
things that can be counted on to stand the test of
time? Where can we turn for peace, for hope and reassurance, in this troubling time? This we know: God
lives and loves his children, the gospel is true, faith
in the Lord Jesus Christ is essential, repentance is
vital, the Atonement is real, Joseph Smith and each
of his successors are authentic prophets who spoke
the truth, the Book of Mormon is the word of God,
and priesthood power has been restored to the earth.
These truths are the foundation of our testimony, the
cornerstone of our faith. We need to stay close to the
Lord every day and thereby strengthen our testimonies and faith if we are to survive the difficulties and
challenges ahead.

*Be faithful and diligent in keeping
the commandments of God, and I will
encircle thee in the arms of my love.*

DOCTRINE & COVENANTS 6:20

God loves all of His children in a perfect, constant, and most miraculous way. Because of our sins, we are separated from our Father, but through the mediation and Atonement of Jesus Christ we are welcomed, received, reconciled, and embraced. Lehi rejoiced that "the Lord hath redeemed my soul from hell; I have beheld his glory, and I am encircled about eternally in the arms of his love" (2 Nephi 1:15). Jesus is our Redeemer, our Savior. To redeem is to purchase, to buy back, to reclaim. To save is to keep, to salvage, to satisfy. Redemption and salvation are miracles. We are redeemed from our sins through the miracle of forgiveness and saved from death and hell through the miracle of the Resurrection. As we come to deeply understand *who* and *whose* we really are and hold fast to the iron rod—we will feel encircled in the love of God.

*For God so loved the world, that he gave his
only begotten Son, that whosoever believeth in him
should not perish, but have everlasting life.*

JOHN 3:16

Our Heavenly Father loves us so much that He gave His only begotten Son, our Savior and Redeemer, as a propitiation—atoning sacrifice—for sin (1 John 4:10). Jesus Christ offered His life willingly and voluntarily for the redemption of mankind. Elder James E. Talmage said of the Savior, "The motive inspiring and sustaining Him through all the scenes of His mission, from the time of His primeval ordination to the moment of victorious consummation on the cross, was twofold; first, the desire to do His Father's will in accomplishing the redemption of mankind; second, His love for humanity, of whose welfare and destiny He had assumed charge" (*Articles of Faith,* 72). Our Heavenly Father loves His children. His greatest gift—the gift of salvation or eternal life (D&C 6:13; 14:7)—has been made available through God's greatest offering—His Beloved Son.

The simple secret is this:
put your trust in the Lord, do your best,
then leave the rest to Him.

JOSEPH B. WIRTHLIN
ENSIGN, NOVEMBER 2008, 28

After leaving his homeland and crossing the great waters to an unknown land, and despite the heartbreaking betrayal, persecution, and apostasy of family and loved ones, Nephi remained ever steadfast in his faith. He knew that his strength came from the Lord: "O Lord, I have trusted in thee, and I will trust in thee forever. I will not put my trust in the arm of flesh; for I know that cursed is he that putteth his trust in the arm of flesh" (2 Nephi 4:34). With courage and devotion, Nephi moved forward with his life, created a nation of believers, and looked ahead to the coming day of the Lord. We, as well, despite the challenges and vicissitudes of life, can move forward with our lives, do our best, and put our trust in the Lord. His ways are higher than our ways, His thoughts and purposes higher than ours (Isaiah 55:8–9).

No matter how strong your faith is,
God will not always reward you immediately
according to your desires. Rather He will respond
with what in His eternal plan is best for you.

RICHARD G. SCOTT
ENSIGN, JANUARY 2007, 12

Our faith, like our character, is woven over time from threads of doctrine, principle, correct choices, and obedience. Elder Richard G. Scott said, "Your exercise of faith will forge strength of character available to you in times of critical need. Such character is not developed in moments of great challenge or temptation. That is when it is used. The bedrock of character is integrity. Worthy character will strengthen your capacity to recognize the direction of the Spirit and be obedient to it. It is more important than what you own, what you have learned, or what goals you have accomplished. Your consistent exercise of faith builds strong character. In turn, fortified character expands your ability to exercise faith, thereby enhancing your capacity and confidence in conquering the trials of life. And this strengthening cycle continues. The more your character is fortified, the more enabled you are to exercise the power of faith" (*Ensign,* Jan. 2007, 12).

If every husband and every wife would constantly do whatever might be possible to ensure the comfort and happiness of his or her companion, there would be very little, if any, divorce. . . . Rather, love and concern would replace abuse and meanness.

GORDON B. HINCKLEY
ENSIGN, NOVEMBER 2004, 84

President Gordon B. Hinckley, who was married on this date in 1937, said, "After dealing with hundreds of divorce situations through the years, I am satisfied that the application of a single practice would do more than all else to solve this grievous problem" (*Ensign,* Nov. 2004, 84). That practice is to do whatever might be possible to ensure the comfort, well-being, and happiness of his or her marriage companion. To focus on the happiness of our spouse is both an attitude and an action; it is a habit of the heart and behavior. The root cause for most marital discord is selfishness and pride; the cure, according to President Hinckley, "for most marital troubles does not lie in divorce. It lies in repentance and forgiveness, in expressions of kindness and concern. It is to be found in application of the Golden Rule" (*Ensign,* Nov. 2004, 84). President and Sister Hinckley were outstanding examples of happiness in marriage.

The time is soon coming, when no man
will have any peace but in Zion.

JOSEPH SMITH
TEACHINGS OF THE PROPHET JOSEPH SMITH, 161

The world seems to ever be darkening in wickedness. As such, we may sometimes be filled with fear and uncertainty, and feel surrounded by sin and evil. Where can we turn for peace and protection? Isaiah prophesied, "Upon all the glory of Zion shall be a defence. And there shall be . . . a place of refuge, and a covert from storm and from rain" (2 Nephi 14:5–6). A *defence* is a bulwark against the invading armies of sin and iniquity; a *place of refuge* is a sanctuary of safety and security from the enemies of righteousness; a *covert* is a shelter from the storms and whirlwinds of the adversary. Zion is the safe haven for the righteous, the place where the pure in heart dwell (D&C 97:21). We can trust that the Lord reigns in Zion; He is our rock and sure foundation (Helaman 5:12).

MAY

*There is a law, irrevocably decreed in heaven
before the foundations of this world, upon which
all blessings are predicated—And when we
obtain any blessing from God, it is by obedience
to that law upon which it is predicated.*

D&C 130:20–21

*I promise you that as you consistently and fervently pray
as a family, and as each member takes his or her turn
and sincerely prays for others, impressions will come as
to what you individually should do to help others.*

JOHN H. GROBERG
ENSIGN, MAY 1982, 50

We have been counseled to have regular family prayers. "Satan will do everything he can to keep us from family prayer, or at least to see that our prayers are only intermittent and mechanical and without sincerity," said Elder John H. Groberg. "If Satan can get us thinking that our children are too young or too old, or if he can get us angry with one another or pre-occupied with TV programs or over-crowded sched-ules or caught up in some other aspect of the press of modern life so that we do not have family prayer, he has effectively won on that point—even though many of the other things we do may be good in and of themselves. Satan doesn't care how he stops us—just so he stops us. Ask yourself: How many times did you have family prayer this last week? Who is winning in your home? What's the score? Don't let the evil one win" (*Ensign,* May 1982, 50).

As we search, pray, and believe, we will recognize miracles in our lives and become miracle workers in the lives of others. We will be persuaded of His promise that all things shall work together for our good.

SUSAN W. TANNER
ENSIGN, MAY 2004, 107

The Lord gave us this promise: "Search diligently, pray always, and be believing, and all things shall work together for your good, if ye walk uprightly and remember the covenant" (D&C 90:24). The promise that things shall work together for our good is repeated many times in the scriptures, particularly to those who are suffering through trials—and to some degree that's every one of us. We can trust the Lord. As we diligently search for truth, as we pray continually and seek the Lord's help, and as we have the courage to exercise faith and hope, we will find the peace that passeth understanding (Philippians 4:7), and we will bless others in the process. As part of our covenant with Christ, we are to be instruments in the Lord's hands. We can be the miracle workers and earthly angels who play supporting roles in the blessing and lifting of others. Those promises will surely be fulfilled for those who sincerely search, pray, and believe.

The Book of Mormon is another testament of
Jesus Christ. . . . It has the power to change lives.
It has the power to convert. If you read it with an open
heart, you will know that it is the word of God.

HENRY B. EYRING
ENSIGN, JULY 2005, 24

In the Book of Mormon we learn of Christ, feel the spirit of the Lord, understand gospel principles, recognize that we must repent, and we reaffirm the prophetic mission of Joseph Smith. Within its pages we will find guidance, answers, and peace. President Henry B. Eyring said, "The scriptures were one of the ways God spoke to me—even when I was a child—about my needs, my situation, and my life. They still are. Since our needs change over a lifetime, God has different things to tell us at different times. Sometimes I go to the scriptures for doctrine. Sometimes I go to the scriptures for instruction. I go with a question, and the question usually is 'What would God have me do?' or 'What would He have me feel?' Invariably I find new ideas, thoughts I have never had before, and I receive inspiration and instruction and answers to my questions" (*Ensign,* Jul. 2005, 24).

*With all its troubles life offers us the tremendous
privilege to grow in knowledge and wisdom, faith and
works, preparing to return and share God's glory.*

SPENCER W. KIMBALL
SPENCER W. KIMBALL, 20–21

President Spencer W. Kimball taught that the Lord
has planned our destiny and so we must accept and
magnify each day: "Sometime we'll understand fully,
and when we see back from the vantage point of the
future, we shall be satisfied with many of the happen-
ings of this life that are so difficult for us to comprehend. . . . We knew before we were born that we were
coming to the earth for bodies and experience and
that we would have joys and sorrows, ease and pain,
comforts and hardships, health and sickness, suc-
cesses and disappointments, and we knew also that
after a period of life we would die. We accepted all
these eventualities with a glad heart, eager to accept
both the favorable and unfavorable. . . . We were willing to take life as it came and as we might organize
and control it, and this without murmur, complaint,
or unreasonable demands" (*Teachings of Spencer W.
Kimball*, 37).

And now, O man, remember,
and perish not.

MOSIAH 4:30

The word *remember* is used 352 times in the scriptures. When its variants are counted, that number jumps to more than 500. *Remember* is found in each of the standard works and is surely one of the most important words in the scriptures and in the dictionary. *Remember* is often used in connection with covenants between God and man. In the sacrament prayers, *remember* is used to commemorate the physical body and blood of the Savior. And we are also commanded, among other things, to "always remember Him." If we strive to sincerely remember and think about Jesus, His Atonement and Resurrection, His gospel and abiding love, and we keep our covenants, then we are promised that we will have His spirit to be us (D&C 20: 77, 79). The weekly Sabbath and sacrament, the ordinances and principles of the gospel, are all designed to help us remember the Savior.

*Set your goals—without goals you can't measure your
progress. But don't become frustrated if the victories
don't come quickly or easily. Remind yourself that
striving can be more important than arriving.*

MARVIN J. ASHTON
ENSIGN, FEBRUARY 1993, 64

Not much would be accomplished in life without
worthy goals, desires, aspirations, and aims. Our goals
give us a road map, a direction, and focus; they moti-
vate and inspire our best efforts; they move us forward
on the pathway of life. Of course, it helps to ponder
goals seriously and write them down, to set time-
frames and deadlines, and sometimes share them with
others who can mentor and provide support. But the
most worthwhile and meaningful goals are those not
about *getting* but about *becoming*. A *getting* goal is something you want to obtain, possess, or attain—which
may lead to discouragement and disappointment; *getting* goals may create in us a devil's dissonance of envy
and frustration. A *becoming* goal concerns the person
you want to become and the virtues and attributes of
godliness you desire to expand in your life. These goals
can generate in us divine discontent that moves us forward with a sense of patience, peace, and contentment.

I wonder what will happen to you in the next 10 years. Where will you be? What will you be doing? That will depend on the choices you make, some of which may seem unimportant at the time but which will have tremendous consequences.

GORDON B. HINCKLEY
ENSIGN, MAY 2004, 112–13

The choices we make expand or limit our opportunities. We can use our agency to choose to obey, or we can use our agency to choose to disobey. In every case, we receive blessings and consequences, rewards and punishments based on the choices we make. This eternal truth is given: "There is a law, irrevocably decreed in heaven before the foundations of this world, upon which all blessings are predicated. And when we obtain any blessing from God, it is by obedience to that law upon which it is predicated" (D&C 130:20–21). God will not force us to be righteous and make good choices, and the devil cannot compel us to choose evil—we are free to choose (Helaman 14:30–31). Remember, that which produces a sense of joy and peace and sweet assurance comes of God, and that which confuses and darkens comes of the devil (Moroni 7:12–17). Our future, here and hereafter, depends on the choices we make.

We must be better than we have ever been before.
As we succeed, we have the sure promise
of the Lord that he will prosper us in every
way necessary for our well-being.

DEAN L. LARSEN
ENSIGN, NOVEMBER 1992, 42

Since the beginning of time, people have received promised blessings of the Lord only to soon forget the divine source of those promises. Moses said to ancient Israel: "Beware that thou forget not the Lord thy God, in not keeping his commandments, and his judgments, and his statutes, . . . lest when thou hast eaten and art full, and hast built goodly houses, and dwelt therein; and when thy herds and thy flocks multiply, and thy silver and thy gold is multiplied, and all that thou hast is multiplied; then thine heart be lifted up, and thou forget the Lord thy God" (Deuteronomy 8:11–14). What a tragedy when we forget the God who suspended this beautiful planet in the heavens and placed us upon it, who continues to watch over us as our loving Father. Two things offend God: disobedience and ingratitude (D&C 59:21)—forgetting Him manifests both. We must not forget God and His promises.

There are two influences in the world. The one is the
influence of our Heavenly Father and the other is the
influence of Satan. We can [choose] which territory we want
to live in, that of our Heavenly Father or that of Satan.

GEORGE ALBERT SMITH
CONFERENCE REPORT, OCTOBER 1949, 5

President George Albert Smith, quoting his grandfather George A. Smith, said: "'There is a line of demarcation, well defined. On one side of the line is the Lord's territory. On the other side of the line is the devil's territory. . . . If you will stay on the Lord's side of the line, you are perfectly safe, because the adversary of all righteousness can not cross that line.' What does that mean? It means to me that those who are living righteous lives, keeping all of the commandments of our Heavenly Father are perfectly safe, but not those who trifle with his advice and counsel" (Conference Report, Oct. 1949, 6). Mormon, an ancient prophet, taught a similar principle: whatsoever persuades us to do evil and believe not in Christ is of the devil, and whatsoever persuades us to do good and believe in Christ is of God (Moroni 7:16–17). Let us choose to live on the Lord's side of the line.

No one of us is less treasured or cherished of God than another.
I testify that He loves each of us—insecurities, anxieties,
self-image, and all. . . . He cheers on every runner, calling
out that the race is against sin, not against each other.

JEFFREY R. HOLLAND
ENSIGN, MAY 2002, 64

We are commanded to avoid covetousness, envy, jealousy, and greed. We are to only "covet earnestly the best gifts" (I Corinthians 12:31)—gifts that are given to us to bless and lift another. Elder Jeffrey R. Holland used the parable of the prodigal son to teach us: "Most 'thou shalt not' commandments are meant to keep us from hurting others, but I am convinced the commandment not to covet is meant to keep us from hurting ourselves. How can we overcome such a tendency so common in almost everyone? For one thing, we can do as these two sons did and start making our way back to the Father. We should do so with as much haste and humility as we can summon. Along the way we can count our many blessings and we can applaud the accomplishments of others. Best of all, we can serve others, the finest exercise for the heart ever prescribed" (*Ensign,* May 2002, 64).

*For he will fulfil all his promises
which he shall make unto you,
for he has fulfilled his promises which
he has made unto our fathers.*

Alma 37:17

We can trust, rely on, and count on the Lord's promises. Unlike so many others who disappoint and let us down, we can have perfect confidence in the Lord and His word. He cannot, will not, does not lie. Eternal law binds Him when we do what He says; but when we disobey, ignore, or reject Him we have no such promise (D&C 82:10). He is perfectly trustworthy, honest, and as reliable as the rising sun in the morning; He is dependable, unswerving, and as constant as the setting sun in the evening. The commandments and covenants of the Lord are everlasting unto all generations (Genesis 17:7). Indeed, the promises of the Lord are made to our fathers and to us—through all generations of time.

*Choose good friends. Friends help to determine
your future. You will tend to be like them and to be found
where they choose to go. Remember, the path we follow
in this life leads to the path we follow in the next.*

THOMAS S. MONSON
ENSIGN, MAY 1998, 47

All along our life's course, we can choose to associate with those who build and bless others, or we can choose to associate with the damaging or the apathetic. Especially for adolescents, friends are a vital part of constructive development: they can help us to stay faithful and strong, or they can lead us in a negative, harmful direction. President Thomas S. Monson said, "In a survey made in selected wards and stakes of the Church, we learned a most significant fact: Those persons whose friends married in the temple usually married in the temple, while those persons whose friends did not marry in the temple usually did not marry in the temple. This same fact pertained also to full-time missionary service. The influence of one's friends appeared to be a highly dominant factor—even equal to parental urging, classroom instruction, or proximity to a temple. The friends you choose will either help or hinder your success" (*Ensign,* May 1998, 47).

There is no limit to what a woman with a mother heart can accomplish. Righteous women have changed the course of history and will continue to do so, and their influence will spread and grow exponentially throughout the eternities.

JULIE B. BECK
ENSIGN, MAY 2004, 77

Sister Julie B. Beck spoke of meeting a group of young mothers: "They were bright and had obtained advanced degrees from respected universities. Now they were devoting their considerable gifts to . . . teaching two-year-olds to be kind to one another. They were soothing babies, kissing bruised knees, and wiping tears. I asked one of those mothers how . . . she could transfer her talents so cheerfully into the role of motherhood. She replied, 'I know who I am, and I know what I am supposed to do. The rest just follows.' That young mother will build faith and character in the next generation one family prayer at a time, one scripture study session, one book read aloud, one song, one family meal after another. . . . She knows that the influence of righteous, conscientious, persistent, daily mothering is far more lasting, far more powerful, far more influential than any earthly position or institution invented by man" (*Ensign,* May 2004, 76–77).

*The Lord has promised that he shall have power
over his saints and shall reign in their midst. It takes
real courage and purpose to live a saintly life.*

DELBERT L. STAPLEY
ENSIGN, DECEMBER 1971, 95

Satan and his followers seek to destroy each one of us, but we have reason to rejoice if we trust and follow the Lord. "The true gospel of Christ is the hope of the world," said Elder Delbert L. Stapley. "It is the only plan that will unite the ethnic and national groups and break down the barriers that divide mankind today. History has proven that man cannot forsake God or his Son, our Savior, and live in peace and security. No individual or people can be in rebellion against God's commandments and be in harmony with him. . . . We must be honest with ourselves and others. We must be morally clean and not live a double moral standard. We must not have two personalities—one for Sunday and another for the other six days of the week" (*Ensign,* Dec. 1971, 95–96).

*Whereby are given unto us exceeding great
and precious promises: that by these ye might be
partakers of the divine nature, having escaped the
corruption that is in the world through lust.*

2 PETER 1:4

We are the sons and daughters of God; we are His
spirit offspring. As children of Heavenly Father, we
have something of divinity within us. But despite
our divine parentage, despite our spiritual potenti-
alities and inherent worth as sons and daughters of
God, we cannot save ourselves. We cannot forgive our
own sins or raise ourselves from the dead. We need
a Redeemer. We have the capacity, through access-
ing the powers of the Atonement, to grow in spiritual
grace and in Christlike attributes so as to become like
Christ—to partake of His nature, become like Him,
and live the quality of His life.

*The scriptures . . . have had a more powerful effect
upon my mind than the sword or anything else which
has happened unto me; therefore I have tried the
virtue of the word of God. (See Alma 31:5.)*

JAY E. JENSEN
ENSIGN, NOVEMBER 1992, 80

Said Elder Jay E. Jensen: "I have found repeated in different places in the scriptures two major promises for reading and studying the scriptures that pertain to the next life: one is exaltation, and the other is eternal life. . . . Nephi said: 'Wherefore, if ye shall press forward, feasting upon the word of Christ, and endure to the end, behold, . . . Ye shall have eternal life.' (2 Ne. 31:20.) The surprising discovery was that most promises that come to us for reading and studying the scriptures pertain to mortality. Three categories of promises to consider are promises of power, promises of increase, and 'other promises'" (*Ensign,* Nov. 1992, 81). Elder Jensen taught that "promises of power" include power to overcome evil, live righteously, teach convincingly, and change our heart and disposition; "promises of increase" include an increase of joy, hope, knowledge, understanding, spirituality, and discernment; and "other promises" include faith and other blessings.

*The kind of life you live, your disposition, your very nature,
will be determined by your thoughts, of which your acts
are but the outward expression. Thought is the seed of action.*

DAVID O. MCKAY
DAVID O. MCKAY, 217

We know that as we think in our heart, so are we (Proverbs 23:7). "Thoughts make us what we are," President David O. McKay said. "Thoughts lift your soul heavenward, or drag you toward hell. . . . Character springs from the depths of the soul. You tell me what you think about when you do not have to think, and I'll tell you what you are" (*David O. McKay,* 217–18). Our actions reside in our thoughts and in our hearts. We possess an inner zone over which we are sovereign—we can control our thoughts, decide our actions, educate our conscience. To be Christlike requires self-regulation, which is always available to us as agents. Our character is defined by our willingness to live by our ideals and to honor our beliefs and commitments.

We must study and understand the truths and commandments found in the scriptures. We must listen carefully to the words of our latter-day prophets, whose teachings will give us guidance, direction, and protection.

MARY N. COOK
ENSIGN, MAY 2009, 118

We need the iron rod of truth and virtue to safely guide us through life. Wise counsel given to the young women of the Church by Sister Mary N. Cook is good advice for each of us: "Daily habits of righteous behavior will also help you to *continually* hold fast to the [iron] rod. As a Young Women general presidency we have invited all of the young women in the world to develop three daily habits: First, pray to your Father in Heaven, morning and night, every day. Second, read the Book of Mormon for at least five minutes every day. And third, smile! Why? We have the restored gospel of Jesus Christ, which brings us true happiness" (*Ensign,* May 2009, 118).

*The sealing of family units can be continued until
the family of God is made perfect. This is the great
work of the dispensation of the fulness of times.*

HOWARD W. HUNTER
ENSIGN, DECEMBER 1971, 71

Does it seem reasonable that persons who have
lived upon the earth and died without the opportunity of baptism should be deprived throughout eternity?" said Elder Howard W. Hunter. "Is there anything unreasonable about the living performing the
baptisms for the dead? Perhaps the greatest example
of vicarious work for the dead is the Master himself.
He gave his life as a vicarious atonement, that all who
die shall live again and have life everlasting. He did
for us what we could not do for ourselves. In a similar way we can perform ordinances for those who did
not have the opportunity to do them in this lifetime"
(*Ensign*, Dec., 1971, 71). We live in a blessed time when
more temples dot the earth than in any time in the
world's history—their purpose is to redeem the dead,
unite families for eternity, and give us opportunity to
provide vicarious service.

I am the resurrection, and the life: he that believeth
in me, though he were dead, yet shall he live:
And whosoever liveth and believeth in me shall never die.

JOHN 11:25–26

Jesus Christ is *the* way, *the* truth, and *the* life (John 14:6), not merely a way, a truth, or a life. He is the means through which we come unto the Father and through which salvation comes (Acts 4:12); He is our advocate and mediator, our Savior and Redeemer, the great hope of Israel. It is only through the name of Jesus Christ—meaning His power or authority, His atoning mission and work—that redemption and salvation come to the children of men (2 Nephi 9:24; Mosiah 3:17; 26:22, Alma 22:13). It is through the atoning grace of our Lord that we are liberated from falsehood and iniquity, through the transforming power of the Holy One of Israel that we become sanctified and holy. Peace and strength here and salvation and eternal life hereafter come through the merits and mercy of Jesus Christ, the author and finisher of our faith (Moroni 6:4).

MAY 21

Give God your best, and
His best will come back to you.

EZRA TAFT BENSON
ENSIGN, DECEMBER 1988, 6

Our loving Heavenly Father and innumerable heavenly hosts are pulling for us to succeed. President Ezra Taft Benson said, "Nothing is going to startle us more when we pass through the veil to the other side than to realize how well we know our Father and how familiar His face is to us. God loves us. He is watching us. He wants us to succeed. We will know some day that He has not left one thing undone for the eternal welfare of each of us. If we only knew it, heavenly hosts are pulling for us—friends in heaven that we cannot now remember who yearn for our victory. This is our day to show what we can do—what life and sacrifice we can daily, hourly, instantly make for God. If we give our all, we will get His all from the greatest of all" (*Ensign,* Dec. 1988, 6).

*Gratitude is . . . the foundation upon which
repentance is built. The Atonement brought mercy
through repentance to balance justice. How thankful
I am for the doctrine of repentance.*

ROBERT D. HALES
ENSIGN, MAY 1992, 63–64

How blessed we are to have the doctrine of repentance to use every day of our lives. The Lord knows full well that we are imperfect mortals living in a fallen world, that we will make mistakes and stumble along the pathway of life. For us, He sent His Son, the Lord Jesus Christ, who offered His life as ransom for all: "Though your sins be as scarlet, they shall be as white as snow; though they be red like crimson, they shall be as wool" (Isaiah 1:18). We are washed clean, sanctified through the blood of Christ. Moroni taught that the Atonement removes the stain of sin: "If ye by the grace of God are perfect in Christ, and deny not his power, then are ye sanctified in Christ by the grace of God, through the shedding of the blood of Christ, which is in the covenant of the Father unto the remission of your sins, that ye become holy, without spot" (Moroni 10:33).

*I will go and do the things which the Lord
hath commanded, for I know that the Lord giveth no
commandments unto the children of men, save he shall
prepare a way for them that they may accomplish
the thing which he commandeth them.*

1 NEPHI 3:7

Prophets of God know and teach from experience and inspiration that the Lord gives commandments unto His children that can be followed, obeyed, accomplished, and lived. Humble and faithful believers also know that the Lord is not capricious or whimsical in His commands; He does not want us to jump through a set of hoops just for the fun or the pain of it. He is truly our loving Father; He wants for us eternal life and happiness, and He knows what will bring to us the greatest measure of peace in this life and eternal felicity in the world to come. When we have a calling in the Church that seems overwhelming, when we face doubts and questions as to gospel standards and expectations, when we wonder if we can do all that the Lord requires—know this: The Lord will sustain us and prepare a way to do all that He asks.

*Don't forget that every blessing promised
to you in the temple, whether individually or
jointly, is conditioned upon your faithful obedience
to the covenants you make in the temple.*

CREE-L KOFFORD
ENSIGN, JUNE 1998, 12

Elder Cree-L Kofford taught that in the temple marriage ceremony, "each of you will *individually* and *separately* make promises, commitments, and covenants with your Heavenly Father and will *individually* receive promises of blessings conditioned on your individual worthiness. The individual nature of these promises is such that even if one of you were to cease being obedient . . . , the other partner who remained faithful would continue to be eligible to receive the promised blessings. . . . The two of you *jointly* will make promises, commitments, and covenants with your Heavenly Father and will make covenants to receive each other as husband and wife. You then will *jointly* receive promises of blessings conditioned upon your joint faithfulness. The continued faithful obedience of both of you is essential if the promised blessings are to be received jointly . . . —that is, as a single unit consisting of two halves" (*Ensign,* Jun. 1998, 10).

*Pride and vanity, the opposites of humility,
can destroy our spiritual health as surely as
a debilitating disease can destroy
our physical health.*

JOSEPH B. WIRTHLIN
ENSIGN, NOVEMBER 1990, 65

Our strengths can become weaknesses that lead to our downfall. We may ambitiously succeed so well in worldly ways that we lose track of gospel verities and no longer put first things first. Our hearts may become centered on worldly treasures (Matthew 6:19–21). Elder Joseph B. Wirthlin said, "[One] temptation to detour us is placing improper emphasis on the obtaining of material possessions. For example, we may build a beautiful, spacious home that is far larger than we need. We may spend far too much to decorate, furnish, and landscape it. And even if we are blessed enough to afford such luxury, we may be misdirecting resources that could be better used to build the kingdom of God or to feed and clothe our needy brothers and sisters" (*Ensign*, Nov. 1990, 65). Let us remember that if we are humble and exercise faith, the Lord's grace can make our weaknesses become strengths and help us stay on the gospel path (Ether 12:27).

My heart goes out to conscientious Saints who, because
of their shortcomings, allow feelings of depression to
rob them of happiness in life. We all need to remember:
men are that they might have joy—not guilt trips!

RUSSELL M. NELSON
ENSIGN, NOVEMBER 1995, 86

Life is meant to be happy and joyful. "Let us do the best we can and try to improve each day," said Elder Russell M. Nelson. "When our imperfections appear, we can keep trying to correct them. We can be more forgiving of flaws in ourselves and among those we love. We can be comforted and forbearing. The Lord taught, 'Ye are not able to abide the presence of God now . . . ; wherefore, continue in patience until ye are perfected' [D&C 67:13]. We need not be dismayed if our earnest efforts toward perfection now seem so arduous and endless. Perfection is pending. It can come in full only after the Resurrection and only through the Lord. It awaits all who love him and keep his commandments. It includes thrones, kingdoms, principalities, powers, and dominions [D&C 132:19]. It is the end for which we are to endure. It is the eternal perfection that God has in store for each of us" (*Ensign,* Nov. 1995, 88).

When we remember in God's way,
we overcome our human tendency simply
to gird for the battle of life and actually
engage in the battle itself.

MARLIN K. JENSEN
ENSIGN, MAY 2007, 36

Remembering prophetic admonitions in God's way means that we do more than listen; we hearken, act, do, respond, obey. We not only prepare to battle the fiery darts of the adversary, we engage in the battle by shunning temptation and resisting the tugs and pulls of the world. King Benjamin exhorted his people to remember in God's way: "And finally, I cannot tell you all the things whereby ye may commit sin; for there are divers ways and means, even so many that I cannot number them. But this much I can tell you, that if ye do not watch yourselves, and your thoughts, and your words, and your deeds, and observe the commandments of God, and continue in the faith of what ye have heard concerning the coming of our Lord, even unto the end of your lives, ye must perish. And now, O man, remember, and perish not" (Mosiah 4:29–30).

*I know that our Heavenly Father keeps his promises.
I, like you, have been sorely tried in a variety of
ways. But this kind of seasoning teaches us that every
burden on the back can become a gift in the hand.*

ELAINE CANNON
ENSIGN, MAY 1982, 96

Elaine Cannon, former Young Women general president, said: "One certainty of life is that each of us will meet some mighty test. This is part of the plan. Another thing that we can count on is that neither here nor hereafter are we suddenly going to emerge with qualities we haven't developed or a pattern of living for which we have not prepared ourselves. Adversity is an important part of the preparation for at least three reasons. One, God knows whom he can trust and who, like Job, will stand firm and love him unconditionally. Second, adversity well handled can increase our understanding and compassion. And we will be more effective in helping others when we've had a few challenges of our own. We just may need to be an answer to somebody else's prayer. And third, we draw closer to our Heavenly Father when we are in deep need. . . . Attitude in adversity turns hopeless to hopeful" (*Ensign,* May 1982, 95).

There is only one way provided by the Lord for man to gain salvation and eternal life in the kingdom of God and that is by and through the living, personal Jesus Christ, and by knowing and living his commandments.

BERNARD P. BROCKBANK
ENSIGN, MAY 1977, 27

We know from prophetic teaching that the Father and Son have corporeal bodies (D&C 130:22). "The belief that God has no body, parts, and passions is not a doctrine of Jesus Christ or a doctrine of the holy scriptures but is a doctrine of men, and to worship such a God is in vain," said Elder Bernard P. Brockbank. "From the time when the Lord created man in his own image and likeness, men have created false gods to worship, such as golden calves, sculptured images, etc.; and billions through the centuries including the very elect have been deceived and misled. . . . The message of The Church of Jesus Christ of Latter-day Saints to the people of the world is that God the Eternal Father and Jesus Christ live, that they are personages with immortal bodies of flesh and bones and passions, and that all mankind are children of God and are created in his image and likeness" (*Ensign,* May 1977, 27).

The righteous need not fear.

1 Nephi 22:17

You don't need to fear your past being revealed if you have tried to live a life of honor and character. You don't need to fear the future if you walk in meekness and trust the Lord and His promises. You don't need to fear the present if you are doing your best to live the gospel, repent, sincerely pray, keep the commandments, and honor your covenants. Where there is deep faith and perfect love, there is no fear (1 John 4:18); where there is willing obedience and submission, there is victory over trepidation; where there is righteousness, there is confidence and trust in the Lord. Things will work out; they always do. It may not be just the way we expect, or just the way we want, but the Lord is merciful and kind: he will uphold, sustain, and strengthen us all along life's twists and turns if we truly strive for righteousness. All will be well.

The gospel is so very simple when we understand it properly.
It is always right, it is always good, it is always uplifting.

L. TOM PERRY
ENSIGN, NOVEMBER 1984, 18

This may be the most oft repeated promise in holy writ: "Inasmuch as ye shall keep my commandments ye shall prosper in the land; but inasmuch as ye will not keep my commandments ye shall be cut off from my presence" (2 Nephi 1:20). The Lord's message is simple and clear in all dispensations and places: when we do what God asks of us with sincerity and faith we are blessed, and when we choose not to keep the commandments we are spiritually cut off. Elder L. Tom Perry observed, "The history of mankind bears such strong testimony regarding the blessings which are enjoyed by men and women if they subject themselves to the will of the Lord. And yet, we see in the world so much sorrow and suffering because we are unwilling to be obedient" (*Ensign,* Nov. 1984, 18). Obedience to gospel principles is the one sure path to abiding peace and happiness.

JUNE

*For the eternal purposes
of the Lord shall roll on, until all
his promises shall be fulfilled.*

MORMON 8:22

*The Lord works from the inside out. The world works
from the outside in. The world would take people out
of the slums. Christ takes the slums out of people,
and then they take themselves out of the slums.*

EZRA TAFT BENSON
ENSIGN, NOVEMBER 1985, 6

The ultimate power of change is in our Savior,
Jesus Christ. Surely we must do our part, choose to
be changed, and focus our efforts on humbly striving
to become true disciples of Christ. But it is through
the Atonement of Jesus Christ that we can do more
than enjoy a change of behavior. We have our *nature*
changed. "Therefore if any man be in Christ, he is a
new creature: old things are passed away; behold, all
things are become new" (2 Corinthians 5:17). This
same principle was taught to king Benjamin by an
angel—that the natural man is an enemy to God and
will stay that way unless and until he yields himself to
the enticings of the Holy Spirit (Mosiah 3:19). Christ
and the gospel are all about change: making bad men
good and good men better; helping ordinary women
become extraordinary. Real change, lasting change,
comes in and through Christ and the enabling and
strengthening power of the Atonement.

*The things of this world, from beginning
to end, . . . make little or no difference in
the happiness of an individual.*

BRIGHAM YOUNG
BRIGHAM YOUNG, 235

Over the centuries, prophets have taught that we should set our hearts on the transcendent things of God rather than on fleeting, worldly things. Those worldly things are more than just money—they are possessions, power, prestige, intelligence, accomplishment, appearance, and whatever else turns us to the world and away from God. The things of this world will never truly satisfy, never fulfill our longing for things of deeper worth and greater meaning. Brigham Young observed, "Men and women who are trying to make themselves happy in the possession of wealth or power will miss it, for nothing short of the Gospel of the Son of God can make the inhabitants of the earth happy, and prepare them to enjoy heaven here and hereafter" (*Brigham Young,* 236). This world is but a temporary home, a way station on the path to higher, holier spheres. Let us not be blinded by myopia or sidelined by sin; let us live in the world, yet hold it back.

Remember the worth of souls is great in the sight of
God; For, behold, the Lord your Redeemer suffered death
in the flesh; wherefore he suffered the pain of all men,
that all men might repent and come unto him.

DOCTRINE & COVENANTS 18:10–11

God's work and glory is to bring to pass the immortality and eternal life of His beloved sons and daughters (Moses 1:39). Our loving Heavenly Father gave us life and provided a Savior so that we could be redeemed from this fallen world and return to live with them. "For God so loved the world, that he gave his only begotten Son, that whosoever believeth in him should not perish, but have everlasting life" (John 3:16). The worth of souls is great because Christ suffered and died for each of us. We are not our own. We have been purchased, redeemed, by the precious blood of Christ (1 Corinthians 6:19–20; 7:23; 1 Peter 1:18). "It is the blood that maketh an atonement for the soul" (Leviticus 17:11). We honor our divine endowment of worth by living faithfully and becoming more like the Father and Son.

*Thou shalt love the Lord thy God with all thy heart,
and with all thy soul, and with all thy mind. This is the
first and great commandment. And the second is like
unto it, Thou shalt love thy neighbour as thyself.*

MATTHEW 22:37–39

The gospel hinge swings on the great commandments to love God and others. There is no true gospel without love, no true discipleship, no true happiness or peace. When we truly love God and our fellowman, everything begins to change and fall into place. President Henry B. Eyring taught, "Love is the motivating principle by which the Lord leads us along the way towards becoming like Him, *our perfect example. Our way of life, hour by hour, must be filled with the love of God and love for others. There is no surprise in that, since the Lord proclaimed those as the first and great commandments. It is love of God that will lead us to keep His commandments. And love of others is at the heart of our capacity to obey Him" (*Ensign,* Nov. 2009, 70). Let us try this day in a meaningful way to more fully love God and all others.

Ask, and it shall be given you;
seek, and ye shall find;
knock, and it shall be opened unto you.

MATTHEW 7:7

The Lord answers our prayers if we ask in faith. The Savior said, "Behold, I stand at the door, and knock: if any man hear my voice, and open the door, I will come in to him, and will sup with him, and he with me" (Revelation 3:20). President Spencer W. Kimball said, "The promise is made to everyone. There is no discrimination, no favored few. But the Lord has not promised to crash the door. He stands and knocks. If we do not listen, he will not sup with us nor give answer to our prayers. Do you know how to listen, grasp, interpret, understand? The Lord stands knocking. He never retreats. But he will never force himself upon us. If we ever move apart, it is we who move and not the Lord" (*New Era,* Mar. 1978, 17). Answers to prayers may not come immediately or as desired, but an omnipotent and omni-loving Lord stands ready for those who exercise faith and trust in Him.

*Spirit sons and daughters of God
need not be permanently put down when lifted up
by Jesus' Atonement. Christ's infinite Atonement
thus applies to our finite failures!*

NEAL A. MAXWELL
ENSIGN, NOVEMBER 2000, 37

A Gospel Doctrine teacher asked his class one Sunday morning, "What is the most important message of the gospel?" Hands shot up and many answers were given: Christ died for us, the gospel has been restored, we have a living prophet, priesthood power is again on the earth, we can talk with God through prayer, scriptures are the revealed word of God, and other worthy comments were made. When the comments slowed, and after a moment of silence, one middle-aged brother who had experienced many of life's heartaches and an extended period of inactivity said thoughtfully, "I believe that the most important message of the gospel is that we can change." How true! Through faith in Jesus Christ and by the power of the infinite Atonement, we can change, repent, and move forward into a new future. We can become new creatures in Christ.

*Wherefore, whoso believeth in God might
with surety hope for a better world, yea, even a place at
the right hand of God, which hope cometh of faith, maketh
an anchor to the souls of men, which would make them
sure and steadfast, always abounding in good works.*

ETHER 12:4

A mother, discouraged one day by her less-than-perfect family, grumbled to herself that her family would surely never grace the cover of the *Ensign* magazine. With a plateful of life's challenges and disappointments, she was disheartened by her family reality. She turned to the Lord in sincere and humble prayer, acknowledging to God that she knew her family was far from perfect. Through her tears and pleading for hope, the clear and comforting voice of the Spirit whispered in her soul: "Neither is mine." No family is perfect—not even our Heavenly Father's. All of us are His spirit children, His sons and daughters. He, too, has wayward and rebellious children; He, too, has troubled and disobedient offspring for whom His heart aches. His love for us is perfect; His long-suffering and compassion is flawless. He does not, and will not give up on us. And with faith and hope as our anchor, we must not give up on our children.

No one event may appear to be very impressive or memorable. But just as . . . strokes of paint complement each other and produce an impressive masterpiece, so our consistency in doing seemingly small things can lead to significant spiritual results.

DAVID A. BEDNAR
ENSIGN, NOVEMBER 2009, 19–20

The Lord said to the Prophet Joseph Smith, "Wherefore, be not weary in well-doing, for ye are laying the foundation of a great work. And out of small things proceedeth that which is great" (D&C 64:33). The greatest work we do while in mortality is the foundation we lay to build strong and righteous families that are worthy to return to the Father and live the quality of life that God himself enjoys— eternal life. To do that takes every worthy desire, effort, and action we can muster to build a celestial family. It's not easy, but no one ever said it would be. When it would be easier to forget about family prayer and scripture study, strong families do it. When it would be more convenient to disregard the prophet's call to hold a weekly family home evening, righteous families do it. That which is eternally great proceeds from our consistent efforts to not be weary in doing these seemingly small family things.

When a seal is put upon the father and mother,
it secures their posterity, so that they cannot be lost,
but will be saved by virtue of the covenant
of their father and mother.

JOSEPH SMITH
HISTORY OF THE CHURCH, 5:530

Parents are commanded to plant faith and gospel understanding in the hearts of their children (D&C 68:25–28; 93:40). But despite their best efforts, some parents find their children departing from the example, teachings, and values exemplified at home. Though their hearts ache, faithful parents whose children are heirs of the covenant, but who have wandered, have reason to hope. We must remember that success in our parental stewardship is measured not by our children's choices but by our own best effort in doing God's will. In parenting, we cannot use outcome-based evaluation. The element of control is missing, and individuals have agency to choose for themselves. With renewed hope and reassurance that the Lord is pleased with our efforts, we can go forward. We can learn not to judge ourselves by our children's actions, but instead to put our faith in God—to truly bring our burdens to Him and trust His promises.

God the Father watches over us, fills our hearts with breathtaking joy, brightens our darkest hours with blessed peace, distills upon our minds precious truths, shepherds us through times of distress, rejoices when we rejoice, and answers our righteous petitions.

DIETER F. UCHTDORF
ENSIGN, NOVEMBER 2009, 22

Perhaps the greatest promise we can count on is that God slumbers not nor sleeps as He, with pure love and perfect care, watches over His children (Psalm 121:4). He is our Father, and He has a fatherly interest in each of His children. He gave us this beautiful earth as a place to learn and grow in the lessons of mortality. A great plan of happiness and mercy was put into place that we might gain immortality and eternal life. A Savior, God's only begotten Son, was provided so that we might repent and change. The knowledge of our Father's encompassing love and watchcare can give us hope, solace, and reassurance during the dark nights of mortality. He is not a distant or callous Father. He loves each of His children. We can go to sleep in peace knowing that our Heavenly Father is awake and watching over us.

*How do we glorify Jesus? How do we say thank you
for the Atonement? . . . Of course, we do it by
loving God, by loving our neighbor, by living the
commandments, and also by being one.*

HUGH W. PINNOCK
ENSIGN, MAY 1987, 64

We manifest our love of the Lord by keeping His commandments (John 14:15), and by striving to be unified in love and devoted to the gospel (D&C 38:27). Followers of Jesus Christ are united in "one Lord, one faith, one baptism" (Ephesians 4:5). And the Lord and our leaders will know of our loyalty and unity because we do what they call us to do. Similar principles apply to marriage and family life: we are to be united in purpose, in devotion to truth, in love and righteousness. As a family, are we united in our seeking for that which is virtuous, lovely, or of good report or praiseworthy? Is there peace and love at home? Do we share our testimonies with others so that they may become one with us? Where there is love and unity there is peace and security in the home and in the heart.

There is a law, irrevocably decreed in heaven
before the foundations of this world, upon which all blessings
are predicated—And when we obtain any blessing from God,
it is by obedience to that law upon which it is predicated.

DOCTRINE & COVENANTS 130:20–21

The law of the Lord is not a restriction, it is an opportunity—it is so much more about blessings than prohibition. It is a great blessing to know that we can trust the Lord: "I, the Lord, am bound when ye do what I say; but when ye do not what I say, ye have no promise" (D&C 82:10). It is a great gift to understand that the Lord's purposes will finally triumph, for "there is nothing that the Lord thy God shall take in his heart to do but what he will do it" (Abraham 3:17). To be happy and at peace we must obey the laws and commandments of our loving Father. We may try to reject, ignore, or rationalize away the commands of God, but no true and lasting peace or joy can ever be found in wickedness or disobedience (Alma 41:10). The Lord desires to bless us abundantly, both here and hereafter.

It is not easy to be a Latter-day Saint.
It was not meant to be easy.

QUENTIN L. COOK
ENSIGN, NOVEMBER 2003, 95

The Savior said, "This is my gospel; and ye know the things that ye must do in my church; for the works which ye have seen me do that shall ye also do" (3 Nephi 27:21). As Saints, we want to do what Jesus wants us to do and become what He wants us to become. Our desire and will turns to the Master with sincere devotion and full purpose. We must hold back the world. Elder Quentin L. Cook observed, "We are bombarded with visual images of violence and immorality. Inappropriate music and pornography are increasingly tolerated. The use of drugs and alcohol is rampant. There is less emphasis on honesty and character. Individual rights are demanded, but duties, responsibilities, and obligations are neglected. . . . If we separate ourselves from this worldly conduct, we will have the Spirit in our lives and experience the joy of being worthy Latter-day Saints" (*Ensign,* Nov. 2003, 95).

*Missionary work is the lifeblood of the Church.
There is no greater work, no more important work.
It blesses the lives of all those who participate in it.
It will continue blessing future generations.*

SILVIA H. ALLRED
ENSIGN, NOVEMBER 2008, 12

Sister Silvia H. Allred of the Relief Society general presidency said, "My mission had a great impact on my life. I learned to rely more on the Lord, to seek the guidance of the Spirit, and to feel an overwhelming love for God's children. My knowledge of the scriptures and my understanding of the doctrines increased. So did my desire to be obedient and to keep the commandments with exactness. My testimony of the Savior and His infinite Atonement was strengthened. My missionary experiences became part of who and what I am. Missionary work became my passion. It has impacted my life and that of my family more than anything else" (*Ensign,* Nov. 2008, 11). Missionary work blesses in a wonderful way both those who serve and those who are served; it changes lives for the better and blesses past, present, and future generations. It is at the heart of our Christian discipleship to fulfill the Savior's commission to share the gospel with the world.

Work is . . . good therapy for most problems.
It is the antidote for worry. It is the equalizer for
deficiency of native endowment. Work makes it
possible for the average to approach genius.

J. RICHARD CLARKE
ENSIGN, MAY 1982, 77–78

As we work, we build lives of usefulness, growth, opportunity, and satisfaction. Work is a temporal and spiritual necessity. Bishop J. Richard Clarke taught, "We have a moral obligation to exercise our personal capabilities of mind, muscle, and spirit in a way that will return to the Lord, our families, and our society the fruits of our best efforts. To do less is to live our lives unfulfilled. It is to deny ourselves and those dependent upon us opportunity and advantage" (*Ensign*, May 1982, 77). And the Lord exhorted, "Let every man be diligent in all things. And the idler shall not have place in the church, except he repent and mend his ways" (D&C 75:29). Happiness is not reserved for the chosen, lucky few; peace of mind and heart is not something that happens by chance. Happiness and peace are available to all who diligently labor, to all who learn and grow in honest toil, to all who lose themselves in work that is meaningful.

*Trust in the Lord with all thine heart;
and lean not unto thine own understanding.
In all thy ways acknowledge him,
and he shall direct thy paths.*

PROVERBS 3:5–6

Trusting in the Lord, despite the sorrows and set-backs of life, requires deep faith and resolute hope that God is in His heaven and that if we pray always and are faithful, all things shall work together for our good (D&C 90:24; Romans 8:28). The world and the worldly may mock those who trust in the Lord; they may ridicule believers and scorn those who rely upon the merits and mercy of Jesus. It has been the same in all dispensations of time. What we must do is look heavenward. What we must do is study the gospel of the Master and the words of the proph-ets. What we must do is come to the Lord in mighty prayer, humility, and gratitude, seeking His influence and direction in our lives. If we do so, the Spirit of the Lord and quiet confidence will distill upon us as the dews from heaven and our trust will grow ever brighter until the perfect day (D&C 50:24).

*No matter who you are or what you may have done,
you can always pray. . . . Prayer is your personal key
to heaven. The lock is on your side of the veil.*

BOYD K. PACKER
ENSIGN, NOVEMBER 2009, 45–46

Prayer opens the doors to heaven—heaven's peace, heaven's blessings, heaven's help. The Lord promised, "Draw near unto me and I will draw near unto you; seek me diligently and ye shall find me; ask, and ye shall receive; knock, and it shall be opened unto you" (D&C 88:63). The adversary, on the other hand, wants us not to pray, not to feel worthy, not to desire the doors of heaven to open in our behalf. The evil one desires that we ignore, deny, reject, minimize, or forget the transcendent power of prayer. He knows that prayer is the key to heaven and the passport to peace, and therefore wants us to turn away from prayer and toward sin. We cannot trust Satan at all. We can, however, trust with perfect confidence the Lord and His promises. We must exercise the faith to put the key of prayer into heaven's lock and come to the Lord in meekness, sincerity, and earnest supplication.

*The fruits of eternal progress are manifest in joy,
peace, love, hope, increased confidence in the Lord. . . .
By our good works we magnify what is mighty in us all,
one step at a time, one day at a time, all the time.*

ELAINE L. JACK
ENSIGN, MAY 1994, 16

Focusing on our eternal purposes can ease our burdens and help us to be more contented and productive. Elaine L. Jack said, "So often we go around in a circle, spinning our spiritual wheels while only our temporal treads hit the road. That seems out of step and out of balance with the way the Lord intended. We have knowledge and spiritual power; such momentum far exceeds anything the world has to offer. Putting off to tomorrow is to fall behind, step backward, and open the door to the subtle influences of Satan. . . . There are diversions which attempt to lure us from the straight and narrow. It is our covenants that are the road signs to eternal life. Just as it is more difficult to read the signs on the main road from a side street, so too it is more difficult to hear the still, small voice of warnings, rough road ahead, when we have distanced ourselves from our covenants" (*Ensign,* May 1994, 15).

*Tithing is a token of gratitude, obedience, and
thanksgiving—a token of our willingness and dedication.
Paying tithing, willingly, develops an honest and pure
heart. Paying tithing increases our love for the Lord.*

YOSHIHIKO KIKUCHI
ENSIGN, MAY 2007, 98

In the book of Malachi, the Lord asks: "Will a man
rob God? Yet ye have robbed me. But ye say, Wherein
have we robbed thee? In tithes and offerings." After
the Lord's exhortation, he then gives the promise,
"and prove me now herewith, saith the Lord of hosts,
if I will not open you the windows of heaven, and
pour you out a blessing, that there shall not be room
enough to receive it" (Malachi 3:8–10). Tithing opens
the windows of heaven and the doors of our hearts as
it works a mighty change. Only a humble and believing heart would willingly, happily pay offerings to the
Lord; only a trusting and obedient heart would pay an
honest tithe to the Lord. Tithing is a principle with a
promise; it is manifestation of our faithfulness, gratitude, and desire to trust, follow, and serve the Lord
with "full purpose of heart" (Mosiah 7:33).

*The nearer men and women live unto God in keeping
his commandments, the greater is the love in the home and
the greater appreciation of the knowledge that that love can
continue throughout the eternities that are to come.*

LEGRAND RICHARDS
ENSIGN, DECEMBER 1971, 84

Beloved apostle LeGrand Richards said, in his last general conference address, "I just can't imagine living on forever and forever after I pass out of this life without the companionship of my sweet wife and my children. How I thank God for them. . . . I think of my children one by one (and I have over a hundred descendants!), and I see what they are accomplishing and the nobility of their lives, and I can hardly realize that I can be their daddy. I feel that that is nearer to becoming a god than anything else I can do here in mortality. And from the days of my youth and young manhood, I have tried to live before those children and descendants of mine so that if they walked in my footsteps they would be honoring their second estate and preparing themselves to have glory added upon their heads forever and forever" (*Ensign,* May 1982, 30).

Therefore go, my son,
and thou shalt be favored of the Lord,
because thou hast not murmured.

1 NEPHI 3:6

The Lord asked hard things of Lehi and his sons. Some of his sons responded in faith and courage, and others responded in a continuous murmur. To murmur is to find fault, complain, criticize, grumble, and groan; it is to distrust the Lord's purposes, plans, and goodness; it is to give in to the natural man of fear, doubt, and weakness. Murmuring can become a loud roar, either verbally or festering in the heart, which can crowd out the whisperings of the Spirit and the humility of obedience. Those who murmur pit their will against the will of God; they become prophets unto themselves. We, too, experience hard things, but as we exercise faith and, like Lehi's faithful sons, refrain from murmuring, we lay claim to the promise of being favored of the Lord, a promise that will sustain us all throughout life. We are to be builders, not murmurers.

How do you overcome [temptation]? One of my simple answers tonight is to constantly remember your covenants, to act on them, and to commit to them. This sequence . . . is a classic, spiritual teaching pattern to prepare us for eternal life.

CHARLES DIDIER
ENSIGN, MAY 1994, 44

Elder Charles Didier, who served as a General Authority for nearly thirty-five years, was baptized as a young college student in Brussels, Belgium. He said: "I can see how remembering my covenants helped me to honor and magnify my priesthood calling, to keep the commandments, and to bring spiritual happiness into my life in preparation for eternal life. During those trial years, many of my young friends in the Church forgot their covenants and one by one returned to the world. The world always stands between man and God, representing two alternatives but only one true choice. How can we be strengthened in making the choice to serve the Lord? By simply focusing on the doctrine of Jesus Christ that will ensure the salvation of those who remember it, accept it, and act upon it" (*Ensign,* May 1994, 43). The key to staying true to the faith is to always remember and live our covenants.

*The year was 1820, the season spring. The boy with
questions walked into the grove. . . . He beheld the
Father and the Son, the great God of the universe
and the risen Lord, both of whom spoke to him.*

GORDON B. HINCKLEY
ENSIGN, NOVEMBER 1984, 52

Speaking of the First Vision, President Gordon B.
Hinckley (who was born on this day in 1910) said,
"This transcendent experience opened the marvelous work of restoration. It lifted the curtain on the
long-promised dispensation of the fulness of times.
. . . There had been nothing of comparable magnitude since the Son of God walked the earth in mortality. Without it as a foundation stone for our faith
and organization, we have nothing. With it, we have
everything. Much has been written, much will be
written, in an effort to explain it away. The finite
mind cannot comprehend it. But the testimony of
the Holy Spirit, experienced by countless numbers of
people all through the years since it happened, bears
witness that it is true, that it happened as Joseph
Smith said it happened, that it was as real as the sun-
rise over Palmyra" (*Ensign*, Nov., 1984, 52).

Gratitude is a Spirit-filled principle. It opens our minds to a universe permeated with the richness of a living God. Through it, we become spiritually aware of the wonder of the smallest things, which gladden our hearts with their messages of God's love.

BONNIE D. PARKIN
ENSIGN, MAY 2007, 35

Our world seems to feed on negativism and criticism, and so often we are ungrateful for or oblivious to the countless blessings all around us. But those who complain and find fault do not know "the dealings of that God who had created them" (1 Nephi 2:12). Like Laman and Lemuel, they are in danger of the sins of pride, murmuring, and ingratitude. Murmuring closes the door to humility, thankfulness, service, and the promptings of the Lord. Gratitude, on the other hand, fills our hearts with faith, hope, and charity. Sister Bonnie D. Parkin, former general president of the Relief Society said, "When we communicate gratitude, we can be filled with the Spirit and connected to those around us and the Lord. Gratitude inspires happiness and carries divine influence. . . . Gratitude is our sweet acknowledgement of the Lord's hand in our lives; it is an expression of our faith" (*Ensign,* May 2007, 35).

And many nations shall come, and say,
Come, and let us go up to the mountain of
the Lord . . . and he will teach us of his ways,
and we will walk in his paths.

MICAH 4:2

A few days after arriving in the Salt Lake Valley, Brigham Young and several others walked to a spot of ground nestled between the great Wasatch Mountains to the east and the Oquirrh Mountains to the west and exclaimed, "Here we will build the Temple of our God" (quoted in David B. Haight, *Ensign,* Oct. 1993, 9). Said Elder Haight, "We may ask ourselves why the Saints—who had already been driven from their homes (and temples) at Kirtland and Nauvoo—would be so willing, even eager, to build another temple. I believe the answer lies in their conviction that the Lord had commanded them to build it so they could receive the ordinances of salvation therein. . . . I am convinced those rugged pioneers knew in their hearts that the ordinances of the temple would actually bind (seal) them to their spouses, children, and parents (living and dead) and provide them an eternal home in the presence of our Heavenly Father and Jesus Christ" (ibid.).

None of us are secure except we keep
the commandments of our Heavenly Father.
The pathway of righteousness is the highway of happiness.
There is no other way to happiness.

GEORGE ALBERT SMITH
CONFERENCE REPORT, APRIL 1950, 168

A young woman, once faithful and strong in the Church, now wanders as a prodigal in darkness and hopelessness because of her rejection of gospel light. She continually tells her family that she's never been happier, but her countenance and actions reveal otherwise. From time to time, in moments of truth when she has come to herself (Luke 15:17), she will confess to loved ones that she knows she will not find abiding happiness in the ways of the world. But, she says, life is short, and she wants to have fun. Her quest for happiness leads always to disappointment; her desire for joy ends up only in heartache. Momentary pleasure may be found, transitory gratification may be experienced, but real and lasting joy comes in obedience, in righteousness, in virtue and truth. The world calls out with empty enticements; the Lord beckons with eternality.

*For the eternal purposes
of the Lord shall roll on, until all
his promises shall be fulfilled.*

MORMON 8:22

Nothing and no one can stop the work of the Lord. There may be temporary setbacks and momentary difficulties, but the eternal purposes and promises of the Lord will roll forth and be fulfilled in remarkable ways. We know which side will ultimately triumph—it is up to us to decide which team we will be on: the side of truth and the Lord, or the side of evil and the adversary. Remember this great prophecy of the Prophet Joseph Smith: "The Standard of Truth has been erected; no unhallowed hand can stop the work from progressing; persecutions may rage, mobs may combine, armies may assemble, calumny may defame, but the truth of God will go forth boldly, nobly, and independent, till it has penetrated every continent, visited every clime, swept every country, and sounded in every ear, till the purposes of God shall be accomplished, and the Great Jehovah shall say the work is done" (*History of the Church,* 4:540).

To be angry is to yield to the influence of Satan.
No one can make us angry. It is our choice.
If we desire to have a proper spirit with us at all times,
we must choose to refrain from becoming angry.

THOMAS S. MONSON
ENSIGN, NOVEMBER 2009, 68

It may not be easy at times, but we can choose to control our emotions and not become angry at people, events, and circumstances. Sometimes people believe their agency or accountability can be suspended when experiencing the heat of an emotion. However, we are still agents, even when we experience life as though we were victims of our emotions. The apostle Paul exhorted, "Let all bitterness, and wrath, and anger, and clamour, and evil speaking, be put away from you, with all malice: And be ye kind one to another, tenderhearted, forgiving one another, even as God for Christ's sake hath forgiven you" (Ephesians 4:31–32). To be Christlike requires self-regulation. Being agents and being accountable signifies that self-regulation is always available to us, as are repentance and forgiveness. With the Lord's divine assistance and loving grace, we can change, overcome bad habits, put off the natural man, and refrain from becoming angry.

*If we must give all that we have, then our
giving only almost everything is not enough.
If we almost keep the commandments,
we almost receive the blessings.*

BRUCE C. HAFEN
ENSIGN, MAY 2004, 98

True disciples strive to follow the Lord in all ways and all times. "Some people want to keep one hand on the wall of the temple while touching the world's 'unclean things' [see Alma 5:57] with the other hand," said Elder Bruce C. Hafen. "We must put both hands on the temple and hold on for dear life. One hand is not even *almost* enough. . . . We can have eternal life if we want it, but only if there is *nothing else* we want more. So we must willingly give everything, because God Himself can't make us grow against our will and without our full participation. Yet even when we utterly spend ourselves, we lack the power to create the perfection only God can complete. Our *all* by itself is still only *almost* enough—until it is finished by the *all* of Him who is the 'finisher of our faith' [Hebrews 12:2; see also Moroni 6:4]." (*Ensign,* May 2004, 98–99).

Service gives us purpose and courage in life. It brings us closer to God and helps us refine our divine nature. It teaches us to love and understand our fellowmen, and it helps us forget about our personal desires, eliminating selfishness, pride, and ingratitude.

CARLOS H. AMADO
ENSIGN, MAY 2008, 36

Those who serve will always seek to please God and live in harmony with Him," taught Elder Carlos H. Amado. "They will be full of peace; they will have a cheerful countenance and a spirit of kindness. Those who serve will strive to ennoble, build, and lift their fellowmen; therefore, they will find the good in others, and they will not find reason or have time to become offended. They develop the virtue of praying for those who criticize. They don't expect recognition or reward. They possess the love of Christ. Those who serve will always be willing to share what they possess and what they know at all times, in all places, and with all people. Those who serve even in adversity will maintain a living hope of a better future. They will continue to be firm in the midst of a crisis because their hope is in Christ" (*Ensign,* May 2008, 36–37).

JULY

*The song of the righteous
is a prayer unto me, and it shall be
answered with a blessing
upon their heads.*

<small>DOCTRINE & COVENANTS 25:12</small>

JULY 1

*I would exhort you that ye would ask God, the
Eternal Father, in the name of Christ, if these things
are not true; and if ye shall ask with a sincere heart, with
real intent, having faith in Christ, he will manifest
the truth of it unto you, by the power of the Holy Ghost.*

MORONI 10:4

Speaking of Moroni's well-known and powerful promise at the conclusion to the Book of Mormon, Elder L. Aldin Porter said, "This is the promise, that our Eternal Father will give us a manifestation of truth—a personal revelation of eternal consequence. The Book of Mormon was given to the convincing of the Jew and Gentile that Jesus is the Christ, manifesting Himself unto all nations. Do not treat lightly the revelations of God. Do not treat lightly this astonishing promise. I bear a solemn testimony to you that this promise has been fulfilled not only in my life but in the lives of hundreds of thousands, even millions, of people. . . . When this sacred witness comes, our love for Him will increase without bounds; our desire to know of Him will increase" (*Ensign,* May 2001, 31).

*If you will make your first concern the comfort, the
well-being, and the happiness of your companion, sublimating
any personal concern to that loftier goal, you will be happy,
and your marriage will go on throughout eternity.*

GORDON B. HINCKLEY
ENSIGN, DECEMBER 1995, 67

Why all of these broken homes?" asked President
Gordon B. Hinckley. "What happens to marriages
that begin with sincere love and a desire to be loyal
and faithful and true one to another? . . . I find selfishness to be the root cause of most of it. I am satisfied that a happy marriage is not so much a matter of
romance as it is an anxious concern for the comfort
and well-being of one's companion. Selfishness so often is the basis of money problems, which are a very
serious and real factor affecting the stability of family
life. Selfishness is at the root of adultery, the break-
ing of solemn and sacred covenants to satisfy selfish
lust. Selfishness is the antithesis of love. It is a can-
kering expression of greed. It destroys self-discipline.
It obliterates loyalty. It tears up sacred covenants. It
afflicts both men and women" (*Ensign,* May 1991, 73).

In times of distress, let your covenants
be paramount and let your obedience be exact.
Then you can ask in faith, nothing wavering,
according to your need, and God will answer.

D. TODD CHRISTOFFERSON
ENSIGN, MAY 2009, 22

Making and honoring our covenants will help us build our faith and moral character. Elder D. Todd Christofferson said: "We need strong Christians who can persevere against hardship, who can sustain hope through tragedy, who can lift others by their example and their compassion, and who can consistently overcome temptations. We need strong Christians who can make important things happen by their faith and who can defend the truth of Jesus Christ against moral relativism and militant atheism. What is the source of such moral and spiritual power, and how do we obtain it? The source is God. Our access to that power is through our covenants with Him. A covenant is an agreement between God and man, an accord whose terms are set by God. In these divine agreements, God binds Himself to sustain, sanctify, and exalt us in return for our commitment to serve Him and keep His commandments" (*Ensign*, May 2009, 19–20).

Men may fail in this country, earthquakes may come,
seas may heave beyond their bounds, there may be great drought,
disaster, and hardship, but this nation, founded on principles
laid down by men whom God raised up, will never fail.

HAROLD B. LEE
THE TEACHINGS OF HAROLD B. LEE, 365

America was formed with freedom at its core, a freedom that enabled the gospel to be restored to the Earth. President Harold B. Lee said, "May I voice a plea for all Americans to love this country with a fervor that will inspire each to so live as to merit the favor of the Almighty during this time of grave uncertainties [World War II], as well as in times to come. I would that all men could believe in the destiny of America as did the early pioneers. . . . I make a further plea that the citizens of this favored land live righteously that they might enjoy the fruits of their righteousness in this land of promise" (*The Teachings of Harold B. Lee,* 365). May God always bless America.

*And the Spirit giveth light to every man
that cometh into the world; and the Spirit enlighteneth
every man through the world, that hearkeneth to the
voice of the Spirit. And every one that hearkeneth to the
voice of the Spirit cometh unto God, even the Father.*

DOCTRINE AND COVENANTS 84:46–47

The Light of Christ is what we call a conscience; it is the divine power that gives life and light to all things; it influences people for good and prepares them to receive the greater light of the Holy Ghost: "The Spirit of Christ is given to every man, that he may know good from evil; wherefore, I show unto you the way to judge; for every thing which inviteth to do good, and to persuade to believe in Christ, is sent forth by the power and gift of Christ" (Moroni 7:16). President Boyd K. Packer taught, "No Father would send His children off to a distant, dangerous land for a lifetime of testing where Lucifer was known to roam free without first providing them with a personal power of protection. He would also supply them with means to communicate with Him from Father to child and from child to Father. . . . We are, none of us, left here alone without hope of guidance and redemption" (*Ensign,* Nov. 2009, 43).

And be not conformed to this world:
but be ye transformed by the renewing of your mind,
that ye may prove what is that good, and acceptable,
and perfect, will of God.... Rejoicing in hope; patient
in tribulation; continuing instant in prayer.

ROMANS 12:2, 12

Those who choose to live not after the manner of the world strive to put off the natural man and become, in the process of time, new creatures in Christ. When we hold back the world, where wickedness prevails, we become saints in very thought, desire, and deed. John taught, "Love not the world, neither the things that are in the world. If any man love the world, the love of the Father is not in him. For all that is in the world, the lust of the flesh, and the lust of the eyes, and the pride of life, is not of the Father, but is of the world. And the world passeth away, and the lust thereof: but he that doeth the will of God abideth for ever" (1 John 2:15–17). How do we overcome a world filled with fleshly allurements and tempting enticements? Love, believe, and trust the Lord; be constant in prayer and patient in tribulation; rejoice always in the hope of the Lord.

Joy in the gospel is . . . our privilege now, this very day.
We must never allow our burdens to obscure our blessings.
There will always be more blessings than burdens—
even if some days it doesn't seem so.

JEFFREY R. HOLLAND
ENSIGN, OCTOBER 2006, 15

Some things don't change; they are true always and forever. One of those vital sureties of life is that the Lord will stand by us, uphold and sustain us, if we turn to Him, trust Him, and rely upon the enabling power of His grace. He will surely bless us. The Savior said, "I am come that they might have life, and that they might have it more abundantly" (John 10:10). We are here to have "life more abundantly" here and now, not just hereafter in the heavenly realm. An abundant life is one that sees the blessings of the Lord and the gospel all around; a life that recognizes that blessings far outnumber burdens even at those times when it doesn't seem so; a life that has enough faith and confidence in the Lord and His heart to know that the Lord will not abandon or forsake us. "[We] are, that [we] might have joy" (2 Nephi 2:25), right here, right now, this day and always.

And whoso receiveth you, there I will be also,
for I will go before your face. I will be on your right hand
and on your left, and my Spirit shall be in your hearts,
and mine angels round about you, to bear you up.

DOCTRINE & COVENANTS 84:88

When missionaries are filled with the spirit of their callings and go forward on the Lord's errand with faith, they will be magnified in those callings and strengthened and guided all along the way. Sharing the gospel with others is a sacred trust, a holy responsibility, a consecrated stewardship filled with promises, blessings, and opportunities. The missionary and those receiving the gospel message have the sweet opportunity to become forever changed for the better, as the apostle Paul said: "And be not conformed to this world: but be ye transformed by the renewing of your mind, that ye may prove what is that good, and acceptable, and perfect, will of God" (Romans 12:2). Whenever the message of salvation is brought into our hearts and homes and lived in sincerity and truth, heaven's angels will surround and bear us up.

From the beginning of recorded religious history,
God has required His people not only to confess Him
as their God, acknowledging His wisdom
and power, but also to confess to Him.

DENNIS B. NEUENSCHWANDER
ENSIGN, DECEMBER 1999, 13

Our sincere confession reflects a godly sorrow which "worketh repentance to salvation" (2 Corinthians 7:10) and indicates that we are striving to overcome pride and the desire to hide our sins. A confession involves recognizing God's power in our lives, acknowledging that without God we are nothing, and learning from God and his authorized representatives. Elder Dennis B. Neuenschwander said: "The rewards of confession are many. . . . Confession helps us to assume responsibility and accountability for our actions. Confession initiates the healing process. Confession removes adversarial relationships. And confession is the key to forgiveness and compassion, which all of us desire from our Father in Heaven and from those who surround us" (*Ensign,* Dec. 1999, 17). Confession is a vital part of the humble disposition of a disciple.

*When we obey as did Adam, endure as did Job, teach
as did Paul, testify as did Peter, serve as did Nephi, give of
ourselves as did the Prophet Joseph, respond as did Ruth,
honor as did Mary, and live as did Christ, we are born anew.*

THOMAS S. MONSON
ENSIGN, JULY 1991, 4

President Thomas S. Monson spoke of a personal
hall of fame reserved for those leaders and mentors
who have influenced the direction of our lives (*Ensign,*
Jul. 1991, 4). These faithful men and women have led
us to become more devoted to the truth, more dutiful
in our obedience, and more dedicated to living a life
of righteousness. Who would you place in your personal hall of fame? Popular figures seem to emerge on
the world's stage, attract attention for a moment, and
then, almost as quickly as they appeared, fade into
distant memory. But fame is not admiration; prominence is not a measure of respect. A hall of fame truly
worthy of the name—and one that stands the test of
time—is not fleeting, it's never forgotten, and it has
the power to change our lives for the better.

*That we as a people may be prepared not only for
the judgments, but for the glory and coming of our Lord,
. . . and be counted worthy to stand in the presence of
the Lord in his glorious kingdom, is my prayer.*

JOSEPH F. SMITH
JOSEPH F. SMITH, 393

The Lord has assured us that if we are prepared we need not fear (D&C 38:30). President Joseph F. Smith said: "We are in perilous times, but I do not feel the pangs of that terror. It is not upon me. I propose to live so that it will not rest upon me. I propose to live so that I shall be immune from the perils of the world, if it be possible for me to so live, by obedience to the commandments of God and to his laws revealed for my guidance. No matter what may come to me, if I am only in the line of my duty, if I am in fellowship with God, if I am worthy of the fellowship of my brethren, if I can stand spotless before the world, without blemish, without transgression of the laws of God, what does it matter to me what may happen to me? I am always ready" (*Joseph F. Smith,* 393–94).

You have a loving Heavenly Father who hears and answers
your prayers. He wants you to be worthy to return and
live with Him someday. Knowing this can help you plan for
your earthly and eternal future with a brightness of hope

COLEEN K. MENLOVE
ENSIGN, MAY 2003, 115

Coleen K. Menlove, who served as general president of the Primary from 1999 to 2005, shared truth with children and adults: "You are a child of God. . . . As you look to the future, look far beyond tomorrow. The scriptures, the teachings of latter-day prophets, and even the Primary songs can help you understand and prepare to reach your eternal potential. Jesus Christ set the example for us of how to live worthy so we may return to the presence of our Heavenly Father. Each of you will have opportunities to learn about Jesus Christ and then follow Him in faith. We show we know how to follow Him by making and keeping baptismal covenants and by receiving and listening to the Holy Ghost. We show we know how to follow Him each time we worthily partake of the sacrament and remember Jesus. . . . We show we know—by keeping the commandments" (*Ensign,* May 2003, 115).

*The song of the righteous is a prayer
unto me, and it shall be answered with
a blessing upon their heads.*

DOCTRINE & COVENANTS 25:12

Music and singing have always been a vital part of the legacy of the people of God from the beginning and will be through all eternity (Job 38:4–7; Mormon 7:7). Just before the most important event of all time—the Savior's suffering in Gethsemane—Jesus and His disciples sang a hymn together (Matthew 26:30; Mark 14:26). We sing in our homes and church meetings, at temple dedications, at all times and places where we want the Spirit of the Lord. Singing is an act of worship, of gratitude and praise, of communion with God that delights God and should delight us. Music can be a prayer that calls forth the blessings of heaven; it invigorates and calms the soul, it can inspire us to deeper spirituality and bring the Spirit mightily into our heart. Music and singing are integral to true righteousness and sincere worship, and those who refuse to sing in some sense refuse to worship and thereby lose heaven's blessings.

We remind you that where much is given, much is required.
We issue the call again for all spiritually, physically,
and emotionally qualified young men to come forth prepared
to become missionaries in the Church of Jesus Christ.

L. TOM PERRY
ENSIGN, NOVEMBER 2007, 49

To serve the Lord in fulltime missionary service is a sacred trust that calls for the best-prepared qualified prospective missionaries in the history of the Church. Apostles and prophets have raised the missionary bar in these challenging latter days when gospel light is needed more than ever. Elder L. Tom Perry said: "Personal worthiness is the minimum spiritual standard for serving a mission. This means that you are worthy in every way to make and to keep sacred temple covenants. Do not disqualify yourself from the blessings bestowed on those who serve in this very special calling by committing acts of transgression which will make you ineligible to serve. . . . Prepare yourself to be more effective in this great calling. May God bless you that this will be your desire. . . . Start now to prepare yourself for the glorious service which is ahead of you as a missionary of the Lord Jesus Christ" (*Ensign,* Nov. 2007, 49).

*The Christ-centered life produces in us,
not a woeful countenance, but a disciplined
enthusiasm to work righteousness.*

NEAL A. MAXWELL
ENSIGN, AUGUST 1981, 14

True spirituality is not so much what we feel but how we live. Enduring and staying faithful will give us the peace and confidence of the Spirit. Elder Neal A. Maxwell observed, "The Lord is preparing a very particular people for very particular chores in the next and everlasting world. Our schooling here cannot be a casual thing, or we would not be able to have immense joy there. One day, some of the challenges, the imponderables, and the incongruities that chafe and frustrate us now (and which are sufficient to deflect the weak from the path of duty) will be seen as having been necessary to our eternal happiness. Then we will even find ourselves thanking the Lord for not removing the thorns in the flesh which we wish so desperately could be removed now. Those who have coped with thorns in the flesh will one day repose in an everlasting rose garden; this rose garden was promised!" (*Ensign,* Aug. 1981, 17).

Neither the President of the Church, nor the First Presidency,
nor the united voice of the First Presidency and the Twelve
will ever lead the Saints astray or send forth counsel to the
world that is contrary to the mind and will of the Lord.

JOSEPH FIELDING SMITH
ENSIGN, JULY 1972, 88

We are promised that the Lord will never permit the united voice of the living prophets, seers, and revelators to lead us astray or send forth false teachings. The Lord will not allow His church to be led into darkness and apostasy. To avoid being deceived, we must evaluate what we hear in light of the standard works of the Church, listen to the confirming voice of the Spirit, and verify that the teaching comes through authorized channels from the leaders of the Church by common consent. The preaching of false doctrine usually comes from the lazy and indolent, or from the proud and self-vaunting ones who become prophets unto themselves. We must be wise, in tune with the Spirit, and constantly on guard so that we can resist, avoid, and discern the craftiness of those who lie in wait to deceive (Ephesians 4:14; D&C 123:12).

*[God] never will institute an ordinance
or give a commandment to His people
that is not calculated in its nature to promote
that happiness which He has designed.*

JOSEPH SMITH
HISTORY OF THE CHURCH, 5:135

All of us want to be happy. The Prophet Joseph Smith said: "Happiness is the object and design of our existence; and will be the end thereof, if we pursue the path that leads to it; and this path is virtue, uprightness, faithfulness, holiness, and keeping all the commandments of God" (*Teachings of the Prophet Joseph Smith,* 255–56). Happiness comes to those who strive to truly live the gospel, those who enter into and keep sacred covenants, those who center their lives on Jesus Christ and manifest integrity, goodness, and holiness in their lives. God wants for us happiness, the deep kind of happiness that is closer to abiding joy. Our Father in Heaven has a love for us that is perfect and never-ending. Our vision and understanding is limited, but our Father knows what will promote our greatest happiness and eternal joy (Isaiah 55:8–9).

[Abraham] staggered not at the promise of God
through unbelief; but was strong in faith,
giving glory to God; And being fully persuaded that,
what he had promised, he was able also to perform.

ROMANS 4:20–21

Abraham, the "father of the faithful," who lived some 2000 years before Christ, was one of the greatest prophets who ever lived. He staggered not at the promises of God as his faith was tested throughout his life. He believed that God would give his wife Sarah a son, though they were both too old to bear children, and he believed that God would raise Isaac from the dead, if need be, to fulfill the promise, "in Isaac shall thy seed be called" (Genesis 21:12; Hebrews 11:17–18). We, too, must not stagger at the promises of God: if we keep the commandments and honor our covenants, trust the Lord and His grace as we access the power of the Atonement, go forward with faith and hope and endure to the end, we will receive God's greatest promise—the gift of eternal life (D&C 14:7). God will surely fulfill His word to all those who believe and stagger not at the promises.

And hallow my sabbaths; and they shall be a sign
between me and you, that ye may know
that I am the Lord your God.

Ezekiel 20:20

When the Lord gave the Ten Commandments to Moses, among the ten was the command to: "Remember the sabbath day, to keep it holy. Six days shalt thou labour, and do all thy work: But the seventh day is the sabbath of the Lord thy God: in it thou shalt not do any work. . . . wherefore the Lord blessed the sabbath day, and hallowed it" (Exodus 20:8–11). As in obedience to all God's commands, actions speak louder than words. Do you want to show the Lord how you feel about Him? Do you want to be an example of the believers in word, thought, and deed (1 Timothy 4:12)? Do you hallow the Sabbath as a day set apart, a day to rest from your labors, a day to more fully keep yourself unspotted from the world (D&C 59:9–10)? One sure measure of your love of the Lord and your authentic desire for righteousness is how holy you keep the Sabbath.

Go forward in faith in keeping your covenants with God and so claim the promise He has made to you with an oath. You can do it in simple things. When you meet with your quorum, you can decide to see them as brothers in the family of God.

HENRY B. EYRING
ENSIGN, MAY 2008, 63

The oath and covenant of the priesthood is a sacred promise—a holy contract—that we will receive everlasting rewards if we honor our priesthood covenants, keep the commandments, and live by every word of God (D&C 84:44). In turn, the Lord promises us all that He hath (D&C 84:38). President Henry B. Eyring said: "I testify that God the Father lives. You have made covenants with Him. He offers you an oath, a promise of eternal life, which He cannot break. I testify to you that the priesthood is the power by which God through His Son, Jesus Christ, created the worlds. I testify that God wants you to succeed and to come home again to live with Him in families forever. I testify to you that this is the true Church of Jesus Christ. In it are the keys of the priesthood. It is that priesthood with which God has honored you" (*Ensign,* May 2008, 64).

Blessed is the man that resisteth temptation:
for when he is tried, he shall receive the crown of life,
which the Lord hath promised to them that love him.

JST, JAMES 1:12

Our Father in Heaven permits temptation to occur so we can be tested and tried in all things (Abraham 3:25). "When we give thanks in all things, we see hardships and adversities in the context of the purpose of life," said Elder Dallin H. Oaks. "We are sent here to be tested. There must be opposition in *all* things. We are meant to learn and grow through that opposition, through meeting our challenges, and through teaching others to do the same" (*Ensign,* May 2003, 97). As we resist and overcome temptation we become stronger and stronger, our faith and trust grow deeper and deeper, our reliance on the Lord and His sustaining hand becomes firmer and firmer. Prayer and scripture study are an armor of protection; faithfulness and humility are a refuge of safety. The crown of righteousness, which is eternal life, is given to those who resist temptation and hold fast to the Iron Rod.

*The small and simple things you choose to do today
will be magnified into great and glorious blessings tomorrow.*

ANN M. DIBB
ENSIGN, MAY 2009, 116

We are to be "examples of the believers" in thought, word, and deed (1 Timothy 4:12). Sister Ann M. Dibb, counselor in the Young Women general presidency and daughter of President and Sister Thomas S. Monson, said: "When I was a young girl, the Young Women program and Mutual were an important part of my life. I loved my friends, the lessons we were taught, youth conferences, and camp. My leaders loved me and taught me the truths of the gospel. They served as second witnesses to the gospel principles my parents had taught. . . . I recognize that I did not understand the magnitude of what was happening in my life. I did not realize that my participation in each and every Church activity was helping me develop a lifelong pattern and commitment to follow the teachings of Jesus Christ. . . . But in very small, incremental steps, I was becoming a believer—and 'an example of the believers'" (*Ensign,* May 2009, 114–15).

I will tell you in your mind and in your heart,
by the Holy Ghost, which shall come upon you
and which shall dwell in your heart.

DOCTRINE & COVENANTS 8:2

We can be blessed with the feelings of the Spirit as we daily walk through life. Joseph Smith said, "When you feel pure intelligence flowing into you, it may give you sudden strokes of ideas" (*History of the Church,* 3:381). President Henry B. Eyring described the influence of the Holy Ghost as "peace, hope, and joy." He added, "Almost always I have also felt a sensation of light" (*Ensign,* Jun. 2007, 18). Being guided by the Spirit isn't about sudden, overwhelming, dramatic experiences; rather, it is about trying day in and day out to do things you know are right. The sincere desire to do what's right and stay faithful are key indicators that a person is on the right track and being led by the Spirit.

*None [of my ancestors] were among those who lived
in Nauvoo or Winter Quarters, and none made the journey
across the plains. But as a member of the Church, I claim
with gratitude and pride this pioneer legacy as my own.*

DIETER F. UCHTDORF
ENSIGN, MAY 2008, 70

Though our journey is different from that of the stalwart pioneers who preceded us, we likewise are pioneers to future generations. President Gordon B. Hinckley said, "This great pioneering movement of more than a century ago goes forward with latter-day pioneers. Today pioneer blood flows in our veins just as it did with those who walked west. It's the essence of our courage to face modern-day mountains and our commitment to carry on. The faith of those early pioneers burns still, and nations are being blessed by latter-day pioneers who possess a clear vision of this work of the Lord. The footsteps that made such a deep impression over the heartland of America make similar impressions in countries across the world— from Belgium to Brazil and France to the Philippines. Step by faithful step, we walk together toward a glorious destiny, building the kingdom of God on earth" (*Ensign,* May 1997, 64).

Be honest with yourselves, honest before God. Be virtuous, be truthful and full of integrity, and fear the Lord your God in your hearts, and his blessing will be with you, and his Spirit will attend you, and your generations after you, worlds without end.

JOHN TAYLOR
JOHN TAYLOR, 64

John Taylor, third president of the Church, passed into eternity on this day in 1887. He joined the Church in Canada in 1836 and was called to the Twelve in 1838, becoming the leader of the Church with the passing of Brigham Young. He was a prominent Church author and editor, and was known for his fervent faith and testimony, his integrity and commitment to the truth. He would not yield on gospel principles; he was not ashamed of the gospel of Jesus Christ (Romans 1:16). And now, many generations after his death, we remember his resolute dedication to the truth. The dishonest, the weak and deceitful, are long since forgotten, but the truth and those who adhere to true principles stand the test of time. Those who are honest and virtuous, those with integrity and humility of heart, will be blessed with the companionship of the Spirit, peace in the soul, and generations yet unborn will rise up and call them blessed (Psalm 72:17).

Counsel with the Lord in all thy doings,
and he will direct thee for good.

ALMA 37:37

Alma counseled his son Helaman, "O, remember, my son, and learn wisdom in thy youth; yea, learn in thy youth to keep the commandments of God. Yea, and cry unto God for all thy support; yea, let all thy doings be unto the Lord, and whithersoever thou goest let it be in the Lord; yea, let all thy thoughts be directed unto the Lord; yea, let the affections of thy heart be placed upon the Lord forever" (Alma 37:35–36). All through the day we can think, *What would I do if the Savior stood beside me?* or *What wouldst Thou have me do?* or *How can I more fully receive and heed the whisperings of the Spirit in my life?* With a prayer in our hearts at all times and places, we continually think of the Lord, place our affections upon Him, and seek His direction, comfort, and influence. The Lord will surely guide and bless us if we turn to Him with full purpose of heart.

As we draw close to God, He will show us our
weaknesses and through them make us wiser, stronger [Ether
12:27]. If you're seeing more of your weaknesses, that just
might mean you're moving nearer to God, not farther away.

BRUCE C. HAFEN
ENSIGN, MAY 2004, 97

Adam and Eve's fall was not a mistake, accident, or disaster. It was a deliberate, necessary part of the great plan of salvation. They could understand the sweet only if they tasted the bitter; they could know true joy only if they had felt heartbreaking sorrow. Elder Bruce C. Hafen taught, "Adam and Eve learned constantly from their often harsh experience. They knew how a troubled family feels. Think of Cain and Abel. Yet because of the Atonement, they could *learn from their experience without being condemned by it.* Christ's sacrifice didn't just erase their choices and return them to an Eden of innocence. That would be a story with no plot and no character growth. His plan is *developmental*—line upon line, step by step, grace for grace" (*Ensign,* May 2004, 97). Having challenges and problems is part of life's purpose. We learn from our growing pains and mistakes, our heartache and sorrow, in a continual process made possible by the Savior's grace.

*Remember that this work is not yours and mine
alone. It is the Lord's work, and when we are on the
Lord's errand, we are entitled to the Lord's help.*

THOMAS S. MONSON
ENSIGN, NOVEMBER 2008, 62

A recently called bishop was overwhelmed with feelings of inadequacy. He felt unprepared spiritually, lacking in wisdom and depth, and worried about the time commitment. He knew that of his own accord he was insufficient for the task. But in process of time, he came to trust and feel inspired by the Lord's promise: when we are on the Lord's errand we are entitled to His help. This story has been experienced by countless others who have felt inadequate for the task. Church members and missionaries, leaders and teachers, mothers and fathers—all have experienced it. But the Lord will not leave us alone, comfortless, and without aid. He is our Savior and Master, to whom we look for solace, direction, and reassurance. When we feel inadequate and unprepared for our callings and responsibilities, trust the Lord. When we feel we can't do our part because we're not smart enough, spiritual enough, or capable enough, trust the Lord.

*If you will live the gospel, nearly everything
else will eventually take care of itself.*

GORDON B. HINCKLEY
STAND A LITTLE TALLER, 226

When all is said and done, it's really quite simple: if we live the gospel, things will eventually work out. That doesn't mean life will be easy or pain free, it doesn't mean all sunshine, lollipops, and happy faces throughout mortality. It does, however, mean that if we exercise robust hope during the dark days, we can go forward with faith. It means that if we rely on the merits and mercy of the Lord and have confidence in His plan of happiness and the infinite Atonement, we will find a promise of sweet reassurance (2 Nephi 2:8). It means that if we choose to stay obedient and submissive even during deepening trials and heartbreak, the Lord will whisper peace to our souls (D&C 121:7–8). Remember the Lord's declaration: "Search diligently, pray always, and be believing, and all things shall work together for your good, if ye walk uprightly and remember the covenant wherewith ye have covenanted one with another" (D&C 90:24).

*I, the Lord, forgive sins unto those who confess
their sins before me and ask forgiveness.*

DOCTRINE & COVENANTS 64:7

Sin is our common lot as fallen humanity. The
apostle Paul observed, "For all have sinned, and come
short of the glory of God" (Romans 3:23). Indeed, it
is impossible to get through mortality without sin.
But the gospel, its ordinances and covenants, gives us
hope. For each of us, sins of personal weakness can be
forgiven through confession, repentance, and the re-
newal of covenants available in taking the sacrament.
God said to Adam, "If thou wilt turn unto me, and
hearken unto my voice, and believe, and repent of all
thy transgressions, and be baptized, even in water, in
the name of mine Only Begotten Son, who is full of
grace and truth, which is Jesus Christ, the only name
which shall be given under heaven, whereby salvation
shall come unto the children of men, ye shall receive
the gift of the Holy Ghost, asking all things in his
name, and whatsoever ye shall ask, it shall be given
you" (Moses 6:52).

Men and women who turn their lives
over to God will discover that He can make a
lot more out of their lives than they can.

Ezra Taft Benson
Ensign, December 1988, 4

Those whose hearts and faith are centered in Christ become forever changed. "Some men are willing to die for their faith, but they are not willing to fully live for it," said President Ezra Taft Benson. "Christ both lived and died for us. Through His atonement and by walking in His steps, we can gain the greatest gift of all—eternal life, which is that kind of life of the great Eternal One—our Father in Heaven. Christ asked the question, 'What manner of men ought [we] to be?' He then answered by saying we ought to be even as He is. (3 Nephi 27:27.) That man is greatest and most blessed and joyful whose life most closely approaches the pattern of the Christ. This has nothing to do with earthly wealth, power, or prestige. The only true test of greatness, blessedness, joyfulness is how close a life can come to being like the Master, Jesus Christ" (*Ensign,* Dec. 1988, 2).

August

Have not I commanded thee?
Be strong and of a good courage;
be not afraid, neither be thou dismayed:
for the Lord thy God is with thee
whithersoever thou goest.

JOSHUA 1:9

*If you will prayerfully read the Book of Mormon, . . .
there will come into your hearts an added measure
of the Spirit of the Lord. There will come a strengthened
resolution to walk in obedience to His commandments.*

GORDON B. HINCKLEY
STAND A LITTLE TALLER, 324

A remarkable event occurred when many thousands of believers choose to follow President Gordon B. Hinckley's August 2005 challenge to read the Book of Mormon before the end of the year. Countless people, young and old and everything in between, could testify of that experience in willingly following the prophet. How testimonies were strengthened, how faith was fortified, how marriages and families were blessed! The Book of Mormon testifies and teaches of Christ; reading it will fill our hearts with the Spirit of the Lord, enlighten our minds, and imbue our souls with joy (D&C 11:13). These two things—choosing to humbly follow the prophet and reading this other testament of Jesus Christ—will produce profound experiences and mighty miracles.

By participating weekly and appropriately in the ordinance
of the sacrament we qualify for the promise that we will
"always have his Spirit to be with [us]" (D&C 20:77).
That Spirit is the foundation of our testimony.

DALLIN H. OAKS
ENSIGN, NOVEMBER 2008, 17

Elder Dallin H. Oaks said, "The ordinance of the sacrament makes the sacrament meeting the most sacred and important meeting in the Church. It is the only Sabbath meeting the entire family can attend together. Its content in addition to the sacrament should always be planned and presented to focus our attention on the Atonement and teachings of the Lord Jesus Christ. . . . During sacrament meeting—and especially during the sacrament service—we should concentrate on worship and refrain from all other activities. . . . Sacrament meeting is not a time for reading books or magazines. Young people, it is not a time for whispered conversations on cell phones or for texting persons at other locations. When we partake of the sacrament, we make a sacred covenant that we will always remember the Savior. How sad to see persons obviously violating that covenant in the very meeting where they are making it" (*Ensign,* Nov. 2008, 17–19).

*Some think of happiness as a glamorous life of ease, luxury,
and constant thrills; but true marriage is based on a
happiness which is more than that, one which comes from
giving, serving, sharing, sacrificing, and selflessness.*

SPENCER W. KIMBALL
ENSIGN, MARCH 1977, 3

Marriage is perhaps the most vital of all the decisions and has the most far-reaching effects, for it has
to do not only with immediate happiness, but also
with eternal joys," said President Spencer W. Kimball.
"It affects not only the two people involved, but also
their families and particularly their children and their
children's children. . . . In true marriage there must be
a union of minds as well as of hearts. Emotions must
not wholly determine decisions, but the mind and the
heart, strengthened by fasting and prayer and serious
consideration, will give one a maximum chance of
marital happiness. It brings with it sacrifice, sharing,
and a demand for great selflessness. Many of the TV
screen shows and stories of fiction end with marriage:
'They lived happily ever after.' . . . Happiness does not
come by pressing a button, as does the electric light;
happiness is a state of mind and comes from within. It
must be earned" (*Ensign,* Mar. 1977, 3).

Our spiritual journey is the process of a lifetime.
We do not know everything in the beginning or even along
the way. Our conversion comes step-by-step, line upon line.

NEIL L. ANDERSEN
ENSIGN, NOVEMBER 2008, 13

True conversion is a lifelong process. Little by little, with faith, and as we make and keep sacred our covenants with the Lord, we can become disciples who desire righteousness with heart, mind, and soul. We will come to realize that our fears have been replaced with faith, our worries with hope, our selfishness with pure love. Elder Neil L. Andersen said, "We first build a foundation of faith in the Lord Jesus Christ. We treasure the principles and ordinances of repentance, baptism, and receiving the gift of the Holy Ghost. We include a continuing commitment to prayer, a willingness to be obedient, and an ongoing witness of the Book of Mormon. . . . We then remain steady and patient as we progress through mortality. At times, the Lord's answer will be, 'You don't know everything, but you know enough'—enough to keep the commandments and to do what is right" (*Ensign*, Nov. 2008, 13). The Lord will help us every step along the way.

*Sooner or later, either privately or publicly, we will all be
tested. We must be prepared to defend our values, our
standards, our commitments, and our covenants to stand as a
witness of God at all times, in all things, and in all places.*

ARDETH G. KAPP
ENSIGN, NOVEMBER 1990, 93

Sister Ardeth Kapp, former general president of the
Young Women, said, "The crickets of our day are different than in times past. They are powerful, more
dangerous and less noticeable. . . . At first, things may
appear to be very innocent. Thoughts, words, and pic-
tures are placed into our minds through very subtle
and sophisticated ways. Thoughts come first and are
then expressed through words. No one uses vulgar,
crude words without first having the same kind of
thoughts. Can you see how damaging such innocent
beginnings are? If we are not watchful, the crickets will
creep into our safe places, our homes, our hearts, and
our minds. Through TV, radio, magazines, movies, literature, music, and fashions, these evil influences will
aggressively begin their silent destruction, multiplying
their forces as they go" (*Ensign,* Nov. 1990, 94). We
must reject the cunning influence of the adversary and
stand steadfast as witnesses of God and His gospel.

*You need have no fear, my dear brothers and sisters,
that any man will ever stand at the head of the Church of Jesus
Christ unless our Heavenly Father wants him to be there.*

HEBER J. GRANT
HEBER J. GRANT, 74

The men who have served as presidents of this
Church are called of God and guided by the inspiration of heaven. They were not just in the right place
at the right time to be called; not simply from the
right family or from the right pedigree; not examples
of mere coincidence or happenstance. They were appointed from the foundations of the world to serve
for a season and move forward the work of the Lord
in their own inimitable way (Abraham 3:22–23;
Jeremiah 1:5). Each one has been different, with distinct personalities and preferences. But each has been
thoroughly consecrated to the work of the Lord, each
has been motivated by the desire to testify and bring
people unto Christ, each has done his best to spread
the gospel and lead us to peace and happiness here
and exaltation hereafter. It is our duty to support the
Lord's anointed prophet by praying for him, following
his inspired counsel, and sustaining him in his labors.

*Be merciful and you shall find mercy. Seek to help save souls,
not to destroy them: for verily you know, that "there is more
joy in heaven, over one sinner that repents, than there is over
ninety and nine just persons that need no repentance."*

JOSEPH SMITH
TEACHINGS OF THE PROPHET JOSEPH SMITH, 77

It has been said that there are only two things we do in life: repent and forgive. Both of these are possible because of the enabling power of the Atonement. We all need to be forgiven, we all need mercy; we all need to forgive, we all need to extend mercy. As disciples of the Lord we have entered into a sacred covenant to "mourn with those that mourn; yea, and comfort those that stand in need of comfort, and to stand as witnesses of God at all times and in all things, and in all places" (Mosiah 18:9). We witness our belief in and determination to follow the Savior by how we treat others. It's not how many daily verses of scripture we read, how long our prayers, or what callings we hold, although those things may manifest a changed heart. The measure of our devotion to the Lord is how we love and forgive, how we reach out to lift and bless, how we show mercy and compassion.

As General Authorities of the Church, we are just the
same as you are, and you are just the same as we are.
You have the same access to the powers of revelation for your
families and for your work and for your callings as we do.

BOYD K. PACKER
ENSIGN, NOVEMBER 2007, 9

There is the natural tendency to look at those who are sustained to presiding positions, to consider them to be higher and of more value in the Church or to their families than an ordinary member," said President Boyd K. Packer. "Somehow we feel they are worth more to the Lord than are we. It just does not work that way! It would be very disappointing to my wife and to me if we supposed any one of our children would think that we think we are of more worth to the family or to the Church than they are, or to think that one calling in the Church was esteemed over another or that any calling would be thought to be less important. . . . No member of the Church is esteemed by the Lord as more or less than any other. It just does not work that way! Remember, He is a father—our Father." (*Ensign,* Nov. 2007, 8–9). If we are worthy, each one of us is entitled to promptings and guidance from the Lord.

Nothing will bring greater joy and success than to live according to the teachings of the gospel. Be an example; be an influence for good; be prepared and worthy to accept any call that comes from the Lord.

N. ELDON TANNER
ENSIGN, NOVEMBER 1975, 74

We are to be "an example of the believers, in word, in conversation, in charity, in spirit, in faith, in purity" (1 Timothy 4:12). As followers of Jesus Christ and believers in His restored gospel, we are always under surveillance, always being watched by others to see if we are walking the talk, practicing what we preach, and striving to live what we teach. Ours is the great and covenantal opportunity to be an influence for good. President N. Eldon Tanner, during the October 1975 general conference, said, "Always remember that people are looking to you for leadership and you are influencing the lives of individuals either for good or for bad, which influence will be felt for generations to come" (*Ensign,* Nov. 1975, 74). We have the ability to influence in a positive way all with whom we come in contact.

*The distance to "a far country" is not to be
measured by miles but by how far our hearts and minds are
from Jesus! (Mosiah 5:13). Fidelity, not geography,
really determines the distance!*

NEAL A. MAXWELL
ENSIGN, NOVEMBER 2000, 36

The world and worldly will increasingly intrude upon our lives; the clarion calls of materialism, skepticism, and cynicism will ever resound around us. But rising above it all—for all those with the spark of the Holy Ghost and the Light of Christ within—will come spiritual feelings and promptings from the Lord to comfort, soften, and guide. As Elder Neal A. Maxwell said, "Doubts of doubt can intrude. All the quick fixes do not really cure the emptiness and boredom of secularism. Further, some who laboriously scale the secular heights find, after all, that they are only squatting atop a small mound of sand! They have worked so hard to get there!" (*Ensign,* Nov. 2000, 36). Those who see things as they really are and as they really will be (Jacob 4:13; D&C 93:24) will give the glory and honor and praise unto God for His great plan of happiness; they will center their energy and devotion on Jesus Christ and His gospel.

*The greatest attainment that we can reach is to preserve our
identity to an eternal duration in the midst of the heavenly hosts.
We have the words of eternal life given to us through the Gospel,
which, if we obey, will secure unto us that precious gift.*

BRIGHAM YOUNG
BRIGHAM YOUNG, 89

Eternal life is the greatest gift that can be given
to us (D&C 14:7). Eternal life is the ability to progress and increase forever; it is the name given to the
kind of life that God lives; it is to live everlastingly,
to never be destroyed, to live the quality of life that
God himself enjoys. Our Heavenly Father's work and
glory is to bring about the immortality and eternal
life of His children (Moses 1:39). Immortality and
eternal life are not synonymous. Immortality is to
live forever in the resurrected state; and by the benevolent grace of God all people will attain this endless continuance of life. But only those who obey the
fullness of the gospel law and endure to the end will
inherit eternal life (D&C 29:43–44). Those who
gain eternal life receive exaltation, they are joint-heirs
with Christ (Romans 8:17), they overcome all things,
have all power, and receive the fullness of the Father.

Self-reliance is taking responsibility for our own spiritual and temporal welfare and for those whom Heavenly Father has entrusted to our care. Only when we are self-reliant can we truly emulate the Savior in serving and blessing others.

ROBERT D. HALES
ENSIGN, JANUARY 2010, 9

As followers of the Lord, our quest is to become more like Him. To choose Christ is to choose to become different, to become a new creature, to become forever changed. Indeed, the glorious message of the gospel of Jesus Christ is that we can change and become better than we are. To become more like our Savior is to become more spiritually attentive; more humble and selfless; more grateful and gracious; more desirous to live providently, increase our gifts and talents, and serve others. The Lord has given us the divine endowment of agency—we are free to act, to choose, to do, and therefore become. Elder Robert D. Hales said, "It is important to understand that self-reliance is a means to an end. Our ultimate goal is to become like the Savior, and that goal is enhanced by our unselfish service to others. Our ability to serve is increased or diminished by the level of our self-reliance" (*Ensign,* Jan. 2010, 9).

Every time that I have listened to the counsel of prophets,
felt it confirmed in prayer, and then followed it, I have found
that I moved toward safety. . . . I have found that the way had
been prepared for me and the rough places made smooth.

HENRY B. EYRING
ENSIGN, JUNE 2008, 6

Looking for the path to safety in the counsel of prophets makes sense to those with strong faith," said President Henry B. Eyring. "When a prophet speaks, those with little faith may think that they hear only a wise man giving good advice. Then if his counsel seems comfortable and reasonable, squaring with what they want to do, they take it. If it does not, they either consider it faulty advice or they see their circumstances as justifying their being an exception to the counsel. . . . The choice not to take prophetic counsel changes the very ground upon which we stand. That ground becomes more dangerous. The failure to take prophetic counsel lessens our power to take inspired counsel in the future. The best time to have decided to help Noah build the ark was the first time he asked. Each time he asked after that, each failure to respond would have lessened sensitivity to the Spirit" (*Ensign*, Jun. 2008, 6).

Honour thy father and thy mother:
that thy days may be long upon the land
which the Lord thy God giveth thee.

EXODUS 20:12

The law dealing with family relationships was identified by Paul as the "first commandment with promise" (Ephesians 6:2). The commandment is to "honour thy father and mother," and the associated promise is that "it may be well with thee, and thou mayest live long on the earth" (Ephesians. 6:2–3). We best honor our parents by living an honorable life. Elder Dallin H. Oaks said, "If you honor your parents, you will love them, respect them, confide in them, be considerate of them, express appreciation for them, and demonstrate all of these things by following their counsel in righteousness and by obeying the commandments of God" (*Ensign,* May 1991, 15). We are under no obligation to follow parents in sin, to allow wickedness or evil in any form under the guise of honoring parents. We honor righteousness and truth. We also have heavenly parents, and as we honor them we will find that our days will indeed be long—even throughout eternity.

For ye are all the children of God by faith in Christ Jesus. For as many of you as have been baptized into Christ have put on Christ.

Galatians 3:26–27

Our own experience tells us that the apostle Paul taught truth: "The Spirit itself beareth witness with our spirit, that we are the children of God" (Romans 8:16). As children of a loving Heavenly Father, we are endowed with the seeds of divinity. He is not a Father removed and disconnected from His children, or a spirit essence, unembodied and without affection. He is our Father; He knows us, He loves us, He wants for us eternal happiness. His greatest joy and ultimate glory come from seeing His children become like Him. He has provided the means by which we can overcome the world: His Son, our Savior. Through the mediation and Atonement of Jesus we can become new creatures, forgiven, redeemed (Mosiah 27:23–26). As we do so, we become changed in Christ. We take a new name: Christ. We receive a new image and countenance: Christ (Alma 5:14, 19). We make a new covenant: Christ.

You all have inquiring minds and are seeking truth in many fields. I sincerely hope your greatest search is in the realm of spiritual things, because it is there that we are able to gain salvation and make the progress that leads to eternal life.

JOSEPH FIELDING SMITH
ENSIGN, MAY 1971, 2

In the hierarchy of knowledge, some knowledge matters more than other knowledge. It's interesting to understand the laws of nature; it's essential that we understand the nature of God. It's worthwhile to know the principles of physics; it's imperative to know the principles of the gospel. There is knowledge that is important, and there is other knowledge that is absolutely vital. "The most important knowledge in the world is gospel knowledge," said President Joseph Fielding Smith. "It is a knowledge of God and his laws, of those things that men must do to work out their salvation with fear and trembling before the Lord. One of our revelations tells us that if we are to be glorified in Christ, as he is in the Father, we must understand and know both how to worship and what we worship (D&C 93:19–20.)" (*Ensign*, May 1971, 2). The knowledge and truth that leads us along the pathway to eternal life is of greatest worth.

At times the statement is made, "I never can forgive [this person or that person]." Such an attitude . . . can canker the soul and ruin one's life. In other instances, an individual can forgive another but cannot forgive himself. Such a situation is even more destructive.

THOMAS S. MONSON
ENSIGN, MAY 1995, 59

The Savior's life was filled with touching examples of mercy and forgiveness. The only perfect person to walk the earth was ever willing to extend mercy, ever ready to offer forgiveness. His example of compassion echoes down the centuries as a model of pure love and perfect kindness. Unlike the Savior, we are stained by worldly susceptibilities and natural-man tendencies; we may hold on to grudges and withhold forgiveness, we may let pride get the best of us and refuse to change or let go or repent. President Thomas S. Monson said, "Should you or I have erred or spoken harshly to another, it is good to take steps to straighten out the matter and to move onward with our lives. 'He [who] cannot forgive others breaks the bridge over which he himself must pass if he would ever reach heaven; for every one has need to be forgiven' [George Herbert]" (*Ensign,* May 1995, 60). We who so desperately need mercy and forgiveness must extend the same to others.

All the imponderable blessings of the Atonement can be given only to those who live the principles and receive the ordinances of the gospel—faith in Jesus Christ, repentance, baptism, receiving the Holy Ghost, and enduring to the end.

L. TOM PERRY
ENSIGN, MAY 2009, 110

As followers of the Lord and beneficiaries of His infinite Atonement, we are under solemn covenant to open our mouths and share with others the good news of the gospel (D&C 33: 7–10). "Our great missionary message to the world is that all mankind is invited to be rescued and to enter the fold of the Good Shepherd, even Jesus Christ," said Elder L. Tom Perry. "Our missionary message is strengthened by the knowledge of the Restoration. We know that God speaks to His prophets today, just as He did anciently. We also know that His gospel is administered with the power and authority of the restored priesthood. No other message has such great eternal significance to everyone living on the earth today. All of us need to teach this message to others with power and conviction. . . . We must warn our neighbors" (*Ensign*, May 2009, 110–11).

*Our Heavenly Father asks His daughters to walk
in virtue, to live in righteousness so that we can fulfill
our life's mission and His purposes. He wants us to
be successful, and He will help us as we seek His help.*

Margaret D. Nadauld
Ensign, November 2000, 14

Women of God can never be like women of the
world," said former Young Women general president
Margaret Nadauld. "The world has enough women
who are tough; we need women who are tender. There
are enough women who are coarse; we need women
who are kind. There are enough women who are rude;
we need women who are refined. We have enough
women of fame and fortune; we need more women of
faith. We have enough greed; we need more goodness.
We have enough vanity; we need more virtue. We
have enough popularity; we need more purity" (*Ensign,*
Nov. 2000, 15). Sister Nadauld said that you can recognize women who are grateful to be daughters of
God by their outward appearance, their attitude and
abilities, their reverence for motherhood, their love
of God, and their kindness, gentleness, and strength.
These women, who are so desperately needed today,
will be beacons of light to the rest of the world.

Prayer is for the uplifting of the suppliant. God without our prayers would be God; but we without prayer cannot be admitted to the kingdom of God.

JAMES E. TALMAGE
JESUS THE CHRIST, 238

It is a transcendent blessing to be able to approach our Father in prayer, to acknowledge Him as the Giver, to express our heartfelt gratitude, desires, and concerns. Just as food is indispensable to life, so too is prayer to our spiritual life. Elder James E. Talmage said, "It is well to know that prayer is not compounded of words, words that may fail to express what one desires to say, words that so often cloak inconsistencies, words that may have no deeper source than the physical organs of speech, words that may be spoken to impress mortal ears. . . . Prayer is made up of heart throbs and the righteous yearnings of the soul, of supplication based on the realization of need, of contrition and pure desire. If there lives a man who has never really prayed, that man is a being apart from the order of the divine in human nature, a stranger in the family of God's children" (*Jesus the Christ*, 238).

*When we truly understand what it means to love as Jesus
Christ loves us, the confusion clears and our priorities
align. Our walk as disciples of Christ becomes more joyful.
. . . Obedience becomes a joy rather than a burden.*

DIETER F. UCHTDORF
ENSIGN, NOVEMBER 2009, 21

President Dieter F. Uchtdorf powerfully taught us
of divine love: "[God] doesn't care one bit if we live
in a castle or a cottage, if we are handsome or homely,
if we are famous or forgotten. Though we are incom-
plete, God loves us completely. Though we are imperfect, He loves us perfectly. Though we may feel
lost and without compass, God's love encompasses us
completely. He loves us because He is filled with an
infinite measure of holy, pure, and indescribable love.
We are important to God not because of our résumé
but because we are His children. He loves every one
of us, even those who are flawed, rejected, awkward,
sorrowful, or broken. . . . No matter our distress, no
matter our sorrow, no matter our mistakes, our in-
finitely compassionate Heavenly Father desires that
we draw near to Him so that He can draw near to us
[D&C 88:63]" (*Ensign,* Nov. 2009, 22–23).

Should the commandments be rewritten?
No, they should be reread and become the guide
and standard of our lives, if we want health and
happiness and peace and self-respect.

RICHARD L. EVANS
ENSIGN, DECEMBER 1971, 58

Elder Richard L. Evans gave this wise counsel to the youth of the Church: "Respect parents. Confide in them. Respect yourselves. Respect God and the knowledge he has given. Don't gamble with life. It is all we have. Don't tempt temptation. Don't foolishly see how close you can come to danger or evil, how close you can come to a precipice. Stay away from what you shouldn't do or where you shouldn't go, or what you shouldn't partake of. And if you've turned toward some dead-end or down some wrong road, turn back as quickly as you can—not later than right now—and thank God for the principle of repentance. Don't run aimlessly looking to and fro for what has already been found. Don't live by the sophistries and temptations of these times. Don't tamper with the degrading soul- and body-destroying things of life. Don't deliberately look less than your best, or grubby or unclean, physically or morally" (*Ensign,* Dec. 1971, 58).

If I had a sufficient power for reasonable argument,
I would try to persuade everyone in the world, both in
and out of the Church, to live the law of the fast.

STERLING W. SILL
ENSIGN, JULY 1974, 9

The first Sunday of each month is set aside as fast Sunday, wherein we are invited to abstain from two meals and then give the monetary value of those meals to the bishop. Our fast offerings go to provide food, clothing, and other help for those in need. Fast Sunday is also a day where we go to church and share our testimonies, express appreciation, and encourage one another. Fasting helps us to develop greater self-discipline and deeper spirituality; it is good for our health and well-being. It reminds us how dependent we are upon the Lord, how grateful we should be for the bounties of life. Elder Sterling W. Sill taught, "This law of the fast can also be a kind of schoolmaster. If we can learn to live it effectively, it will help us to keep every other law better because of the power and faith that will be generated in us as a natural consequence of our living this important law" (*Ensign,* Jul. 1974, 11).

After they had spoken these words the Spirit of the Lord
came upon them, and they were filled with joy,
having received a remission of their sins, and having peace
of conscience, because of the exceeding faith which
they had in Jesus Christ who should come.

MOSIAH 4:3

The scriptures link our happiness in this life and the next with peace of conscience. Alma taught that the opposite of joy is remorse of conscience (Alma 29:5). Other prophets tie the torment of the wicked following this life to the fear, guilt, and pain they feel (2 Nephi 9:14, 46; Mosiah 2:38; 3:24–25; Mormon 9:5). Joseph Smith said: "A man is his own tormentor and his own condemner. Hence the saying, They shall go into the lake that burns with fire and brimstone. The torment of disappointment in the mind of man is as exquisite as a lake burning with fire and brimstone" (*History of the Church*, 6:314). The righteous, on the other hand, are those who exercise faith and repent, continually strive to overcome the world and put off the natural man. As the apostle Paul taught, "For to be carnally minded is death; but to be spiritually minded is life and peace" (Romans 8:6).

*The Atonement not only benefits the sinner but also benefits
those sinned against. . . . By forgiving "those who trespass against
us" the Atonement brings a measure of peace and comfort to those
who have been innocently victimized by the sins of others.*

JAMES E. FAUST
ENSIGN, NOVEMBER 2001, 20

President James E. Faust said the Savior "knows our
mortal trials by firsthand experience. It is a bit like us
trying to climb Mount Everest and only getting up
the first few feet. But He has climbed all 29,000 feet
to the top of the mountain. He suffered more than
any other mortal could" (*Ensign,* Nov. 2001, 19–20).
Although we cannot fully comprehend the magnitude of the Atonement, we can come to fully appreciate the perfect and encompassing love the Savior has
for each of us. His love, which is everlasting, is full
of mercy, long-suffering, and grace. We can trust the
promise that through our repentance and the gift of
the Atonement, we can be healed, we can be forgiven,
and we can prepare to be worthy to stand in the
Lord's presence. If we are quick to repent and quick
to forgive, we will come to fully understand the sweet
joy of the infinite Atonement.

*Cheating in academic work is unprincipled, dishonest,
and a form of self-deception and betrayal. No student
can hope to ultimately succeed in a career or profession
if he or she builds upon a foundation of fraud.*

DAVID A. BEDNAR
NEW ERA, OCTOBER 2005, 6

A recent nationwide survey of high school and university students found that a large proportion had cheated in school. Even more discouraging was that most students felt satisfied with their personal character and ethics and believed that cheating or lying wasn't a big deal, that everyone does it, and that it isn't necessarily an indication of lack of integrity. Prophets and the Spirit of the Lord tell us otherwise. Dishonesty in any form is self-deception and a betrayal of the best within us, the Spirit, and our sacred covenants. Yes, we all make mistakes; we're all far from perfect. But we can sincerely strive in our conversations and interactions, in our school and occupational endeavors, to be people of honor, character, and integrity. If we do so, we build foundations of truth and relationships of trust.

In one who is wholly converted, desire for things inimical to the gospel of Jesus Christ has actually died, and substituted therefor is a love of God, with a fixed and controlling determination to keep his commandments.

MARION G. ROMNEY
ENSIGN, NOVEMBER 1975, 72

Those who are converted have beating in their hearts a love of God, a fixed determination to keep His commandments, and a testimony of the living reality of the Savior and the restored gospel. Paul told the Romans that such a one would walk in newness of life: "Know ye not, that so many of us as were baptized into Jesus Christ were baptized into his death? Therefore we are buried with him by baptism into death: that like as Christ was raised up from the dead . . . even so we also should walk in newness of life" (Romans 6:3–4). Peter taught that by walking in the newness of life one escapes "the corruption that is in the world through lust," and by developing within himself faith, virtue, knowledge, temperance, patience, godliness, brotherly kindness, and charity, he becomes a partaker "of the divine nature" (2 Peter 1:4–7). To walk in newness of life is to be truly converted.

Have not I commanded thee?
Be strong and of a good courage; be not afraid,
neither be thou dismayed: for the Lord thy God
is with thee whithersoever thou goest.

JOSHUA 1:9

Moses spoke to ancient Israel, saying, "Be strong and of a good courage, fear not, nor be afraid of them: for the Lord thy God, he it is that doth go with thee; he will not fail thee, nor forsake thee" (Deuteronomy 31:6). Referencing this bold statement from Moses, a latter-day prophet, Thomas S. Monson, said, "It is this sweet assurance that can guide you and me—in our time, in our day, in our lives. Of course, we will face fear, experience ridicule, and meet opposition. Let us have the courage to defy the consensus, the courage to stand for principle. Courage, not compromise, brings the smile of God's approval. Courage becomes a living and an attractive virtue when it is regarded not only as a willingness to die manfully, but also as a determination to live decently. . . . All men have their fears, but those who face their fears with dignity have courage as well" (*Ensign,* May 2004, 55–56).

*A temple recommend is one of the highest accolades
we may receive. To use it regularly permits us to participate
in the choicest gifts within the keeping of the Church.
Those who attend feel a special spirit there. Peace comes.*

A. THEODORE TUTTLE
ENSIGN, MAY 1982, 66

Temple work and temple building are spreading across the earth in a remarkable and miraculous way. How blessed we are to have so many houses of the Lord on the earth today—more than at any time in the world's history. But, in a sense, we are just beginning. So much is yet to be done. It is we—the living—who have the responsibility to be worthy of a temple recommend and do our part to redeem the dead. Everything that goes on inside the temple is about eternity and about family. Temples are houses of instruction, places of covenants and promises, sanctuaries of peace, havens of blessings, and the link between heaven and earth. As we attend the temple and participate in sacred ordinances, we can glimpse a bit of heaven and savor the sweet serenity of the Lord's spirit. Blessings flow from temple work to those on both sides of the veil.

*Behold, I, the Lord, have brought you together that
the promise might be fulfilled, that the faithful among
you should be preserved and rejoice together. . . . I,
the Lord, promise the faithful and cannot lie.*

DOCTRINE & COVENANTS 62:6

Some elders of the Church were commanded in 1831 to travel from Kirtland to Missouri and, preaching the gospel along the way, there hold a conference. The Lord promised that he would "crown the faithful with joy and with rejoicing" (D&C 52:43). We, too, travel the roads of life with a promise: we will be blessed and preserved if we are faithful. Sometimes the road is long and hard, sometimes it seems impossible to travel, but we can trust the Lord and His promise: He will ever attend those who follow Him in humility, faith, and righteousness. He is a God of His word, a God of truth, a God of exactness and honor. He cannot, does not, and will not, lie. As the Lord said anciently, and the same promise is true in our day: "I the Lord have spoken it, and I will do it" (Ezekiel 36:36).

There are no shortcuts to eternity. Thus,
extreme patience becomes another key factor as
we develop our testimony over a lifetime.

ROBERT L. SIMPSON
ENSIGN, MAY 1987, 41

The process of developing a testimony comes in process of time, "line upon line, precept upon precept; here a little, and there a little" (D&C 128:21). Elder Robert L. Simpson said, "Now, whether it be a testimony about the Book of Mormon, tithing, the Word of Wisdom, the law of the fast, keeping the Sabbath day holy, or any other principle, the process is exactly the same. First we must understand it through the scriptures and then we live it to the best of our ability; then we ask Heavenly Father with a sincere heart, with faith in Christ; then the truth of that principle will be manifest to us by the power of the Holy Ghost. If you want to know the truth, you become informed, you be willing, and you be available" (*Ensign,* May 1987, 42). The Holy Ghost will confirm the truth to our hearts and lead us to that which is true; it will give us the strength and understanding to go forward with faith.

SEPTEMBER

See that ye do all things in worthiness,
and do it in the name of Jesus Christ,
the Son of the living God; and if ye do this,
and endure to the end, ye will
in nowise be cast out.

MORMON 9:29

Marriage is the closest and most intimate relationship one makes in this life, and the most serious and sacred decision. If you haven't been to the Lord's house, get ready, be clean, prepare to come to establish the foundation for a special, happy, eternal marriage.

MARION D. HANKS
ENSIGN, NOVEMBER 1984, 38

Marriage has been described as a marathon, not a sprint. It takes effort and work, commitment and dedication. Speaking of eternal marriage, Elder Marion D. Hanks said: "It is simple to see, isn't it, that the kind of marriage we're talking about doesn't just happen? The foundation is laid in the House of the Lord. The marriage is pronounced by authority of God. And then it is fashioned by two who are wholesome, prepared emotionally and practically, and who are honest. It requires being *ready* to go to a temple, being mature enough to make promises and keep them and to receive holy promises and qualify for them. So wherever we are with respect to marriage— years from it, close to it, or deeply committed in it—we must be wise, be faithful to the commandments of God, be true" (*Ensign,* Nov. 1984, 37–38).

[The Lord] commands, and to those who obey Him, whether they be wise or simple, He will reveal Himself in the toils, the conflicts, the sufferings that they shall pass through in His fellowship; and they shall learn by their own experience who He is.

THOMAS S. MONSON
ENSIGN, MAY 1986, 39

The word of the Lord to each of us is this: "Wherefore, now let every man learn his duty, and to act in the office in which he is appointed, in all diligence" (D&C 107:99). Whatever our calling at present, we are to be anxiously engaged in doing our duty, magnifying our calling, and serving others in love and kindness. We don't need a specific calling to fulfill our covenant duty to be "willing to bear one another's burdens" and "mourn with those that mourn" and "comfort those that stand in need of comfort" and "stand as witnesses of God at all times and in all things" (Mosiah 18:8–9). "Let us, in the performance of our duty, follow in the footsteps of the Master," encouraged President Thomas S. Monson (*Ensign,* May 1986, 39). True disciples follow the Lord every time they sincerely love, serve, and lift others.

The challenge before us is great. It will require us to
exercise increased faith, energy, and commitment
if we are to reach [our] brothers and sisters. But we
must do it. The Lord is counting on us to do it.

BEN B. BANKS
ENSIGN, NOVEMBER 1999, 10

President Gordon B. Hinckley taught us that every new convert needs a friend, a responsibility, and continued nourishing by the good word of God to remain active in the Church. The lost sheep among us need that same care and concern to help them back to the fold. Elder Ben B. Banks said, "We must remember that change occurs slowly. We all need to have patience, offer fellowship and friendship, learn to listen and love, and be careful not to judge. In every ward and branch there are good, honest men and women. Many don't know how to come back to church. There are good fathers and mothers among them. Many have one thing in common: they are not the spiritual leaders in their homes. When men and women of faith visit these individuals and become their friends and love them and teach them the gospel, I believe they and their families will come back" (*Ensign,* Nov. 1999, 10).

The forces of life are always stronger than the forces of death. If we choose, if we even desire to choose, if we even hope for the desire to choose, we set in motion powerful forces for life that are led by Jesus Christ himself.

CHIEKO N. OKAZAKI
ENSIGN, NOVEMBER 1996, 90

Sister Chieko N. Okazaki, former first counselor in the general Relief Society presidency, said, "Choose life even though the forces of death seem strong! Choose hope even though despair seems close! Choose to grow even though circumstances oppress you! Choose to learn even though you must struggle against your own ignorance and that of others! Choose to love, even though ours are days of violence and vengeance. Choose to forgive, to pray, to bless another's life with simple kindness. Choose to build the sisterhood of the Relief Society by lifting and strengthening one another with love, testimony, faith, and service. I promise that you will feel the abundant love of the Savior. He receives each act of mercy to one of the least as one done to Himself. And in return He defies hopelessness, weariness, despair, and meaninglessness on our behalf" (*Ensign*, Nov. 1996, 91).

*When we undertake to cover our sins, or to gratify our pride,
our vain ambition, or to exercise control or dominion or
compulsion upon the souls of the children of men, . . . the heavens
withdraw themselves; the Spirit of the Lord is grieved.*

DOCTRINE & COVENANTS 121:37

The finest guide for priesthood leadership and service in the kingdom is found in the Lord's words of peace to the Prophet Joseph in Liberty Jail in 1839: "No power or influence can or ought to be maintained by virtue of the priesthood, only by persuasion, by long-suffering, by gentleness and meekness, and by love unfeigned; By kindness, and pure knowledge, which shall greatly enlarge the soul without hypocrisy, and without guile" (D&C 121:41–42). Man has no priesthood power or authority where there is arrogance and vain ambition, unrighteous dominion and hypocrisy, sinfulness and deceit. Righteousness comes of humility and long-suffering, kindness and care, love and compassion. Power in the priesthood cannot be forced, manipulated, or borrowed in the hour of need. It is developed over time in daily efforts to serve the Lord and "do justly, and to love mercy, and to walk humbly with thy God" (Micah 6:8).

*We're all on a journey. Dads are a little further down
the road, but none of us has yet arrived at our final
destination. . . . Fathers and sons can play a critical role
in helping each other become the best that they can be.*

M. RUSSELL BALLARD
ENSIGN, NOVEMBER 2009, 47

Fatherhood is a sacred stewardship. Speaking to
fathers, President Ezra Taft Benson emphasized,
"Remember your sacred calling as a father in Israel—
your most important calling in time and eternity—a
calling from which you will never be released" (*Ensign,*
Nov. 1987, 51). Fathers serve essentials roles in the
home as teachers, examples, breadwinners, protectors,
companions, friends, spouses, and moral guides. They
are to preside, protect and provide for the family, and
partner with their spouses in rearing a family in love
and righteousness (see "The Family: A Proclamation
to the World"). Although father-child relationships
are never perfect, fathers and children help each other
to learn and grow, to love and forgive, to develop attributes of godliness and become strong men and women
of Christ. Faithful fathers seek to follow the divine
example of their Heavenly Father—a sacred appren-
ticeship in the process of becoming like God.

*Doesn't it make you deeply grateful to belong to a church
with apostles and prophets at the head . . . ? As the
world moves deeper and deeper into sin, this wonderful
Church stands like a giant granite boulder.*

VAUGHN J. FEATHERSTONE
ENSIGN, NOVEMBER 1999, 13

The light of the restored gospel will never be extinguished even as the world moves ever deeper in darkness and sin. But that strong link to the faith of our fathers and to a robust future for the Church is dependent upon our youth. It has been said that the Church is only one generation away from apostasy. Elder Vaughn J. Featherstone taught, "Beloved youth, be grateful for parents who have prayer and read the scriptures. Prize family home evening. Be grateful for those who teach and train you. . . . Young men and young women, raise the standard; carry the torch for your generation. We have absolute confidence you will. I thank God for the one link that still holds, the one light that will not go out. Remember how blessed you are to have prayer in your homes. And always try to put lights in your mothers' eyes. That's the least we can all do for them" (*Ensign*, Nov. 1999, 16).

*Individual worth is intrinsic, it is internal; it is eternal. It . . .
cannot be taken from us when the blossom of youth fades, when
economic conditions leave us desolate, when sickness or handicaps
befall us, or when prominence and visibility are obscured.*

JOANNE B. DOXEY
ENSIGN, NOVEMBER 1987, 91

Recognition of our inherent, divine endowment of worth is the key to building a secure relationship with God and the key to walking the pathway of life with faith, hope, and courage. Sister Joanne B. Doxey, then a member of the Relief Society general presidency, said: "If we rely on the Lord, follow the map, and watch the road signs, without making a lot of unnecessary detours, we can navigate through mortality and reach our destination safely, in the Lord's due time. Decisions determine destiny. What are some of the road signs or guides that help us through this earthly life? A living prophet, who speaks the mind and will of God; prayer, whereby we can speak to God and be directed by the Holy Spirit; the scriptures, wherein God speaks to us; the priesthood, with power to act for God; and sacred covenants and ordinances, which offer us family life with our Heavenly Father forever" (*Ensign,* Nov. 1987, 91).

Great rewards will come when we persevere.

W. CRAIG ZWICK
NEW ERA, MAY 2007, 43

When we allow the Lord to be the architect of our life plan," said Elder W. Craig Zwick, "long-term benefits result and connect us to additional opportunities and experiences that accelerate our capacity for growth. . . . Sometimes we need a tangible way to measure success. If we can feel good about our efforts every day, then even in the most difficult circumstances we can have that tangible feeling of success. Being 'steadfast and immovable' and not letting anything get in our way 'in keeping the commandments of God' (Alma 1:25) is a tangible outcome that provides an enduring foundation to grow on. We grow when we have to overcome pains of endurance—that's perseverance. Impressive results may not come every day or even every week, but we need to hang in there. That's the steadfast and immovable side of it. Great rewards will come when we persevere"(*New Era,* May 2007, 42–43).

*Character is the aim of true education; and science,
history, and literature are but means used to accomplish
the desired end. Character is not the result of chance work
but of continuous right thinking and right acting.*

DAVID O. MCKAY
GOSPEL IDEALS, 440–41

In the hierarchy of truth, some truths matter more than others. The aim of knowledge and education is to make of us people of character and wisdom, people who think and do the right thing. "Gaining knowledge is one thing and applying it, quite another," said President David O. McKay. "Wisdom is the right application of knowledge; and true education—the education for which the Church stands—is the application of knowledge to the development of a noble and Godlike character. A man may possess a profound knowledge of history and of mathematics; he may be authority in psychology, biology, or astronomy; he may know all the discovered truths pertaining to geology and natural science; but if he has not with this knowledge that nobility of soul which prompts him to deal justly with his fellow men, to practice virtue and holiness in personal life, he is not a truly educated man" (*Gospel Ideals*, 440).

Which now of these three, thinkest thou,
was neighbour unto him that fell among the thieves?
And he said, He that shewed mercy on him.
Then said Jesus unto him, Go, and do thou likewise.

LUKE 10:36—37

The Savior's parable of the good Samaritan is a commission with a promise: if we treat others with mercy and kindness, we too will be shown mercy and kindness at the day of judgment. Bishop H. David Burton said, "To help relieve suffering is to cultivate a Christlike character. We are charged, as were those who listened at the feet of the Savior 2,000 years ago, to *'go, and do thou likewise.'* The Prophet Joseph Smith taught that it is our responsibility 'to feed the hungry, to clothe the naked, to provide for the widow, to dry up the tear of the orphan, to comfort the afflicted, whether in this church or in any other, or in no church at all, wherever he finds them' (*Times and Seasons,* 15 Mar. 1842, 732). May we be generous with our time and liberal in our contributions for the care of those who suffer" (*Ensign,* May 1997, 77).

The Lord knows both what He will need you to do and what you will need to know. He is kind and He is all-knowing. So you can with confidence expect that He has prepared opportunities for you to learn.

HENRY B. EYRING
ENSIGN, OCTOBER 2002, 18

The Lord in His mercy, understanding, and encompassing love knows us better than we know ourselves. He knows how to customize our learning experiences so that we have the greatest opportunity to become more like Him. "The Lord loves you and watches over you," said Elder Henry B. Eyring. "He is all-powerful, and He promised you this: 'But seek ye first the kingdom of God, and his righteousness; and all these things shall be added unto you' (Matthew 6:33). That is a true promise. When we put God's purposes first, He will give us miracles. If we pray to know what He would have us do next, He will multiply the effects of what we do in such a way that time seems to be expanded. He may do it in different ways for each individual, but I know from long experience that He is faithful to His word" (*Ensign,* Oct. 2002, 20).

Just being a member of this Church is not enough.
Nor is merely going through the motions of membership
sufficient in this day of cynicism and unbelief.
The spirituality and vigilance of a saint are required.

KEITH B. MCMULLIN
ENSIGN, MAY 2001, 62

Bishop Keith B. McMullin of the Presiding Bishopric spoke of what it means to be a saint: "Being saintly is to be good, pure, and upright. For such persons, virtues are not only declared but lived. For Latter-day Saints, the kingdom of God, or the Church, is not a byline; rather, it is the center and the substance of their lives. Home is 'a bit of heaven,' [David O. McKay, in Conference Report, Apr. 1964, 5] not a hotel. The family is not merely a societal or biological entity. It is the basic eternal unit in God's kingdom wherein the gospel of Jesus Christ is taught and lived. Indeed, Latter-day Saints diligently strive to become a little better, a little kinder, a little nobler in the daily affairs of life. . . . Holding to this course provides Latter-day Saints the means for avoiding the treacherous shoals of worldliness. Living this way enables members of the Church to become the covenant people of the Lord" (*Ensign,* May 2001, 62).

It is contrary to the order of heaven for any soul
to be locked into compulsive, immoral behavior
with no way out! It is consistent with the workings of the
adversary to deceive you into believing that you are.

BOYD K. PACKER
ENSIGN, NOVEMBER 1986, 18

We will not and cannot be tempted above that which we are able to resist and bear (1 Corinthians 10:13). We are sovereigns over our ability to choose, our ability to stand firm, our ability to withstand the workings of the adversary. It may not be easy due to the insidious and unprecedented evil spreading across the earth before the final winding up scenes; but with the Lord's help and by His merciful atoning sacrifice we can become strong and resolute, we can repent and be made clean. Our challenges and susceptibilities may be great, our weaknesses and imperfections real, but we are never victims, never without the hope and faith and strength that comes of the Lord. There is always a way out of sin and immorality, and that is the Lord and the enabling power of His redeeming grace.

The scriptures speak of [the Lord's] arms being open, extended, stretched out, and encircling. They are described as mighty and holy, arms of mercy, arms of safety, arms of love. . . . We have each felt to some extent these spiritual arms around us.

NEIL L. ANDERSEN
ENSIGN, NOVEMBER 2009, 40

Revealed in Nephi's psalm is a heart full of meekness, faith, and hope in the Lord: "O Lord, I have trusted in thee, and I will trust in thee forever. I will not put my trust in the arm of flesh. . . . I will lift up my voice unto thee; yea, I will cry unto thee, my God, the rock of my righteousness" (2 Nephi 4:34–35). Those who trust the Lord will find that His arms are ever open, stretched out to us in mercy and love. We feel the Lord's encircling arms when in heartache and anguish, when we feel alone and afraid, whenever we sincerely pray, repent, and desire to change for the better. The prophet Mormon spoke of the eventual sorrow of people who "might have been clasped in the arms of Jesus" had they repented (Mormon 5:11). The love of our Savior is perfect, constant, and all-encompassing—His mighty arms forever stretch out to us.

See that ye do all things in worthiness, and do it
in the name of Jesus Christ, the Son of the living God;
and if ye do this, and endure to the end,
ye will in nowise be cast out.

MORMON 9:29

When Jesus instituted the sacrament among the Nephites, He taught them that it was to be done in remembrance of His Atonement, and if it was partaken of worthily we would be blessed with the Spirit: "And this shall ye do in remembrance of my body, which I have shown unto you. And it shall be a testimony unto the Father that ye do always remember me. And if ye do always remember me ye shall have my Spirit to be with you. . . . And this shall ye always do to those who repent and are baptized in my name; and ye shall do it in remembrance of my blood, which I have shed for you, that ye may witness unto the Father that ye do always remember me" (3 Nephi 18: 7, 11). Each week we are blessed to have an occasion to examine ourselves, to renew our covenants, to reaffirm our commitment to always remember the Savior.

*I know of no experience more sweet
or feeling more precious than to heed a prompting
only to discover that the Lord has answered
another person's prayer through you.*

THOMAS S. MONSON
ENSIGN, NOVEMBER 2002, 55

The Lord has promised that He will bless His faithful and humble followers with promptings of the Spirit. He knows whom He can trust, whom He can count on to respond, whom He can rely upon to heed a whispering of the Spirit, take action, follow through, and obey. If we heed those promptings, our Heavenly Father will inspire our direction in life and guide our footsteps to bless others. Those flashes of inspiration come not in a strong wind, earthquake, or fire, but in a still small voice (1 Kings 19:11–12). That quiet voice of the Spirit is prompting us whenever we reach out in love and kindness to others, whenever we yearn to do good, whenever we desire to follow the Lord and become more like Him, whenever we seek "to do justly, and to love mercy, and to walk humbly with . . . God" (Micah 6:8).

Lift up your voices unto this people;
speak the thoughts that I shall put into your hearts,
and you shall not be confounded before men;
For it shall be given you in the very hour, yea,
in the very moment, what ye shall say.

DOCTRINE & COVENANTS 100: 5–6

Countless individuals have experienced the remarkable feeling of having words come out of their
mouths that they had neither prepared, anticipated,
or even fully understood. They were guided by the
Lord to lift up their voices because they were humble,
desirous, faithful, and obedient. We have the promise that we will not be confounded if we speak the
thoughts that God puts into our hearts. We will know
what to say, how to say it, and when to say it. The
Lord said, "But a commandment I give unto you, that
ye shall declare whatsoever thing ye declare in my
name, in solemnity of heart, in the spirit of meekness,
in all things. And I give unto you this promise, that
inasmuch as ye do this the Holy Ghost shall be shed
forth in bearing record unto all things whatsoever ye
shall say" (D&C 100:7–8). The Spirit will quietly,
without drama or fanfare, inspire our thoughts, our
words, and our actions.

When in situations of stress we wonder if there is any more
in us to give, we can be comforted to know that God,
who knows our capacity perfectly, placed us here to succeed.
No one was foreordained to fail or to be wicked.

NEAL A. MAXWELL
ENSIGN, FEBRUARY 1990, 31

We are in mortality to be tried and tested, to learn and grow and progress toward the goals Heavenly Father has outlined for us. We must proceed diligently along life's pathway "in wisdom and order," yet not run faster than we have strength, neither be so overzealous that we miss the essence of gospel living (Mosiah 4:27). We must be realistic, patient, and kind in our expectations of others and ourselves. Elder Neal A. Maxwell said, "When we have been weighed and found wanting, let us remember that we were measured before and we were found equal to our tasks; and, therefore, let us continue, but with a more determined discipleship. When we feel overwhelmed, let us recall the assurance that God will not overprogram us; he will not press upon us more than we can bear" (D&C 50:40; *Ensign,* Feb. 1990, 31). We are not expected to become perfect in mortality but to succeed in our progression toward eternal life.

*No Latter-day Saint who is true and faithful in all things
will ever pursue a course, or espouse a cause, or publish an
article or book that weakens or destroys faith. There is, in fact,
no such thing as neutrality where the gospel is concerned.*

BRUCE R. MCCONKIE
ENSIGN, NOVEMBER 1984, 84

Elder Bruce R. McConkie said: "The Church is
like a great caravan—organized, prepared, following an appointed course, with its captains of tens
and captains of hundreds all in place. What does it
matter if a few barking dogs snap at the heels of the
weary travelers? . . . The caravan moves on. Is there
a ravine to cross, a miry mud hole to pull through, a
steep grade to climb? So be it. The oxen are strong
and the teamsters wise. The caravan moves on. Are
there storms that rage along the way, floods that wash
away the bridges, deserts to cross, and rivers to ford?
Such is life in this fallen sphere. The caravan moves
on. Ahead is the celestial city, the eternal Zion of our
God, where all who maintain their position in the
caravan shall find food and drink and rest. Thank
God that the caravan moves on!" (*Ensign,* Nov. 1984,
85).

*Moses never entered the promised land. Joseph Smith never saw
Zion redeemed. Some of us may not live long enough to see the day
when the Book of Mormon floods the earth. . . . But, God willing,
I intend to spend all my remaining days in that glorious effort.*

EZRA TAFT BENSON
ENSIGN, NOVEMBER 1988, 6

President Ezra Taft Benson said, "I have a vision
of the whole Church getting nearer to God by abiding by the precepts of the Book of Mormon. Indeed,
I have a vision of flooding the earth with the Book
of Mormon. My beloved Saints, I am now entering
my ninetieth year. I am getting older and less vigorous and am so grateful for your prayers. . . . I do not
know fully why God has preserved my life to this age,
but I do know this: That for the present hour He has
revealed to me the absolute need for us to move the
Book of Mormon forward now in a marvelous manner. You must help with this burden and with this
blessing which He has placed on the whole Church,
even all the children of Zion" (*Ensign,* Nov. 1988, 6).
The Book of Mormon changes lives; we will be richly
blessed as we work to share its powerful message of
Jesus Christ with others.

Now, this restoration shall come to all, both old and young, both bond and free, both male and female, both the wicked and the righteous; and even there shall not so much as a hair of their heads be lost; but every thing shall be restored to its perfect frame.

Alma 11: 44

It was in contention with Zeezrom that Amulek powerfully taught the doctrine of resurrection: Jesus Christ shall loose the bands of temporal death, all shall rise in immortality, a restoration shall come to all, and there is no more death after the resurrection (Alma 11:42–45). Later, Amulek's missionary companion, Alma, would teach the same truths: "The soul shall be restored to the body, and the body to the soul; yea, and every limb and joint shall be restored to its body; yea, even a hair of the head shall not be lost; but all things shall be restored to their proper and perfect frame" (Alma 40:23). These truths concerning the resurrection are among the most glorious of all the promises of God—they give us hope in our mortal trials and adversities, courage for the temporal challenges and disappointments we face, and sweet expectation and assurance of that magnificent day of restoration and resurrection.

Parents have a sacred duty to rear their children in love and righteousness, to provide for their physical and spiritual needs, to teach them to love and serve one another, observe the commandments of God, and be law-abiding citizens wherever they live.

"THE FAMILY: A PROCLAMATION TO THE WORLD"
ENSIGN, NOVEMBER 1995, 102

On this day in 1995, President Gordon B. Hinckley issued to the world a proclamation that clarified doctrine and provided a clarion call to dedicate our best efforts in strengthening the family. Family life is the essence of the gospel plan. Parents are given a sacred responsibility—a stewardship with a promise. If they give their best efforts in teaching their children the doctrines and commandments of the gospel (D&C 68:25–28) and rear them in love and righteousness, then the Lord will magnify and consecrate their efforts unto Him. They will be magnified in that the Lord will enhance their capacities, inspire their endeavors, and enlarge their love, understanding, and compassion. And they will be consecrated in that the Lord sanctifies, or makes holy, those who dedicate their time, energy, and actions to upholding and strengthening the family. Family work is holy work of the most sacred kind.

*Once a person is true and obedient to the light and knowledge
received, he not only develops the ability to use that which
has been given but the capacity to receive more knowledge
increases, for he now understands and appreciates the gift.*

DAVID B. HAIGHT
ENSIGN, MAY 1988, 23

If we truly love the Lord, we will keep His commandments (John 14:15). Elder David B. Haight said,
"People learn obedience by being obedient. We see
its fruits. Halfhearted obedience is without reward.
The gospel invites vigorous participation in living its
principles. . . . If we could feel or were sensitive even in
the slightest to the matchless love of our Savior and his
willingness to suffer for our individual sins, we would
cease procrastination and 'clean the slate,' and repent
of all our transgressions. This would mean keeping
God's commandments and setting our lives in order,
searching our souls, and repenting of our sins, large
or small. It means loving our neighbor, living an ex-
emplary life, and—high on the list—being good husbands and good wives. . . . It means being honest in
our affairs, and serving others, which includes sharing
the gospel of Jesus Christ to all the world, and—with
love—to succor those in need" (*Ensign,* May 1988, 23).

*For his word ye shall receive, as if from mine own mouth,
in all patience and faith. For by doing these things the
gates of hell shall not prevail against you; yea, and the Lord
God will disperse the powers of darkness from before you.*

DOCTRINE & COVENANTS 21:5–6

When the prophet speaks to us in his capacity as the Lord's spokesman, we are under obligation to, as the Lord said on the day the Church was organized in 1830, "give heed unto all his words and commandments which he shall give unto you as he receiveth them, walking in all holiness before me" (D&C 21:4). On another occasion, in the Lord's dictated preface to the Doctrine & Covenants, He said, "What I the Lord have spoken, I have spoken, and I excuse not myself; and though the heavens and the earth pass away, my word shall not pass away, but shall all be fulfilled, whether by mine own voice or by the voice of my servants, it is the same" (D&C 1:38). Transcendent promises await those who obey the law of the prophets and hearken unto their words: the gates of hell will not prevail, darkness will be dispersed, and heaven will pour out blessings upon us.

Remember: the heavens will not be filled with those
who never made mistakes but with those who recognized
that they were off course and who corrected their
ways to get back in the light of gospel truth.

DIETER F. UCHTDORF
ENSIGN, MAY 2008, 60

Among life's greatest blessings is the opportunity for second chances. A disobedient child says to his mother, "I promise I'll do better next time" or "Can I try again?" All of us fall short, make mistakes, commit sin, and long for a fresh start. And while justice and fairness always have their claims, mercy and second chances also have their places. The theme of second chances is as old as time. We know the story of the prodigal son who came home again and the story of the reluctant prophet Jonah, who got a second chance to overcome his fears. And we all have personal and family stories of making mistakes but then trying anew. It is comforting to know that neither mortality nor heaven is a monastery for perfect people. We are here to learn and grow, make course corrections, repent, and get back on the gospel track in following the Lord. We all have second chances.

Every day each of us is implicated in obscuring
the light or in chasing away the darkness.
We have been called to invite the light and to be a
light, to sanctify ourselves and edify others.

ROBERT S. WOOD
ENSIGN, NOVEMBER 1999, 84

James wrote of the attributes of holiness, including the control of language and conversation. He said, "If any man offend not in word, the same is a perfect man, and able also to bridle the whole body" (James 3:2). He used a seagoing analogy to note that as a small helm can drive a great ship, so the tongue might also set our course and fate (James 3:4–5); used improperly, the tongue "defileth the whole body, and setteth on fire the course of nature" (James 3:6). In our day, Elder Robert S. Wood said: "When we speak and act, we should ask whether our words and expressions are calculated to invite the powers of heaven into our lives and to invite all to come unto Christ. We must treat sacred things with reverence. We need to eliminate from our conversations the immodest and the lewd, the violent and the threatening, the demeaning and the false" (*Ensign*, Nov. 1999, 84).

*It is so important in this day that we each build an
inner core of spirituality. As you exercise your faith
and feel that spirituality grow, you will begin to feel
more secure. You will feel more confident.*

JANETTE C. HALES
ENSIGN, MAY 1994, 98

A young man questions the faith of his fathers in
light of recent faultfinding from associates. A young
woman wonders if it is really possible to stay true to
the Church in this day of great temptation. Both ask
if it's realistic in the twenty-first century to trust in
God and stand as a witness to the truthfulness of
the gospel. Yes, it is! Today, as in times past, we each
need a deep inner core of spirituality to hold onto in
stormy, difficult days. Sister Janette C. Hales, former
Young Women general president, said, "I have a testimony of our Savior's love for us. He understands our
challenges. He will help us. We were intended to have
experiences that will help us know good from evil.
Most of us make mistakes. We can't be perfect alone.
The atoning gift of Jesus Christ allows us to let go of
our weaknesses and be strengthened by His perfection" (*Ensign,* May 1994, 98).

*Our Father in Heaven has promised us peace in
times of trial and has provided a way for
us to come to Him in our need. He has given
us the privilege and power of prayer.*

REX D. PINEGAR
ENSIGN, MAY 1993, 66

Our Heavenly Father knows our thoughts and the
intents of our hearts (D&C 6:16). He knows what
we're worried about, what we wonder about, and what
we want and need in life. He is our Father, our loving and perfect Father, and His ways and thoughts
are higher than ours (Isaiah 55:8–9). Thanks be to
God that we can come to Him in humble prayer and
sincere supplication; we can call upon Him anytime,
anywhere, and speak to Him in the quiet thoughts of
our minds and from the deepest feelings of our souls.
We can carry at all times a prayer in our hearts. So
when you are concerned and afraid—pray for peace
and understanding; when you are feeling good about
life and all is well—pray with thanksgiving; when you
are discouraged or overwhelmed—pray for strength
and perspective. God will not forsake those who remember Him in prayer.

*He who doeth the works of righteousness
shall receive his reward, even peace in this world,
and eternal life in the world to come.*

DOCTRINE & COVENANTS 59:23

Tough times can teach us great truths. They give us opportunity to reflect on our values and what's most important in life. These challenging times raise important questions about our priorities, our measures of success, our temporal and spiritual well-being, and the ultimate goals and purposes of life. Now is a good time to rediscover timeless virtues and divine promises. Among the Savior's most comforting words are these: "Come unto me, all ye that labour and are heavy laden, and I will give you rest. Take my yoke upon you, and learn of me; for I am meek and lowly in heart: and ye shall find rest unto your souls. For my yoke is easy, and my burden is light" (Matthew 11:28–30). Those who sincerely strive for righteousness will receive everlasting rewards. Those who trust and obey the Lord, and truly come unto Him in meekness and devotion, will find rest and peace to their souls, here and hereafter.

OCTOBER

Search diligently, pray always, and be believing,
and all things shall work together for your good,
if ye walk uprightly and remember the covenant
wherewith ye have covenanted one with another.

DOCTRINE & COVENANTS 90:24

*Covenants remembered by parents will be remembered
by God. The children may thus become the beneficiaries
and inheritors of these great covenants and promises.
This is because they are the children of the covenant.*

JAMES E. FAUST
ENSIGN, NOVEMBER 1990, 35

To be born under the covenant is to be part of an eternal family; it is to be born to parents who have been sealed by the authority of the holy priesthood for time and eternity. There is no greater blessing than to have the promise that your posterity are sealed to you and that you are bound together as a family throughout eternity. Children of the covenant are rightful heirs to all the promises made to father Abraham and have rightful claim upon all the ordinances of salvation. Converts to the Church are able to receive the same blessings as those who were born into the Church—it is for this purpose that families are sealed together in the temple. The transcendent promises of eternal sealings carry obligations and responsibilities of the covenant. Truly, where much is given much is expected. We can trust that God will honor the covenants kept by faithful parents and watch over the children of the covenant.

*Along with losing the Spirit, pornography users also lose
perspective and proportion. . . . Real consequences start to
accumulate as self-respect ebbs away, sweet relationships sour,
marriages wither, and innocent victims begin to pile up.*

L. WHITNEY CLAYTON
ENSIGN, NOVEMBER 2007, 52

Nothing is hidden from the Lord (2 Nephi 27:27).
He knows our thoughts, our actions, and our desires.
He also knows of the great evil that surrounds us,
and He wants to help us resist iniquity and choose
the right. Elder L. Whitney Clayton spoke to those
caught in the trap of pornography: "Now is the time
to free yourself with the help of the Savior. There is
a way out, but you will need His help to escape. Your
complete recovery will depend upon your complete
repentance. Go to your bishop immediately. Seek his
inspired guidance. He will help you put in place a
plan of repentance that will restore your self-esteem
and bring the Spirit back into your life. The healing
power of the Atonement of the Lord Jesus Christ
reaches all afflictions, even this one. If you will turn
to the Savior with all of your heart and follow the
counsel of your bishop, you will find the healing you
need" (*Ensign,* Nov. 2007, 53).

If ye do not watch yourselves, and your thoughts, and your words, and your deeds, and observe the commandments of God, and continue in the faith of what ye have heard concerning the coming of our Lord, even unto the end of your lives, ye must perish.

MOSIAH 4:30

King Benjamin taught an eternal truth more than two millennia ago: we need to watch ourselves to make sure that we keep the commandments and continue in the faith. A century and a half later, the apostle Paul exhorted followers of Jesus, "Examine yourselves, whether ye be in the faith; prove your own selves" (2 Corinthians 13:5). We must be ever vigilant in watching our thoughts, actions, and desires; we must be honest in our self-examination to see that we are strong in the faith. We cannot let our guard down and become lax in our efforts to follow Jesus and live the gospel. We cannot rationalize our way out of faithful obedience or justify disobedience to God's laws by thinking that we are the exception to the rule. Watching and examining ourselves is part of remembering the covenants we have made, the commandments we have promised to obey, and the blessings we have received.

*It was meant to be that life would be a challenge. To suffer
some anxiety, some depression, some disappointment,
even some failure is normal. . . . Things will straighten
out. There is great purpose in our struggle in life.*

BOYD K. PACKER
ENSIGN, MAY 1978, 93

We relentlessly hear that materialism is what life
is about, that instant gratification and continual happiness are rights, that hard times and heartache mean
life is neither good nor fair. The world says that anything less than "eat, drink, and be merry" signifies we
are being unfairly cheated and not living life to the
fullest. How sad, how shortsighted, to see so myopically both life in the present and the unfolding future.
All of us know life is difficult. If we try to remember
that simple fact and understand we are here to learn
and grow, we will come to know that all these things
will give us experience and be for our good (D&C
122:7). Challenges, trials, sorrow, and disappointment are part of living in this fallen world. But they
are also part of the Lord's plan of happiness. If God
would remove all these from our lives we could not,
would not, develop strength of character or the attributes of godliness.

The more we are blessed with means, the more we are blessed with responsibility; the more we are blessed with wisdom and ability, the more we are placed under the necessity of using that wisdom and ability in the spread of righteousness.

BRIGHAM YOUNG
BRIGHAM YOUNG, 240

Although we have different temporal resources and means, we have equal responsibility to do what we can. We are to open our hearts to others, share what we are able, and set our hearts upon the things of God rather than on worldly things. Brigham Young observed, "Though I possessed millions of money and property, that does not excuse me from performing the labor that it is my calling to perform, so far as I have strength and ability, any more than the poorest man in the community is excused. . . . If we have a world of means, we have a world of responsibility" (*Brigham Young,* 240). Both rich and poor can do their part to contribute to building the kingdom. Our contributions will vary, but they need only to come from the heart, not the pocketbook. As we strive to live the gospel, as we share our temporal possessions with others, we know true joy and fulfill our sacred stewardship.

*No part of walking by faith is more difficult than walking the
road of repentance. However, with "faith unto repentance,"
we can push the roadblock of pride away and beg God for mercy.
One simply surrenders, worrying only about what God thinks.*

NEAL A. MAXWELL
ENSIGN, MAY 1991, 91

Repentance signifies a change of heart; it means
turning away from sin and toward faith, away from
pride and toward meekness. Elder Neal A. Maxwell
said, "When you and I make unwise decisions, if
we have frail faith, we not only demand to be rescued but we want to be rescued privately, painlessly,
quickly—or at least to be beaten only 'with a few
stripes' (2 Nephi 28:8). Brothers and sisters, how can
we really feel forgiven until we first feel responsible?
How can we learn from our own experiences unless
these lessons are owned up to? In the trial of faith, we
may sometimes feel God has deserted us. The reality
is that our behavior has isolated us from Him. It is
when we first feel the consequences of our mistakes
and are just turning away from these, but have not yet
turned fully to God, that we may have these feelings
of being forsaken" (*Ensign,* May 1991, 91).

Let us love one another: for love is of God;
and every one that loveth is born of God, and knoweth God.
He that loveth not knoweth not God; for God is love.

1 JOHN 4:7–8

Love is a gift of God. When we feel God's love in our lives, we know abiding happiness and we wish to extend that love to others. True love of God fills us to overflowing with love for others. Indeed, love changes everything; it gives meaning to life and keeps us going when we feel like giving up, it can be what awakens us in the morning and what settles us into sweet dreams when we sleep. Our efforts to nurture love would fail were it not for infusions of divine love along the way. Ultimately, all love comes from God—who is the embodiment of love. He loves us, His children, with a perfect, constant, and unchanging love. The more we sincerely seek Him, the more we will feel His love working a mighty change in our hearts—and in the hearts of those we love.

[The Lord] expects us to have family home evening—one night a week to gather our children together and teach them the gospel.

GORDON B. HINCKLEY
ENSIGN, MARCH 2003, 3

The inspired family home evening program of the Church began in 1915, when President Joseph F. Smith encouraged members to set aside one night a week devoted specifically to the family. It was to be a time of teaching and singing, of sharing and reading the scriptures, of cultivating talents and having some fun, of discussing family matters and going over the week's schedule. President Gordon B. Hinckley said, "We have a family home evening program once a week across the Church in which parents sit down with their children. They study the scriptures. They talk about family problems. They plan family activities and things of that kind. I don't hesitate to say if every family in the world practiced that one thing, you'd see a very great difference in the solidarity of the families of the world" (*Ensign,* Mar. 2003, 3). Great blessings will come to those families who take seriously the charge to hold a weekly family home evening.

*In a world of turmoil and uncertainty, it is more
important than ever to make our families the center of
our lives and the top of our priorities. Families lie
at the center of our Heavenly Father's plan.*

L. TOM PERRY
ENSIGN, MAY 2003, 40

The gospel is a family plan of happiness. Elder L. Tom Perry observed, "In recent meetings with the First Presidency, they have expressed concern about the deterioration of the family. Their mandate to the Priesthood Executive Council was to concentrate on the family in our assignments. In response to the First Presidency, many plans and efforts are already in place. We will use all of the resources we have to encourage greater harmony, greater love, and greater influence in the Lord's special designated unit—the family. We need to make our homes a place of refuge from the storm, which is increasing in intensity all about us. Even if the smallest openings are left unattended, negative influences can penetrate the very walls of our homes" (*Ensign,* May 2003, 40). For happiness here and joy hereafter, we must focus our greatest attention and expend our best efforts in safeguarding and strengthening our marriages and families.

*There is no Latter-day Saint who dies after having lived
a faithful life who will lose anything because of having failed to do
certain things when opportunities were not furnished him or her.*

LORENZO SNOW
THE TEACHINGS OF LORENZO SNOW, 138

Lorenzo Snow, who died at age eighty-seven on
this day in 1901, gave further clarification regarding
the promise that no faithful Latter-day Saint will lose
anything because of having failed to do certain things
when he or she was not given opportunities: "In other
words, if a young man or a young woman has no opportunity of getting married, and they live faithful
lives up to the time of their death, they will have all the
blessings, exaltation, and glory that any man or woman
will have who had this opportunity and improved it.
That is sure and positive" (*The Teachings of Lorenzo Snow,*
138). The Lord and His gospel are perfectly fair and
just. A loving and compassionate Lord would not pe-
nalize or punish someone who has not had the opportunity to take action, choose, or be accountable for
choices. We are responsible for the choices we make
based on our opportunities, knowledge, and accountability. We believe in a gospel of second chances.

*The Savior gave us the scriptures, paid by prophets at a
price we cannot measure, so that we could know Him.
Lose yourself in them. Decide now to read more and
more effectively than you have ever done before.*

HENRY B. EYRING
SPEECHES, 1999, 94

President Henry B. Eyring gave us a warning and
a promise: "You have the right and the obligation to
choose for yourselves. You can search the scriptures
or not. You can choose to work hard enough, to ponder, and to obey His commandments, so that the
Holy Ghost can be your companion. Then you will
come to know the Savior better and better and your
heart will swell with love for Him, or you can choose
to delay. You can choose to drift, deciding past efforts will be enough. My warning is a simple matter
of cause and effect. Jesus Christ is the light and the
life of the world. If we do not choose to move toward
Him, we will find that we have moved away. . . . If
you will let your heart be drawn to the Savior, to always remember Him, and to our Heavenly Father in
prayer, you will have put on spiritual armor" (*Speeches,*
97).

*The tender mercies of the Lord are over all those
whom he hath chosen, because of their faith, to make
them mighty even unto the power of deliverance.*

1 NEPHI 1:20

The lot of the Lord's chosen people was not meant
to be easy. Yet the hand of the Lord is over His
people and He makes blessings of their afflictions
(D&C 122:7). We can be delivered from our temptations, heartache, and hardship by exercising faith in
the Lord and calling upon His holy name. Amulek
wisely counseled: "Humble yourselves even to the
dust, and worship God, in whatsoever place ye may be
in, in spirit and in truth; and that ye live in thanksgiving daily, for the many mercies and blessings which
he doth bestow upon you. Yea, and I also exhort you,
my brethren, that ye be watchful unto prayer continually, that ye may not be led away by the temptations of
the devil, that he may not overpower you. . . . I would
exhort you to have patience, . . . and bear with those
afflictions, with a firm hope that ye shall one day rest
from all your afflictions" (Alma 34:38–41).

Sacrifice is an amazing principle. As we willingly give
our time and talents and all that we possess, it becomes
one of our truest forms of worship. It can develop within us a
profound love for each other and our Savior, Jesus Christ.

CAROL B. THOMAS
ENSIGN, MAY 2001, 64

When we willingly give of our time, means, effort, and energy to bless and lift others, we know true joy and reap the bounties of eternity; when we serve faithfully in our callings and go on missions, we develop more love, patience, and compassion; when we do our best to live the gospel and love the Lord, we draw closer to the Spirit and hear more clearly its promptings. The Lord surely blesses those who strive to put off the natural man and woman and give of themselves. It's no sacrifice when one loves the Lord with heart, mind, and strength. President Gordon B. Hinckley said, "It is not a sacrifice to live the gospel of Jesus Christ. It is never a sacrifice when you get back more than you give. It is an investment, . . . a greater investment than any. . . . Its dividends are eternal and everlasting" (*Teachings of Gordon B. Hinckley*, 567–68).

Remember, faith and doubt cannot exist in the mind at the same time, for one will dispel the other. Cast out doubt. Cultivate faith. Strive always to retain that childlike faith which can move mountains and bring heaven closer to heart and home.

THOMAS S. MONSON
NEW ERA, SEPTEMBER 2005, 7

Speaking to the young men and women of the Church, President Thomas S. Monson promised, "When firmly planted, your testimony of the gospel, of the Savior, and of our Heavenly Father will influence all that you do throughout your life. It will help to determine how you spend your time and with whom you choose to associate. It will affect the way you treat your family, how you interact with others. It will bring love, peace, and joy into your life. It should help you determine to be modest in your dress and in your speech. In the past year or so we have noticed a dramatic change in the way some of our young people are dressing. Styles in clothing change; fads come and go; but if the dress styles are immodest, it is important that we avoid them. When you dress modestly, you show respect for your Heavenly Father and for yourself" (*New Era*, Sept. 2005, 7–8).

Every sincere prayer is heard and answered by our Heavenly Father, but the answers we receive may not be what we expect or come to us when we want or in the way we anticipate.

DAVID A. BEDNAR
ENSIGN, MAY 2008, 97

How wonderful it is to know that we can talk with our Father in Heaven every day, any time, and continually in our hearts through prayer. The disposition to pray is a sign of our current spiritual state, our direction and desires, our character, humility, and willingness to be submissive. It certainly takes faith and hope to pray to an unseen God, and meekness is needed to trust that the heavens are open and that God loves us and cares about our happiness and welfare. (Remember, it was a prayer that dispelled the darkness and ushered in the glorious morning of the Restoration.) Our perfect, omnipotent, and omni-loving Father knows what is best for each of His children. Our Father, who is patient, understanding, compassionate, and all-knowing, waits to hear from His children in prayer; He yearns to bless and guide us in prayer uttered or expressed silently in the heart.

*When we are true to the sacred principles
of honesty and integrity, we are true to our
faith, and we are true to ourselves.*

RICHARD C. EDGLEY
ENSIGN, NOVEMBER 2006, 74

A person with integrity has inside-out congruence: what they believe and teach and talk about is the way they strive to live. They have so integrated their righteous beliefs and principles into who they are that they walk the walk and, although imperfect, are true to their values at all times and in all places. Honesty and truthfulness are the basis of a true Christian life. Bishop Richard C. Edgley said, "For Latter-day Saints, honesty is an important requirement for entering the Lord's holy temple. Honesty is embedded in the covenants that we make in the temple. Each Sunday as we partake of the holy emblems of the Savior's flesh and blood, we again renew our basic and sacred covenants—which encompass honesty. As Latter-day Saints we have a sacred obligation to not only teach the principles of honesty, but also to live them. . . . Honesty should be among the most fundamental values that govern our everyday living" (*Ensign*, Nov. 2006, 74).

*The Lord will never permit me or any other man
who stands as President of this Church to lead you astray.
It is not in the programme. . . . If I were to attempt
that, the Lord would remove me out of my place.*

WILFORD WOODRUFF
WILFORD WOODRUFF, 199

We have the sure promise that the Lord will not allow His Church to be led astray. That does not mean we believe the Lord's authorized prophets are perfect; neither does it mean we believe in prophetic infallibility. We recognize they are mortal men and that God works through mortals to accomplish His wonderful work. We also know they are called to witness for Christ in all the world and hold the keys of the priesthood. President Wilford Woodruff said: "I say to the Latter-day Saints the keys of the kingdom of God are here, and they are going to stay here, too, until the coming of the Son of Man. Let all Israel understand that. They may not rest upon my head but a short time, but they will then rest on the head of another apostle, and another after him, and so continue until the coming of the Lord Jesus Christ in the clouds of heaven" (*Wilford Woodruff,* 197).

Search diligently, pray always, and be believing,
and all things shall work together for your good,
if ye walk uprightly and remember the covenant
wherewith ye have covenanted one with another.

DOCTRINE & COVENANTS 90:24

If we honor our covenants and hold fast to the iron rod, things will work together for our good. It may not be easy; we'll have our difficult days, months, or years. But our challenges have the capacity to change our hearts, our outlooks, and our relationships for the better—they can strengthen and build us, or they can weaken and destroy us. When we turn to Christ, trust Him and rely on Him, we will not only find the comfort we seek, but in so doing we will gain an increased testimony and conviction of the reality of the Savior and His Atonement, which can heal all suffering and mend all that which is broken. Christ feels our pain (Alma 7:11–12), and His Atonement can heal the effects of pain and affliction, it can cleanse and compensate for the consequences of our sins, it can fill us with the faith and hope to continue remembering our covenants.

Jesus Christ has the power to save. Through His divine sacrifice, He has provided the way for us to gain eternal life. . . . We know Satan will tempt and try us as we seek to do these things, but the Lord has promised that He will strengthen us.

BARBARA THOMPSON
ENSIGN, MAY 2009, 83–84

Sister Barbara Thompson, said, "As a child I was taught by my parents that my Heavenly Father and Jesus Christ love me. . . . They taught me that Jesus Christ is our Savior and only through Him can we be saved. [See Mosiah 3:17.] I was also taught that in order for my faith to increase, I needed to pray every day. . . . I was taught that as I read and studied the scriptures, my knowledge and testimony of the truthfulness of the gospel would grow. I was taught to love God and that I could show my love by keeping His commandments. [See John 14:15.] I also learned as a child about the importance of the temple. In my youth I learned that making and keeping sacred temple covenants would keep me on course to eternal life. Each of us must follow these principles throughout our lives to increase our faith and personal righteousness" (*Ensign,* May 2009, 84).

Moral discipline is the consistent exercise of agency to choose the right because it is right, even when it is hard. It rejects the self-absorbed life in favor of developing character worthy of respect and true greatness through Christlike service.

D. TODD CHRISTOFFERSON
ENSIGN, NOVEMBER 2009, 105

True disciples of Jesus Christ are moral agents who have become people of moral discipline. "The root of the word *discipline* is shared by the word *disciple,* suggesting to the mind the fact that conformity to the example and teachings of Jesus Christ is the ideal discipline that, coupled with His grace, forms a virtuous and morally excellent person," said Elder D. Todd Christofferson. "Moral discipline is learned at home. While we cannot control what others may or may not do, the Latter-day Saints can certainly stand with those who demonstrate virtue in their own lives and inculcate virtue in the rising generation" (*Ensign,* Nov. 2009, 105–07). Moral discipline is lived at home as we teach, mostly by example, the need to keep the commandments and follow the Lord; it is lived outside the home as we manifest in our lives integrity and honor in all our interactions. People of moral character strive to choose the right at all times, in all places.

OCTOBER 21

*Peace of mind comes from strengthened faith in Jesus Christ.
Happiness comes from being diligent in keeping covenants
made at baptism and in the holy temples of the Lord.*

KENT D. WATSON
ENSIGN, NOVEMBER 2009, 39

We live in a day when anger rages in the hearts of many, when incivility and harshness seem to rule. To hold back the world and choose the more excellent way of the Master takes self-control and self-mastery. It means turning our lives more fully over to the Lord, who can change us from the inside out and make of us new creatures. The world may not honor true disciples, but the Lord will exalt them on high; the culture may not appreciate devout Christians who are trying to be like Jesus, but the heavens will open and pour out wisdom, strength, and blessings upon them. Those who resist the clarion call of the world and choose temperance over excess, self-discipline over indulgence, self-control over recklessness, will notice that their faith in the Lord is strengthened and their happiness is deeper—they will experience more peace in the heart and in the home.

*We must never ask the Lord for blessings, then ignore
the answer. And so we pray, "Thy will be done,
O Lord. Thou knowest best, kind Father."*

SPENCER W. KIMBALL
NEW ERA, MARCH 1978, 19

To pray with real intent manifests to the Lord that
we are willing to exercise robust faith, abiding trust,
and heartfelt humility. The proud either see no need
for prayer or rush off a few rote words with little effort or thought; but the faithful, the trusting, the
humble come to prayer with sincerity of intention
and action. Prayer, whether long or short, uttered or
unexpressed, is a holy habit that comes from the heart
as we approach our Maker with purpose, submissive-
ness, and meekness. We can become so infused with
the spirit of prayer that a heavenly petition is constantly in our hearts. And as we ponder the goodness
of God, as we consider His great plan of happiness, as
we think of His unnumbered blessings, we carry always in our hearts, at every moment, a prayer of gratitude and thanksgiving.

I, Nephi, beheld the power of the Lamb of God,
that it descended upon the saints of the church of the Lamb,
and upon the covenant people of the Lord, who were
scattered upon all the face of the earth; and
they were armed with righteousness.

1 NEPHI 14:14

As the world sinks ever deeper into darkness and sin, the humble followers of Christ benefit from the companionship of the Lord and His angels and will wield that power of faith and righteousness by which mighty miracles are wrought. Righteousness generates the power of God in one's life: the power to resist temptation and wickedness and hold back the world, the power to access the infinite Atonement in sincere prayer and repentance, the power to change one's life for the better and reach out in love and service to others. Those who have entered into a covenant with Christ have confidence born of faith, assurance born of hope, and devotion born of charity. They trust the Lord and His plan for the happiness of His children—they know whose side they are on, and they know they are on the winning side. They have cast aside fear and doubt and, armed with righteousness and the power of God, step boldly into the future.

*I told the brethren that the Book of Mormon was
the most correct of any book on earth, and the keystone of
our religion, and a man would get nearer to God by
abiding by its precepts, than by any other book.*

JOSEPH SMITH
TEACHINGS OF THE PROPHET JOSEPH SMITH, 194

There is a spiritual power in the Book of Mormon that can bring us nearer to God. The promised spiritual endowment is associated with faithful study of the scriptures: "Whosoever believeth on my words, them will I visit with the manifestation of my Spirit" (D&C 5:16). The Book of Mormon changes lives: it deepens our desire to follow the Lord, it expands our love for our fellowman, it enlarges our understanding of the doctrines of salvation and the plan of happiness. The Book of Mormon reminds us of God's love, it testifies of Christ as our Redeemer, it is a second witness to the verity of the Bible, and it reveals the divine calling of the Prophet Joseph Smith. If we sincerely make the Book of Mormon a course of study and a way of life—a Liahona for our lives—we will come to truly know the Lord and develop the attributes of godliness. Indeed, there is power in the word of God.

Our Father knew exactly what He was doing when
He created us. He made us enough alike to love each other,
but enough different that we would need to unite our
strengths and stewardships to create a whole.

SHERI L. DEW
ENSIGN, NOVEMBER 2001, 13

Sheri Dew said, "Sisters, we as women are not diminished by priesthood power, we are magnified by it.
. . . Your future husbands and the men with whom you
serve will need the support only you can give. You have
an inner spiritual strength that President James E.
Faust said equals and even surpasses that of men. [See
Ensign, Nov. 1999, 101.] Do not abdicate your spiritual responsibility. Your faith will preach compelling
sermons. No amount of time in front of the mirror
will make you as attractive as having the Holy Ghost
with you. Bless your family and the Church as only a
woman of God can—with virtue, faith, integrity, and
constant compassion. Young men, your ordination to
the priesthood is a grand privilege and responsibility,
and not a license to dominate. Be unfailingly worthy
to exercise this godly power. . . . A man is never more
magnificent than when he is guided by the Spirit to
honor the priesthood he holds" (*Ensign*, Nov. 2001, 13).

There is no peace, saith the Lord, unto the wicked.

ISAIAH 48:22

There can be no real peace when a person carries sinfulness in the heart or mind. We may try to fill our lives to overflowing with activities and pleasure; we may attempt to distract ourselves with the amusements and enticements of the world; we may even endeavor to distance ourselves from the Church and the whisperings of the Spirit, hoping to dull the cognitive and spiritual dissonance gnawing inside us—but no abiding peace will be found. Without humility and repentance there is no lasting peace; without submission and surrender to eternal principles, there is no enduring contentment; without a sincere striving for authentic righteousness and integrity, there is no genuine joy. At the same time, let us remember the words of the apostle Paul, "For all have sinned, and come short of the glory of God" (Romans 3:23). We are imperfect people living in a fallen world, but with the help of our Savior, we can experience true joy, contentment, and peace.

*The purpose of God's creations and of His giving us life is
to allow us to have the learning experience necessary
for us to come back to Him, to live with Him in eternal life.*

HENRY B. EYRING
ENSIGN, OCTOBER 2002, 16

President Henry B. Eyring spoke about the purpose
of learning experiences and education: "When the
Saints in Utah were still struggling to produce enough
food to live, they started schools. They felt driven to
lift their children toward light and to greater usefulness by education. That drive is more than a cultural
tradition passed on through the generations. It is the
natural fruit of living the gospel of Jesus Christ. You
see it today across the world in our missionaries coming home from their brief service in the field. Those
who have planted the good word of God and have
served faithfully invariably have awakened in them
a great desire for self-improvement. And with that
comes a desire to learn more and to gain greater skills.
. . . the drive for learning among our people must have
a powerful spiritual component. That spiritual element, when it is effective, refines and uplifts the aims
of our total education" (*Ensign,* Oct. 2002, 15–16).

The Lord will accept that which is enough,
with a good deal more pleasure and satisfaction
than that which is too much and unnecessary.

JOSEPH F. SMITH
CONFERENCE REPORT, OCTOBER 1912, 134

President Joseph F. Smith said, "There is such a thing as overdoing. A man may fast and pray till he kills himself; and there isn't any necessity for it; nor wisdom in it. . . . The Lord can hear a simple prayer, offered in faith, in half a dozen words, and he will recognize fasting that may not continue more than twenty-four hours, just as readily and as effectually as He will answer a prayer of a thousand words and fasting for a month. . . . The Word of Wisdom dictates that when we become weary we should stop and rest. When we are threatened with exhaustion, through over-exertion, wisdom would caution us to wait, to stop; not to take a stimulant to urge us on to greater extremes, but go where we can retire and rest and recuperate according to the laws of nature" (Conference Report, Oct. 1912, 133–34). We should be faithful, wise, prudent, and use good judgment in all aspects of gospel living.

Honesty is a principle of salvation in the kingdom of God.
Without it there can be no salvation.
Just as no man or woman can be saved without baptism,
so no one can be saved without honesty.

MARK E. PETERSEN
ENSIGN, DECEMBER 1971, 72

Followers of Jesus Christ are people of honor and integrity; they strive always to be people of character who are honest in their endeavors and relations. Elder Mark E. Petersen said, "As God condemns immorality, so he denounces hypocrisy, which is one of the worst forms of dishonesty. When he describes the hell of the world to come, he specifies that dishonest persons will go there. As no unclean thing can enter the presence of the Lord, so no liar nor cheat nor hypocrite can abide in his kingdom. Dishonesty is directly related to selfishness, which is its origin and source. Selfishness is at the root of nearly all the disorders that afflict us, and man's inhumanity to man continues to make countless thousands mourn. If all mankind were honest, we could have heaven here on earth" (*Ensign,* Dec. 1971, 72). Honesty is more than a best policy; it is a principle of salvation in the kingdom of God.

Forget yourself and get lost in this great cause. . . . Look to the Lord and live and work to lift and serve His sons and daughters. You will come to know a happiness that you have never known before if you will do that.

GORDON B. HINCKLEY
STAND A LITTLE TALLER, 192

The secret of happiness is that it is most often found in pursuit of something else. True happiness is most often a by-product of meaningful activities, such as service or working toward a goal or a purpose larger than one's self. Yes, we can get that momentary rush of happiness that comes of winning, of purchasing, of leisure time recreating. But when you ask people to deeply reflect on what makes them truly the happiest, they will often say, "just being with my family" or "working toward a goal" or "serving others." Also, happiness comes of forgiveness and repentance, of service and sacrifice, of reaching out to others in love and kindness, of turning our hearts over to the Lord and trusting His gospel plan, His mercy and grace, His love and compassion. Happiness comes not from acquiring, but in giving; it comes not from focusing on ourselves, but in forgetting ourselves and getting lost in the great cause of Christ.

*To truly be able to feed His lambs and nourish
His sheep with testimony and the Spirit, we must also
cultivate in our homes and classrooms respect
for each other and reverence for God.*

Margaret S. Lifferth
Ensign, May 2009, 11

Sister Margaret S. Lifferth taught that respect for others and reverence for God are close cousins: "As parents and leaders, our examples of respect for each other are critical. . . . Are we the examples we need to be? Ask yourself these questions: Am I an example of respect in my home by the way I treat those I love the most? What is my demeanor during a sports event? If my child has a disagreement with a teacher, coach, or peer, do I listen to both sides of the issue? Do I show respect for the property of others as well as take care of my own? How do I respond to others with whom I disagree in matters of religion, lifestyle, or politics? As parents and leaders exemplify and teach respect for others, we confirm in the hearts of our children that each of us is truly a child of God and all are brothers and sisters through eternity" (*Ensign,* May 2009, 11).

NOVEMBER

Behold, I say unto you that whoso believeth
in Christ, doubting nothing, whatsoever he
shall ask the Father in the name of Christ
it shall be granted him; and this promise is
unto all, even unto the ends of the earth.

MORMON 9:21

*Search these commandments, for they are
true and faithful, and the prophecies and promises
which are in them shall all be fulfilled.*

DOCTRINE & COVENANTS 1:37

On this date in 1831, the Lord dictated a preface to
the Doctrine and Covenants during a special conference of elders held at Hiram, Ohio. The Doctrine &
Covenants is the only book in existence that bears the
honor of a preface given by the Lord himself—which
should be the case, for the book was not written by
Joseph Smith but was dictated by Jesus Christ and
contains true and faithful commandments as well as
the prophecies and promises of eternal life. In that
sacred prologue, the Lord establishes the truth contained within its pages with these resounding words:
"What I the Lord have spoken, I have spoken, and I
excuse not myself; and though the heavens and the
earth pass away, my word shall not pass away, but
shall all be fulfilled, whether by mine own voice or by
the voice of my servants, it is the same" (D&C 1:38).

There are no new or easy ways we earn a relationship [with God]. It is the old ways, the tried-and-true-always-works ways: scripture study, prayer, and living those things you learn through your study and prayers.

SHARON G. LARSEN
ENSIGN, MAY 2000, 89

Speaking to the young women of the Church, Sister Sharon G. Larsen said, "Witnessing is showing by our behavior what we believe, and that can start in our own families. How cheerfully do we contribute to our family? How hard do we work to be successful in our studies? How faithfully do we respond to callings to serve? . . . The way you live your life every day, the words you say and don't say, the people you help, the clothes you wear, your choice of entertainment will show your strength and courage. It will give you confidence to reach out. You don't have the power to make rainbows or waterfalls, sunsets or roses, but you do have the power to bless people by your words and smiles and your sincere interest in them. Think of it—you carry within you the power to make the world better for someone each day! That is standing as a witness of God" (*Ensign,* May 2000, 90).

Pray for guidance and protection from the Lord. He will sustain you. He will become a trusted friend, and you will discover that your example will attract many friends who will take courage from your strength of character.

W. CRAIG ZWICK
ENSIGN, MAY 2008, 98

The world needs young men and women who have strength and character, who stand for truth and righteousness, who are examples to their peers and to the world. Elder W. Craig Zwick said, "Never forget that you are a [child] of God. He loves you. Live by your standards. Stand up for what you believe in. Sometimes it is not easy, and you may be standing alone for awhile. Look for friends with integrity and character, then go to them and express appreciation for their examples. You might even find someone who has been feeling as lonely as you" (*Ensign,* May 2008, 98). The Lord will stand by those youth who stand by Him; He will sustain those who believe and trust Him; He will uphold those who follow Him in humility. Young people are the future of the Church, the future of the world. The Lord, the Church, and generations to come need your example, righteousness, and strength of character.

*Behold, I say unto you that whoso believeth in Christ,
doubting nothing, whatsoever he shall ask the Father
in the name of Christ it shall be granted him; and this
promise is unto all, even unto the ends of the earth.*

MORMON 9:21

We live in a world that seems to be growing darker and more complex. Wickedness spreads, war and upheaval rule, confusion and uncertainty stir in our hearts and our culture. Where can we turn for peace amid the tumult of storms around us? What we can trust to stand the test of time? Who can we rely on to give us the hope and reassurance we seek? In the final analysis it's really quite simple: believe in and exercise faith in Jesus Christ, repent, trust the Lord and His promises, and do all that He asks of us. If we do so, without doubt or fear, His promise of peace and joy in this world and eternal life in the world to come is sure. When we manifest this kind of abiding faith and trust, we can approach our Father in Heaven in humble prayer with the confidence that "all his promises shall be fulfilled" (Mormon 8:22).

Tithing is not a matter of money so much as it is a matter of faith. We take the Lord at His word, and it is my testimony that He keeps His word. . . . He will open the windows of heaven and pour down blessings upon you.

GORDON B. HINCKLEY
ENSIGN, JULY 1998, 4

It is a remarkable thing to trust the Lord and His servants enough to know that our tithing is going to build the kingdom and not to line pockets. When we pay tithes and offerings to the Lord, we acknowledge His hand in our lives, we manifest our faith and humility, and we recognize that we are wholly dependent upon the Lord. The law of tithing reminds the Saints that the Lord's ways are different from those of men. Blessings are promised to those who follow the Lord's law of tithing: the Lord will care for our temporal and spiritual needs, our loyalty to God will deepen, and our faith will increase. God promises that He will open the windows of heaven and "pour you out a blessing, that there shall not be room enough to receive it" (Malachi 3:10). The true wealth promised a tithe payer is spiritual in nature, coming from heaven and not earth.

Look around you and find somebody that is in a worse plight than yourself; go to him and find out what the trouble is, then try to remove it with the wisdom which the Lord bestows upon you; and the first thing you know, your gloom is gone.

LORENZO SNOW
CONFERENCE REPORT, APRIL 1899, 2–3

One of the simplest and surest promises of life is that as we forget about ourselves, reach out to others in love and compassion, and go about looking for and doing good, we will feel better about life. When you feel weighed down by the trials and vicissitudes of life, look for someone you can lift with a compliment, a smile, or a simple word of thanks. When all seems dark and gloomy, extend yourself to another who needs the light of friendship and kindness. The Savior taught, "whosoever will lose his life for my sake shall find it" (Matthew 16:25). It's an amazing, paradoxical process: as we lose ourselves in the blessing and service of others, we truly find ourselves—our very best selves.

*There is no tomorrow to remember
if we don't do something today.*

THOMAS S. MONSON
ENSIGN, NOVEMBER 2008, 85

Today is the day to live and enjoy and do. President Thomas S. Monson said, "If you have children who are grown and gone, in all likelihood you have occasionally felt pangs of loss and the recognition that you didn't appreciate that time of life as much as you should have. Of course, there is no going back, but only forward. Rather than dwelling on the past, we should make the most of today, of the here and now, doing all we can to provide pleasant memories for the future. If you are still in the process of raising children, be aware that the tiny fingerprints that show up on almost every newly cleaned surface, the toys scattered about the house, the piles and piles of laundry to be tackled will disappear all too soon and that you will—to your surprise—miss them profoundly" (*Ensign,* Nov. 2008, 85–86). Life is short; we must cherish every moment, for too soon our days will pass away.

*Frequently, . . . feelings of self-disappointment come not from
wrongdoing, but from stresses and troubles for which we may not
be fully to blame. The Atonement of Jesus Christ applies to these
experiences. . . . The Savior can wipe away all of our tears.*

BRUCE C. HAFEN
ENSIGN, APRIL 1990, 7

The infinite power of the Savior's Atonement provides each of us with healing balm not only for sin but
also for discouragement, carelessness, inadequacy, despair, and bitterness. Elder Bruce C. Hafen said, "A
sense of falling short or falling down is not only natural but essential to the mortal experience. Still, after all
we can do, the Atonement can fill that which is empty,
straighten our bent parts, and make strong that which
is weak. The Savior's victory can compensate not only
for our sins but also for our inadequacies; not only for
our deliberate mistakes but also for our sins committed
in ignorance, our errors of judgment, and our unavoid-
able imperfections. Our ultimate aspiration is more
than being forgiven of sin—we seek to become holy,
endowed affirmatively with Christlike attributes, at
one with him, like him. Divine grace is the only source
that can finally fulfill that aspiration, after all we can
do" (*The Broken Heart*, 19–20).

Kindness is the essence of greatness and the fundamental characteristic of the noblest men and women I have known. Kindness is a passport that opens doors and fashions friends. It softens hearts and molds relationships that can last lifetimes.

JOSEPH B. WIRTHLIN
ENSIGN, MAY 2005, 26

Elder Joseph B. Wirthlin taught: "When we are filled with kindness, we are not judgmental. The Savior taught, 'Judge not, and ye shall not be judged: condemn not, and ye shall not be condemned: forgive, and ye shall be forgiven' [Luke 6:37]. . . .

"'But,' you ask, 'what if people are rude?'

"Love them.

"'If they are obnoxious?'

"Love them.

"'But what if they offend? Surely I must do something then?'

"Love them.

"'Wayward?'

"The answer is the same. Be kind. Love them.

"Why? In the scriptures Jude taught, 'And of some have compassion, making a difference' [Jude 1:22].

"Who can tell what far-reaching impact we can have if we are only kind?" (*Ensign,* May 2005, 28).

*Sometimes it isn't easy as parents to teach our children.
Sometimes we make mistakes. . . . As parents, we should
keep our desire to do our best, constantly show our love, and
not blame ourselves if our children choose another way.*

RUTH B. WRIGHT
ENSIGN, MAY 1994, 84

Parents are instructed to "teach their children to pray,
and to walk uprightly before the Lord" (D&C 68:28).
Ruth B. Wright, then a counselor in the Primary
general presidency, said: "What does it mean to walk
uprightly before the Lord? The word *upright* is defined
as honest, honorable, straightforward. Thus, to walk
uprightly, our children need to choose to live in an
honest, honorable, straightforward manner. Children
who understand and live the gospel today can walk
with assurance and joy and someday will enter the
presence of the Lord, walking uprightly." Sister Wright
continued: "What do we teach our children? It is essential that we teach them the gospel of Jesus Christ.
. . . Where do we teach our children? . . . We teach our
children everywhere we are with them. . . . How do we
teach our children? We teach by example. Our children will learn far more by observing us walk uprightly
than any other way" (*Ensign,* May 1994, 84).

To be humble is to recognize our utter dependence upon the Lord. We are conscious of our strengths, but we do not exalt ourselves and become prideful, for we know that all good things ultimately come from God.

GLENN L. PACE
ENSIGN, JANUARY 2005, 32

Life can sometimes beat us down and fill us with discouragement, despair, and lack of hope or confidence. Conversely, sometimes we may experience success and feel so full of ourselves that we exalt ourselves over others. Both are opposite ends of the same problem—self-absorption—and both forget the hand of the Lord. Elder Glenn L. Pace said, "To *lack confidence* is to have feelings of low self-worth. We are preoccupied with our weaknesses, and we lack faith in the Lord's ability to use those weaknesses for our good. We do not understand our inestimable worth in the eyes of God, nor do we appreciate our divine potential. Ironically, both pride and a lack of self-confidence cause us to focus excessively on ourselves and to deny the power of God in our lives" (*Ensign,* Jan. 2005, 32–33). Those who are weak and disheartened must turn to the Lord for strength; those who are proud must turn to the Lord for humility.

Remember also the promises which were made to you.

DOCTRINE & COVENANTS 3:5

We would do well to continually insert our names as we ponder the promises of the Lord. For example, "Remember, Nancy Jones, the promises which were made to you" (D&C 3:5), or "Remember, Mark Smith, the Lord will fulfil all his promises which he shall make unto you" (Alma 37:17). We each have received abundant promises from the Lord, uttered or unexpressed. We receive promises when we obtain a priesthood or patriarchal blessing; when we are set apart for a calling; when we listen to general conference; when we study the scriptures, seek the Lord in humble prayer, and a host of other ways. We also receive promises that come in the form of quiet whisperings of the Spirit and the still small voice that gently reassures and guides us along life's pathway. As members of the household of faith, we have entered into a covenant with Christ that consists of rich blessings that will surely come to the faithful.

The love of God does not supersede His laws and His commandments, and the effect of God's laws and commandments does not diminish the purpose and effect of His love. . . . God's love for His children is an eternal reality.

DALLIN H. OAKS
ENSIGN, NOVEMBER 2009, 26

Elder Dallin H. Oaks, beloved apostle and retired judge, said: "Some seem to value God's love because of their hope that His love is so great and so unconditional that it will mercifully excuse them from obeying His laws. In contrast, those who understand God's plan for His children know that God's laws are invariable, which is another great evidence of His love for His children. Mercy cannot rob justice [see Alma 42:25], and those who obtain mercy are 'they who have kept the covenant and observed the commandment' (D&C 54:6). . . . God's love is so perfect that He lovingly requires us to obey His commandments because He knows that only through obedience to His laws can we become perfect, as He is. . . . If only we will listen, we can know of God's love and feel it, even when we are disobedient. . . . God's choicest blessings are clearly contingent upon obedience to God's laws and commandments" (*Ensign,* Nov., 2009, 26–27).

If your so-called friends urge you to do anything you know to be wrong, you be the one to make a stand for right, even if you stand alone. . . . There is no friendship more valuable than your own clear conscience, your own moral cleanliness.

THOMAS S. MONSON
ENSIGN, MAY 2008, 65

We need less criticism and more understanding; less condemnation and more comfort. In a word, we all need more friendship. When we're discouraged, a good friend can lift our spirits. When we're struggling with an important decision, a wise friend can help us sort through the options. When all seems dark, a true friend will listen and shed the light of hope. And when we feel alone and anxious, a loyal friend will offer support. Steadfast friends want us to be the best we can be; they encourage us to stay true to gospel standards and do what is right. At times, we may need to leave friends who are negative influences. It would be better to be alone for a time than to stay connected with those who would lead us away from righteousness. Goodness will attract goodness; and eventually good, true, and loyal friends will be found.

*If we could live our religion, fear God, be strictly honest,
observe his laws and his statutes, and keep his commandments
to do them, we should feel very different. Our spirits would
be peaceful and buoyant. . . . Our joys would increase.*

JOHN TAYLOR
JOHN TAYLOR, 64

True joy comes in living our religion; but occasionally we lose sight of our rich blessings. "We forget,
sometimes, that we are engaged, with many others, in
establishing righteousness and planting the kingdom
of God upon the earth; and we condescend to little
meannesses, and become forgetful of the great and
glorious calling to which we are called," said John
Taylor. "Many of us give way to temptation; we falter
and get into darkness, and lose the Spirit of the Lord.
We forget that God and angels are looking upon us;
we forget that the spirits of just men made perfect
and our ancient fathers . . . are gazing upon us, and
that our acts are open to the inspection of all the authorized agencies of the invisible world. And, forgetting these things sometimes, we act the part of fools,
and the Spirit of God is grieved; it withdraws from
us, and we are then left to grope our way in the dark"
(*John Taylor*, 64).

Boldly face disappointments and the pains that
accompany them. If you deny them or hide them from view,
the chances are great that you will become worn out and fail.

JACOB DE JAGER
NEW ERA, MARCH 1984, 7

Elder Jacob de Jager of the Seventy said: "The problem that young people face is maintaining balance and perspective through the inevitable disappointments when they occur. These disappointments may range from nonachievement in school or poor communication in the home to not being able to withstand the great pressure of peer groups and the feelings of self-reproach when giving in to their wishes. There is a great need to examine yourself in these matters and ask yourself the old question, 'Am I part of the problem, or do I contribute to solving the problem?' As honest, good, law-abiding young people, you are faced with many temptations and pressures. But as long as you have come to a firm understanding that your anchor of hope is the gospel of Jesus Christ, then you have already elevated yourselves to a level of understanding that will enable you to overcome many disappointments" (*New Era*, Mar. 1984, 6).

And I will also be your light in the wilderness;
and I will prepare the way before you, if it so be that ye shall
keep my commandments; wherefore, inasmuch as ye shall keep
my commandments ye shall be led towards the promised land.

1 Nephi 17:13

The Lord accompanied Nephi and his extended family as He led them to the promised land. Each day and in every way, Nephi exercised faith in the Lord, trusted His promises, and kept the commandments. We too are on a journey—the journey of life. In this day of darkness and iniquity, we need the light and watchcare of the Lord. Some wander in the wilderness of sin and hopelessness, some are lost in the desert of despair and confusion. We need the guidance and reassurance of the Lord. He has promised if we trust Him and keep His commandments as we journey through life: "Behold, I will go before you and be your rearward; and I will be in your midst, and you shall not be confounded" (D&C 49:27).

*Marriage . . . cannot survive selfishness, impatience,
domineering, inequality, and lack of respect. Marriage . . .
thrives on acceptance, equality, sharing, giving, helping,
doing one's part, learning together, enjoying humor.*

DAVID O. MCKAY
DAVID O. MCKAY, 150

President David O. McKay spoke often about marriage and family life: "Minimize the faults, commend virtues. After the first thrill of the honeymoon is worn off, couples begin to see frailties, idiosyncrasies which they had not noticed before. . . . And so we become prone to find fault. Let us learn to control ourselves in that respect. . . . God help us to build homes in which the spirit of heaven on earth may be experienced. You and I know that that is possible, it is not a dream, it is not a theory. We may have that sweet companionship between husband and wife which grows dearer and dearer as the troubles of life come on. We can have homes in which children will never hear father and mother wrangle or quarrel. God help us . . . to build such homes, and to teach our young men and young women who are anticipating home life, to cherish such an ideal" (*David O. McKay*, 150).

*Knowing and remembering who we are and whose we are, we
become guided by a force affecting our attitude and our conduct.
We draw close to our Father in Heaven through sacred ordinances
and covenants available only through His restored church.*

ARDETH G. KAPP
ENSIGN, MAY 1992, 79

Sister Ardeth G. Kapp related an experience that
speaks of the power of faith and covenants: "I had the
privilege of visiting with a faithful family of Latter-day
Saints in a small nipa hut in the Philippines. In this
humble setting, a beautiful young woman, fourteen
years old, listened intently while her father explained
that by saving all the money they could and selling
everything they owned, the family would one day have
enough to go to the temple where they could be sealed
as a family forever. It is our faith in the importance of
making covenants with God and coming to understand our immense possibilities that the temple, the
house of the Lord, becomes the focus for all that really
matters. In the temple we participate in ordinances
and covenants that span the distance between heaven
and earth. They prepare us to one day return to God's
presence and enjoy the blessings of eternal families
and eternal life" (*Ensign,* May 1992, 79).

The only safe way for us to do, as individuals, is to live so humbly, so righteously and so faithfully before God that we may possess his Spirit to that extent that we shall be able to judge righteously, and discern between truth and error.

JOSEPH F. SMITH
JOSEPH F. SMITH, 270

Joseph F. Smith said, "When we live so that we can hear and understand the whisperings of the still, small voice of the Spirit of God, let us do whatsoever that Spirit directs without fear of the consequences. It does not make any difference whether it meet the minds of carpers or critics, or of the enemies of the kingdom of God, or not. Is it agreeable to the will of the Lord? Is it compatible with the spirit of the great latter-day work in which we are engaged? Is the end aimed at likely to advance the Church and to strengthen it in the earth? If its trend is in that direction, let us do it, no matter what men may say or think" (*Joseph F. Smith,* 269). With the still small voice of the Spirit as our guide, we will have the faith and confidence to follow the Lord and hold back the enticements and mockery of the world.

*Trust is to human relationships what faith is to gospel living.
It is the beginning place, the foundation upon which more can
be built. Where trust is, love can flourish. Then add to love
consecration, the dedication of two lives to a holy purpose.*

BARBARA B. SMITH
ENSIGN, NOVEMBER 1981, 83

Eternal marriage is a commitment of heart, mind, and soul. It is the bringing together of two different people, and—in the spirit of love, harmony, and forgiveness—the creating of a new family unit that will go on into the eternities. In order for a marriage to grow and thrive into something beautiful, husband and wife must build a foundation of trust and faith, as well as an ardent dedication to both the institution of marriage and the preservation of their own marriage. Those who desire a celestial marriage love their spouse with all their hearts and cleave to each other and none else (D&C 42:22). *To cleave* means to adhere to unwaveringly, to be fiercely loyal to one another. Marriage is not easy; but nothing worthwhile and enduring is. Marriage takes effort and work, fidelity and devotion, sacrifice and selflessness. And it's not all serious or onerous—marriage can be the home of our deepest joys and happiest moments.

If we will seek the grace of God, He will come to our aid and the aid of our loved ones in times of need. Let us obey the Lord in all things and offer to Him the ultimate sacrifice of "a broken heart and a contrite spirit."

GENE R. COOK
ENSIGN, MAY 1993, 81

We believe in a living Christ, a living Lord, who is as alive today as when he walked the earth in the meridian of time.

> *I know that my Redeemer lives.*
> *What comfort this sweet sentence gives!*
> *He lives, he lives, who once was dead.*
> *He lives, my ever-living Head.* (Hymns, 136)

As we seek His grace and rely on His mercy and merits, we can feel His sustaining influence and move forward with faith. The Lord reminds us, "Fear thou not; for I am with thee" (Isaiah 41:10). He called himself our "rereward" (Isaiah 52:12), meaning that He would guard our backs and be there for us. We will have true confidence and sweet assurance when we love the Lord with all our hearts and our neighbors, whether they be next door or around the world. That love takes time and practice, but when our conscience is clear and we trust the Lord, we have nothing to fear.

Be strong and of a good courage, fear not,
nor be afraid of them: for the Lord thy God,
he it is that doth go with thee; he will
not fail thee, nor forsake thee.

DEUTERONOMY 31:6

To modern Israel, the Lord has said: "Therefore, fear not, little flock; do good; let earth and hell combine against you, for if ye are built upon my rock, they cannot prevail. . . . Look unto me in every thought; doubt not, fear not" (D&C 6:34, 36). The Lord's promises are sure: He will not fail or forsake those who turn to Him, trust Him, and obey Him. We need not fear the forces of evil around us. We need not be afraid of the adversary and his minions. We need not tremble to go into the world if we have the confidence of the Lord in our hearts and a testimony in our souls. Strength comes from putting our trust in the Lord; courage comes of humbly turning our hearts to God. How comforting to know that in a world of deception and corruption there is a fount of wisdom and light, a reliable source of truth, a trustworthy place to which we can turn!

*In some quiet way, the expression
and feelings of gratitude have a wonderful
cleansing or healing nature. Gratitude brings
warmth to the giver and the receiver alike.*

ROBERT D. HALES
ENSIGN, MAY 1992, 65

Gratitude is the mark of a great soul. Elder Robert D. Hales said, "Gratitude is a state of appreciation, an act of thanksgiving, which causes us to be humble because we recognize an act of kindness, service, or caring from someone else which lifts us and strengthens us. Ingratitude is the attitude of being unaware or not recognizing when someone has assisted us or helped us or, even worse, when we know we have been helped and have not given thanks privately or publicly. . . . Gratitude expressed to our Heavenly Father in prayer for what we have brings a calming peace—a peace which allows us to not canker our souls for what we don't have. Gratitude brings a peace that helps us overcome the pain of adversity and failure. Gratitude on a daily basis means we express appreciation for what we have now without qualification for what we had in the past or desire in the future" (*Ensign,* May 1992, 65).

*Regardless of our trials, with the abundance
we have today, we would be ungrateful if we
did not appreciate our blessings.*

QUENTIN L. COOK
ENSIGN, NOVEMBER 2008, 104

Grateful people are happier and healthier than ungrateful people. They are more inclined to give back
to the world. They gain wisdom and are more apt to
pass that wisdom on to the next generation. Grateful
people are realists. They know that life has its challenges and heartaches, its satisfactions and joys. To
be grateful doesn't mean we don't recognize the difficulties of life. Gratefulness flows from an abundant
heart that rejoices in another day of life, another opportunity to love and interact with God's creations.
Thankfulness flows from wide-open hearts that
perceive beauty, even when it is surrounded by ugli-
ness, and find peace amidst the storms of life. Our
sorrows and trials may even be the very things that
help gratitude grow in our hearts. We can be grateful
that, more often than not, things tend to work out.
We can be thankful for good people and for all those
in the past upon whose shoulders we stand.

We all need guidance through life. We obtain it best from the standard works and teachings of the prophets of God. With diligent effort, we can achieve that guidance and thus qualify for all of the blessings that God has in store for His faithful children.

RUSSELL M. NELSON
ENSIGN, NOVEMBER 2000, 18

Elder Russell M. Nelson said, "In your journey through life, you meet many obstacles and make some mistakes. Scriptural guidance helps you to recognize error and make the necessary correction. You stop going in the wrong direction. You carefully study the scriptural road map. Then you proceed with repentance and restitution required to get on the 'strait and narrow path which leads to eternal life' [2 Nephi 31:18; see also Matthew 7:14; Jacob 6:11; 3 Nephi 14:14, 27:33; D&C 132:22]. Brothers and sisters, our busy lives force us to focus on things we *do* from day to day. But the development of character comes only as we focus on who we really *are.* To establish and accomplish those greater goals, we do need heavenly help" (*Ensign,* Nov. 2000, 17). How reassuring to know that divine help is close by, always ready, just waiting to be obtained by those diligent seekers who desire the guidance and blessings of heaven.

You can have sacred, revelatory, profoundly instructive experiences with the Lord [even] in the most miserable experiences of your life—in the worst settings, while enduring the most painful injustices.

JEFFREY R. HOLLAND
ENSIGN, SEPTEMBER 2009, 28

Elder Jeffrey R. Holland spoke of the sense in which Liberty Jail could be called a temple: "Certainly this prison-temple lacked the purity, beauty, comfort, and cleanliness of our modern temples. The speech and behavior of the guards and criminals who came there were anything but temple-like. In fact, the restricting brutality and injustice of this experience at Liberty would make it seem the very antithesis of the liberating, merciful spirit of our temples and the ordinances performed in them" (*Ensign,* Sept. 2009, 28). And yet in that "temple" the Lord taught the Prophet Joseph Smith in a sacred, profound, and personal way. We too can be taught transcendent truths even in the midst of great suffering and hardship, perhaps even *because* of our suffering and hardship. God's loving arm is always stretched out in our behalf, waiting to tutor and comfort us—wherever we may be, in whatever condition we may find ourselves.

*I would that ye should remember, that as much as ye
shall put your trust in God even so much ye shall be
delivered out of your trials, and your troubles, and your
afflictions, and ye shall be lifted up at the last day.*

ALMA 38:5

Perhaps the most oft repeated promise in the scriptures is that if we trust God and keep His commandments, we will be strengthened and comforted in our
afflictions and lifted up at the last day. That is the
Lord's promise in all dispensations and to all people.
To trust God means that we know enough of His encompassing omnipotence and omniscience—as well
as His loving and compassionate heart—to know that
He has our best interests in mind, He wants for us
eternal joy and everlasting life, He desires that we inherit all that He has. To be lifted up applies both here
and hereafter: it means that we see the light in the
dark tunnels of our lives is the Lord, "the Light of the
World;" it means we hold on to the iron rod of hope
and trust in the Lord through the trials and tribula-
tions of life; it means ultimately to be crowned with
celestial glory and eternal life.

If we live the gospel, people will come into the Church.
They will see the virtue of our lives, and they will be
attracted to the message we have to teach.
That message places great emphasis on the family.

GORDON B. HINCKLEY
ENSIGN, MARCH 2003, 5

The Church is only as strong as its families. That's why prophets have spoken clearly over the generations about the central importance of the family unit in our doctrine and practice. President Gordon B. Hinckley said, "We believe that the family is the basic unit of society. You can't have a strong community without strong families. You can't have a strong nation without strong families—the father, the mother, the children as one unit working together. Now the family is falling apart all over America, all over the world. If we can just cultivate good, wholesome family life among our members, I don't worry very much about the future of this Church" (*Ensign,* Mar. 2003, 5). One of the hallmarks of the Church is the emphasis it places on the family. We know that God himself lives in a family unit, and we wish to live worthy to inherit the kind of eternal family life that He enjoys.

The supreme act of worship is to keep the commandments, to follow in the footsteps of the Son of God, to do ever those things that please Him.

JOSEPH FIELDING SMITH
ENSIGN, DECEMBER 1971, 27

There is nothing new about headlines decrying a lack of integrity in the lives of so many. Some so-called upstanding and active members of the Church are later found to be full of hypocrisy and iniquity (Matthew 23:28)—they talk the talk but they don't walk the walk. And while none of us is perfect, there is a considerable difference between blatant hypocrisy and being imperfect mortals who stumble and falter as we sincerely strive to live the gospel. True discipleship is more than checking off a list of "shalts" and "shalt-nots" at the end of the day. We may miss the whole spirit of the gospel if we focus more on performance and duty than on consecration and genuine devotion; we may miss the essence of gospel living by centering our hearts on checklists and obedience, rather than truly coming to the Lord with broken hearts and contrite spirits. Pride, which is at the heart of hypocrisy, always goes before the fall (Proverbs 16:18).

December

Trust in the Lord with all thine heart;
and lean not unto thine own understanding.
In all thy ways acknowledge him,
and he shall direct thy paths.

PROVERBS 3:5–6

Look for [an eternal companion] who is developing the essential attributes that bring happiness: a deep love of the Lord and of His commandments, a determination to live them, one that is kindly understanding, forgiving of others, and willing to give of self.

RICHARD G. SCOTT
ENSIGN, MAY 1999, 26

Elder Richard G. Scott said: "An essential priority of a prospective wife is the desire to be a wife and mother. She should be developing the sacred qualities that God has given His daughters to excel as a wife and mother: patience, kindliness, a love of children, and a desire to care for them. . . . She should be acquiring a good education to prepare for the demands of motherhood. A prospective husband should also honor his priesthood and use it in service to others. Seek a man who accepts his role as provider of the necessities of life, has the capacity to do it, and is making concerted efforts to prepare himself to fulfill those responsibilities. I suggest that you not ignore many possible candidates who are still developing these attributes. . . . You will likely not find [a] perfect person, and if you did, there would certainly be no interest in you. These attributes are best polished together as husband and wife" (*Ensign,* May 1999, 26).

*I find that when I get casual in my relationships with divinity
and when it seems that no divine ear is listening . . . that
I am far, far away. If I immerse myself in the scriptures
the distance narrows and the spirituality returns.*

SPENCER W. KIMBALL
TEACHINGS OF SPENCER W. KIMBALL, 135

Scripture study brings to our life a powerful dimension that can't be reached in any other way. Sincere scripture study will increase our faith, deepen our testimonies, and bolster our desire to do what is right; it will bless us with a feeling of inspiration, gratitude, and humility; it will strengthen our relationships with others and with Heavenly Father and Jesus Christ. If we are intentional about spending some daily time in the scriptures and in the latest conference report (the May and November issues of the *Ensign*) we will be the beneficiaries of marvelous blessings of wisdom and understanding, light and truth. It matters not the length of the minutes, but the desire and intent of the heart. A few sincere moments with the holy word of God, ancient or modern, will draw heaven closer to us and work a mighty change in our hearts.

*Behold, the time has fully come, which was spoken of by
the mouth of Malachi . . . to turn the hearts of the
fathers to the children, and the children to the fathers,
lest the whole earth be smitten with a curse.*

DOCTRINE & COVENANTS 110:14–15

Elijah the prophet came to the Kirtland Temple
to restore the keys associated with temple work, that
sealing power which binds families for eternity. This
fulfilled Malachi's prophecy and was an essential
event in the restoration of gospel fulness (Malachi
4:6). "So what does this mean? To turn our hearts to
our fathers is to search out the names of our deceased
ancestors and to perform the saving ordinances in the
temple for them. This will forge a continuous chain
between us and our forefathers eventually all the way
back to Father Adam and Mother Eve," said President
James E. Faust. "The process of finding our ancestors
one by one can be challenging but also exciting and
rewarding. We often feel spiritual guidance as we go
to the sources which identify them. Because this is a
very spiritual work, we can expect help from the other
side of the veil" (*Ensign,* Nov. 2003, 55–56).

*I am more concerned about the moral deficit in our nations
than I am about their budget deficits, though that, too, is
a most serious matter. . . . But what [societies] need, above
all else, is a strengthening of the homes of the people.*

GORDON B. HINCKLEY
ENSIGN, SEPTEMBER 1996, 5

President Gordon B. Hinckley outlined four simple
things that will help our families: "Let us teach and
learn goodness together, work together, read good
books together, pray together. These things can be
done notwithstanding the frenetic pressures of our
lives. They can be done with children and particularly
when children are small. . . . I encourage you as one
who has been ordained to the holy apostleship and to
the calling I now hold. That sacred office is not given
as a bestowal of honor. It is given with the responsibility to bless, encourage, strengthen, and build faith
in things good and things divine. In the authority of
that priesthood, my brethren and sisters, I bless you,
that each of you, each of us, feeble as our efforts may
seem to be, may become a factor for good in capturing
the spirit of goodness in our homes and in recaptur-
ing it for our nations" (*Ensign,* Sept. 1996, 8).

*In everything we do and say, in how we dress, in how we
spend our time, in all the choices we make, we demonstrate
what we believe, and that becomes [a] pattern to follow.*

VIRGINIA U. JENSEN
ENSIGN, NOVEMBER 2001, 95

The Lord's promises are sure," said Sister Virginia U.
Jensen. "To maintain a firm stance for ourselves and
help others stand firm, the message of the restored
gospel must be firmly planted in our hearts and
taught in our homes. In your own homes, give your
children and loved ones the spiritual armor they will
need as they leave you each day and venture away
from the safe fortress of your home. Teach your loved
ones how to draw upon the powers of heaven through
fasting and prayer. Teach them that keeping the
Sabbath day holy will insulate them from the world.
Teach them to be obedient. Teach them to seek God's
approval, not man's. . . . The truths of the gospel and
knowledge of the plan of salvation are weapons your
family members can use for victory over Satan's evil
forces" (*Ensign*, Nov. 2001, 94).

Those who have felt the touch of the Master's hand somehow cannot explain the change that comes into their lives. There is a desire to live better, to serve faithfully, to walk humbly, and to live more like the Savior.

THOMAS S. MONSON
ENSIGN, SEPTEMBER 1989, 4

President Thomas S. Monson asks, "How can we account for these miracles? Why the upsurge of activity in brothers and sisters long dormant? The poet, speaking of death, wrote, 'God touched him, and he slept.' I say, speaking of this new birth, 'God touched them, and they awakened.' Two fundamental reasons largely account for these changes of attitudes, of habits, of actions. First, brothers and sisters have been shown their eternal possibilities and have made the decision to achieve them. People cannot really long rest content with mediocrity once they see excellence is within their reach. Second, other men and women and, yes, young people have followed the admonition of the Savior and have loved their neighbors as themselves and helped to bring their neighbors' dreams to fulfillment and their ambitions to realization. The catalyst in this process has been the principle of love, described as the noblest attribute of the human soul" (*Ensign,* Sept. 1989, 4).

God's measure of our worth in His kingdom will
not be the high positions we have held here among men
nor in His church, nor the honors we have won,
but rather the lives we have led and the good we have done.

HAROLD B. LEE
THE TEACHINGS OF HAROLD B. LEE, 75

Our worthiness is measured by how closely we try to live our lives in accordance with the teachings of the Master. As we reach out to others in love and kindness and go about doing good, we are indeed emulating the gift of Jesus Christ and his "more excellent way" (Ether 12:11). Real worth, true success, is manifest more in the heart than in the pocketbook; it's reflected in cherished memories of loved ones; it's defined by making a difference in others' lives. Worth is not dependent on social, economic, or intellectual advantage. You don't have to sit in a corner office, travel to exotic places, or capture headlines to be successful. Our days—whether many or few—will come to an end, and so much of what the world thinks of as success will vanish in time. But a truly successful life is never forgotten. Charity and goodness stand the test of time; generosity and compassion outlive us; decency and integrity are everlasting.

I will give unto the children of men line upon line,
precept upon precept, here a little and there a little; and
blessed are those who hearken unto my precepts, and
lend an ear unto my counsel, for they shall learn wisdom.

2 NEPHI 28:30

The wisdom and treasures of heaven are rationed to those who have proven themselves faithful stewards over the light and truth they have received. To the faithful and those anxiously engaged in righteousness shall be given more and more; to the slothful and wicked shall be taken away that light, truth, and wisdom they once had. The Lord, in His love, mercy, and understanding, grants unto His people "all that he seeth fit that they should have" (Alma 29:8; see also Alma 12:9–11). The riches of heaven are obtained by obedience to the laws of heaven. There are no riches or treasures of wisdom, light, or truth in rebellion and disobedience. We learn little by little, line upon line, precept upon precept, through teaching and testing, doing and becoming, until we receive more light and truth, which grows and grows ever brighter "until the perfect day" (D&C 50:24).

*Oh, how [the Savior] rejoices when a lost soul
is found by a faithful undershepherd and
then is tenderly and lovingly brought home again!*

ALEXANDER B. MORRISON
ENSIGN, MAY 1992, 14

Though our love is not yet perfect, we can be filled with the love of God. Alma departed Zarahemla to seek the apostate Zoramites and bring them back to the fold of Christ: "O Lord, wilt thou grant unto us that we may have success in bringing them again unto thee in Christ. Behold, O Lord, their souls are precious, and many of them are our brethren; therefore, give unto us, O Lord, power and wisdom that we may bring these, our brethren, again unto thee" (Alma 31:34–35). Elder Alexander B. Morrison said, "True undershepherds help others to partake of the bread of life and the living water through selfless service. They know that service solves the seeming paradox of the scriptures: one has to *lose* his or her life to *find* it. Service, wise undershepherds understand, is the golden key which unlocks the doors to celestial halls. For many, Christ is found through serving Him" (*Ensign,* May 1992, 14).

*I again admonish the Latter-day Saints to aim and
diligently endeavor to free themselves from debt.
Get out of debt and keep out of debt, and then you
will be financially as well as spiritually free.*

JOSEPH F. SMITH
JOSEPH F. SMITH, 168

We have been counseled for generations to live
within our means. "Keep your possessions free from
debt," said President Joseph F. Smith. "Get out of
debt as fast as you can, and keep out of debt, for that is
the way in which the promise of God will be fulfilled
to the people of his Church, that they will become
the richest of all people in the world. But this will
not happen while you mortgage your homes and your
farms, or run into debt beyond your ability to meet
your obligations; and thus, perhaps, your name and
credit be dishonored because you overreached yourselves" (*Joseph F. Smith,* 167). There are few things that
will generate more serenity in the heart and home
than being financially solvent and free from debt. A
sense of temporal security and a feeling of spiritual
peace and contentment will come to all who follow
prophetic counsel to get out and stay out of debt.

What progress can there be for a man unconscious of his faults?
Such a man has lost the fundamental element of growth, which
is the realization that there is something bigger, better, and more
desirable than the condition in which he now finds himself.

DAVID O. MCKAY
GOSPEL IDEALS, 12

Failure to recognize our faults closes the door to learning, growth, and true discipleship. Life becomes stagnant when pride and slothfulness combine to produce self-satisfaction. President David O. McKay said, "Heaven pity the man who is unconscious of a fault! Pity him also who is ignorant of his ignorance! Neither is on the road to salvation. . . . Ignorance and sin are man's worst enemies. They are barriers to salvation. Only through repentance and obedience to the gospel can these be eradicated. In the repentant man's soul these evils are supplanted by light and knowledge" (*Gospel Ideals*, 13–14). The gospel is a message of continual growth and change, of learning and developing over the life course—it can make bad people good and good people better. True disciples of the Lord humbly and honestly examine themselves: they are never done but enduringly seek to become more, learn more, and grow more.

There is no organization better able to respond to the challenges of humanity than the priesthood of the Most High God. . . . We now call upon you to mobilize our priesthood quorums in response to the employment and financial challenges facing our members.

RICHARD C. EDGLEY
ENSIGN, MAY 2009, 53

We live in uncertain and challenging times. How blessed we are to belong to a church that has both doctrine and a system in place to assist and support one another. To the brethren of the priesthood, Bishop Richard C. Edgley said, "Among our quorum members, you will likely find those who know of job openings and others who are skilled at writing résumés or assisting in interview preparation. Regardless of titles or skills, you will find a brotherhood committed to bear one another's burdens" (*Ensign,* May 2009, 53). The priesthood organization is ordained of God: stake presidents, bishops, high priest group leaders, and elders quorum presidents, all called to assist members in their quest for eternal life. The brethren of the priesthood are organized to look after one another and their families, to support each other in difficult times. A quorum gives each priesthood holder a place of brotherhood and fellowship.

*Peace, hope, and direction are outcomes of striving
to live the teachings of Jesus and obeying His laws and
commandments. The scriptures teach, "Great peace
have they which love thy law" (Psalm 119:165).*

PATRICIA P. PINEGAR
ENSIGN, NOVEMBER 1999, 67

The story is told of a father and son flying a kite together: "The boy said to his father, 'Daddy, let's cut the string and let the kite go; I want to see it go higher and higher.' His father said, 'Son, the kite won't go higher if we cut the string.' 'Yes, it will,' responded the little boy. 'The string is holding the kite down; I can feel it.' The father handed a pocketknife to his son. The boy cut the string. In a matter of seconds the kite was out of control. It darted here and there and finally landed in a broken heap. That was difficult for the boy to understand. He felt certain the string was holding the kite down. The commandments and laws of God are like the kite string. They lead us and guide us upward. Obedience to these laws gives us peace, hope, and direction" (*Ensign,* Nov. 1999, 67–68).

*Remember, remember that it is upon
the rock of our Redeemer, who is Christ, the Son
of God, that ye must build your foundation.*

HELAMAN 5:12

We must always remember that it is upon the rock
of our Redeemer that we must build our foundation,
so that "when the devil shall send forth his mighty
winds, yea, his shafts in the whirlwind, yea, when all
his hail and his mighty storm shall beat upon you, it
shall have no power over you to drag you down to the
gulf of misery and endless wo, because of the rock
upon which ye are built, which is a sure foundation,
a foundation whereon if men build they cannot fall"
(Helaman 5:12). A foundation built upon Christ will
stand strong through storm and tempest; it will not
be tossed about with every wind of doctrine or the
cunning craftiness of man (Ephesians 4:14). The
principles and standards of the gospel are eternal.
They are given to each of us to keep us on the path
leading back to the presence of our Heavenly Father
and His Son, Jesus Christ.

Immortality or the resurrection will happen to us all. . . .
Eternal life in happiness and glory in association with those
we love will be the reward only of those who exercise faith
in Jesus Christ through obedience to his commandments.

WM. GRANT BANGERTER
ENSIGN, NOVEMBER 1988, 82

Those who qualify for God's greatest gift, even eternal life (D&C 14:7), focus their hearts on the Redeemer, overcome the world by obedience to His commandments, and remain steadfast and immovable in honoring sacred covenants. The great plan of happiness centers on the Atonement and Resurrection of Jesus Christ. Elder Wm. Grant Bangerter testified, "I have known of Jesus Christ since before I can remember. I was taught to pray to God in his name since infancy. I don't believe there has been a single day of my life when I have not openly sought for his blessings, his spirit, and his protection. I want his type of eternal life. It has come to mean everything to me. I know that the gospel is true, since I have heard the voice of God through his Spirit confirm and witness it to me" (*Ensign,* Nov. 1988, 82).

*The greatest security of members of The Church of
Jesus Christ of Latter-day Saints comes from learning
to listen to and obey the words and commandments
that the Lord has given through living prophets.*

ROBERT D. HALES
ENSIGN, MAY 1995, 17

We live in a time when "all things shall be in com-
motion; and surely, men's hearts shall fail them; for fear
shall come upon all people" (D&C 88:91). We wonder about the future and worry about the present—is
there reason for hope? Yes, because God lives and
watches over His faithful people and will not abandon
us. Yes, because Jesus is our Savior and has given us
the means whereby we can be redeemed from the Fall
and, by His grace, overcome the world. Yes, because a
chosen seer who received the priesthood keys necessary for salvation and hence restored the Lord's true
church. Yes, because those same keys are held today by
fifteen prophets, seers, and revelators, who as the living
oracles of God continue to lead and guide the Church
by prophecy and revelation. Security, confidence, and
peace come to those who listen to the words of the living prophets and obey them.

At this season when we usually celebrate the Savior's birth by giving generous gifts to each other, we all would do well to remember his supernal, unparalleled gifts to us. We might think, too, of the gifts we could give to him.

TED E. BREWERTON
ENSIGN, DECEMBER 1994, 7

Elder Ted E. Brewerton said, "It was our Father's plan to provide a Savior for us—his only Begotten Son in the flesh, Jesus Christ—who could pay the atoning price for the sins that we would commit. Our sins would inevitably bring upon us spiritual death, barring us from Heavenly Father's presence. But Christ would intercede in our behalf; his atonement would meet the demands of eternal justice against us. . . . Imagine, for example, that your sins have pulled you into the bottom of a deep pit. From a cliff high above, the Lord tosses a rope to you—the rope of mercy. In order for the rope to be of any help, you must tie it around you and fasten it with the knot of repentance. This is the only way to be pulled free of sin" (*Ensign*, Dec. 1994, 7). Repentance is our gift to the Savior when we offer a broken heart and contrite spirit.

*I promise that if we unclutter our lives a little bit and
in sincerity and humility seek the pure and gentle
Christ with our hearts, we will see Him, we will find
Him—on Christmas and throughout the year.*

DIETER F. UCHTDORF
FIRST PRESIDENCY DEVOTIONAL, DECEMBER 6, 2009

President Dieter F. Uchtdorf said, "Sometimes when we read about people who could not see the Savior for who He was, we marvel at their blindness. But do *we* also let distractions obstruct our view of the Savior—during this Christmas season and throughout the year? Some are external distractions—the gifts we worry about, the decorations, or the clamorous advertising—but often it is what is inside us that blinds us from seeing the Christ. Some may feel a certain level of intellectual aloofness that distances them from Christ. . . . The familiar story of Jesus the Christ can get lost amid the flood of scientific advances, pressing news, or the latest popular movies or books. Some are so caught up in the details of running their lives that they don't make time for much else. . . . Their hearts are so focused on the world that they cannot see the Christ" (First Presidency Christmas Devotional, December 6, 2009).

Our Savior, whose humble birth we celebrate
at this Christmas season, came to earth to dedicate
His whole life as an example of service to others.
If we are wise, we will take Him as our model.

V. DALLAS MERRELL
ENSIGN, DECEMBER 1996, 10

Having the self-discipline to focus our efforts gives us the power to reach our goals and reach out to others in love and service. Each decision to keep moving in the right direction, each effort to follow the Master, each step we take to serve others makes us better, more humble, less selfish, and allows us to do more. There is nothing more restrictive than laziness, sin, or unmet potential. Through self-discipline and service, we discover our true potential and make it a reality. That is true freedom. Those who achieve the most in life include others along the way, they decide what they want to do and then stick to their task. They have learned that self-discipline and service are the keys that unlock the doors to joy and happiness.

Giving, not getting, brings to full bloom the Christmas spirit. Enemies are forgiven, friends remembered, and God obeyed. . . . We look out upon the world's busy life and become more interested in people than things.

THOMAS S. MONSON
ENSIGN, DECEMBER 2008, 5

Christmas is special because our hearts turn more fully to others. During this season, we spend more time thinking of what we can give, what we can share, what we can do for others. That is the sacred spirit of Christmas. President Thomas S. Monson said, "Times change; years speed by; but Christmas continues sacred. In this marvelous dispensation of the fulness of times, our opportunities to give of ourselves are indeed limitless, but they are also perishable. There are hearts to gladden. There are kind words to say. There are gifts to be given. There are deeds to be done. There are souls to be saved. . . . If we are to have the very best Christmas ever, we must listen for the sound of sandaled feet. We must reach out for the Carpenter's hand. With every step we take in His footsteps, we abandon a doubt and gain a truth" (*Ensign,* Dec. 2008, 7–8).

*The greatest gift of this or any other Christmas is
the Atonement of Jesus as the Redeemer, the Son of
God. . . . It is a gift we cannot handle or touch, but
we can feel the immeasurable love of the Giver.*

JAMES E. FAUST
ENSIGN, DECEMBER 2001, 6

The Atonement is the focal point of all history.
Elder Bruce R. McConkie said, "Nothing in the
entire plan of salvation compares in any way in importance with that most transcendent of all events,
the atoning sacrifice of our Lord. It is the most
wwimportant single thing that has ever occurred
in the entire history of created things; it is the rock
foundation upon which the gospel and all other
things rest" (*Mormon Doctrine,* 60). The power and
majesty of the Atonement must be felt, not just ana-
lyzed or studied. To come close to feeling the depth
and meaning of this consummate expression of divine
love, we must seek the Lord with sincerity of heart,
draw ever closer to the Spirit, and strive to more
fully live the gospel. We will find as we do so that we
will become more like the Savior. We will truly and
deeply come to love Him because we will know that
He loved us first (1 John 4:19).

The real Christmas comes to him who has taken Christ into his life as a moving, dynamic, vitalizing force. The real spirit of Christmas lies in the life and mission of the Master.

HOWARD W. HUNTER
ENSIGN, DECEMBER 2005, 24

Christmas is a good season to seriously consider the power and majesty of the baby born in Bethlehem. When we truly take Christ into our lives, we become changed, transformed, regenerated, new creatures. No longer do we look to the world of Babylon for happiness and contentment; we gain the disposition of a disciple in Zion who wants only to do good and no longer wishes to do evil (Mosiah 5:2). Elder Howard W. Hunter said, "During the hurry of the festive occasion of this Christmas season, find time to turn your heart to God. Perhaps in the quiet hours, and in a quiet place, and on your knees—alone or with loved ones—give thanks for the good things that have come to you, and ask that His Spirit might dwell in you as you earnestly strive to serve Him and keep His commandments. He will take you by the hand and His promises will be kept" (*Ensign,* Dec. 2005, 25).

I testify that God will keep His promises to you as you honor your covenants with Him. . . . He will strengthen and finish your faith. He will, by His Holy Spirit, fill you with godly power.

D. TODD CHRISTOFFERSON
ENSIGN, MAY 2009, 22–23

Elder D. Todd Christofferson explained that as we honor covenants, faith expands by three means: "In the first place, the promised fruits of obedience become evident, which confirms our faith. Secondly, the Spirit communicates God's pleasure, and we feel secure in His continued blessing and help. Thirdly, come what may, we can face life with hope and equanimity, knowing that we will succeed in the end because we have God's promise to us individually, by name, and we know He cannot lie (see Enos 1:6; Ether 3:12)" (*Ensign,* May 2009, 21).

*For unto us a child is born, unto us a son is given: and
the government shall be upon his shoulder: and his name
shall be called Wonderful, Counsellor, The mighty
God, The everlasting Father, The Prince of Peace.*

Isaiah 9:6

Isaiah prophesied more than seven hundred years
before the birth of Jesus Christ that the Prince of
Peace would be born. Isaiah spoke Messianically, as
have countless prophets before and since the Savior's
birth. All inspired eyes and hearts of generations
past looked to the glorious meridian day when the
Son of God would take on mortality and be born of
a virgin, would teach His gospel truth, would prof-
fer His life as a vicarious sacrifice for fallen man, and
would be resurrected as the firstfruits of eternal life
(1 Corinthians 15:20). The world and everything in
it changed with the advent of the Savior's mortal life
and with His divine mission and infinite Atonement
for all the sons and daughters of God. We have the
unconditional promise of immortality because of the
life and mission of the Master, and because of Jesus
we have the conditional promise of eternal life if we
are found worthy.

We bear testimony, as His duly ordained Apostles—that Jesus is the Living Christ, the immortal Son of God. He is the great King Immanuel, who stands today on the right hand of His Father. He is the light, the life, and the hope of the world.

"THE LIVING CHRIST:
THE TESTIMONY OF THE APOSTLES"

On January 1, 2000, the First Presidency and Quorum of the Twelve Apostles issued a testimony to the world: "As we commemorate the birth of Jesus Christ two millennia ago, we offer our testimony of the reality of His matchless life and the infinite virtue of His great atoning sacrifice. None other has had so profound an influence upon all who have lived and will yet live upon the earth. . . . He gave His life to atone for the sins of all mankind. His was a great vicarious gift in behalf of all who would ever live upon the earth. We solemnly testify that His life, which is central to all human history, neither began in Bethlehem nor concluded on Calvary. He was the Firstborn of the Father, the Only Begotten Son in the flesh, the Redeemer of the world" ("The Living Christ"). On this day when we celebrate the Savior's birth, let us thank God for the matchless gift of His Son.

The child grew, and waxed strong in spirit, filled with
wisdom: and the grace of God was upon him.

And Jesus increased in wisdom and stature,
and in favour with God and man.

LUKE 2:40, 52

Elder James E. Talmage taught that the Savior "came among men to experience all the natural conditions of mortality; He was born as truly a dependent, helpless babe as is any other child; His infancy was in all common features as the infancy of others; His boyhood was actual boyhood, His development was as necessary and as real as that of all children. Over His mind had fallen the veil of forgetfulness common to all who are born to earth, by which the remembrance of primeval existence is shut off. The Child grew, and with growth there came to Him expansion of mind, development of faculties, and progression in power and understanding. His advancement was from one grace to another, not from gracelessness to grace; from good to greater good, not from evil to good" (*Jesus the Christ,* 105–6). Although we are vastly different from Jesus, we, too, are here in mortality to grow in spirit, wisdom, stature, and favor with God and man.

And this is life eternal,
that they might know thee the only true God,
and Jesus Christ, whom thou hast sent.

JOHN 17:3

Life eternal, the quality of life that God himself enjoys, is possible only to those who come to truly know God and His Son, Jesus Christ. It is not knowing *of* them—it is *knowing* them. To know them is to follow their way, live their truth, and seek to emulate their life (John 14:6); it is to keep the commandments and honor covenants, pray and repent, and live with charity for all. Knowing means doing; truly knowing means a change of life. Elder Robert D. Hales asked, "Some wonder, why is belief in God so important? . . . Without God, life would end at the grave and our mortal experiences would have no purpose. Growth and progress would be temporary, accomplishment without value, challenges without meaning. There would be no ultimate right and wrong and no moral responsibility to care for one another as fellow children of God. Indeed, without God, there would be no mortal or eternal life" (*Ensign,* Nov. 2009, 29).

*Our yearnings for happiness were implanted in our hearts by
Deity. They represent a kind of homesickness, for we have
a residual memory of our premortal existence. They are also a
foretaste of the fulness of joy that is promised to the faithful.*

JACK H. GOASLIND
ENSIGN, MAY 1986, 52–53

We are here in mortality to experience joy and
happiness. The plan of our loving Father is called
"the plan of happiness" (Alma 42:16); and in the
meridian of time, it was heralded by angelic messengers as "good tidings of great joy, which shall be to all
people" (Luke 2:10). Yet how do we find true happiness? Elder Jack H. Goaslind said, "Striving for happiness is a long, hard journey with many challenges.
It requires eternal vigilance to win the victory. You
cannot succeed with sporadic little flashes of effort.
. . . Faith is not a magical formula. It requires that you
make a deliberate decision to do good and then carry
out your decision. Do it. Simply do it, and do it long
enough that you experience success, no matter how
hard it may seem. Your victory over self brings communion with God and results in happiness—lasting
and eternal happiness" (*Ensign,* May 1986, 52–54).

*Let us get on our knees and plead with the Lord
for direction. Then let us stand on our feet, square up our
shoulders, and march forward without fear to enlarge
among people everywhere the righteousness of the Lord.*

GORDON B. HINCKLEY
ENSIGN, MAY 1999, 88

As the year winds down, let us resolve to go forward with faith. President Gordon B. Hinckley said, "Let us return to our homes with resolution in our hearts to do a little better than we have done in the past. We can all be a little kinder, a little more generous, a little more thoughtful of one another. We can be a little more tolerant and friendly to those not of our faith, going out of our way to show our respect for them. We cannot afford to be arrogant or self-righteous. It is our obligation to reach out in helpfulness, not only to our own but to all others as well. Their interest in and respect for this Church will increase as we do so" (*Ensign,* May 1999, 88). We each have a covenant responsibility to be a light instead of a judge, to be an example not a critic, to build and bless everyone with whom we come in contact.

*Many of life's important lessons are not easily learned.
Nevertheless, when properly learned, these lessons
can become stepping-stones toward happiness in this
life and eternal glory in the world to come*

CHRISTOFFEL GOLDEN JR.
NEW ERA, FEBRUARY 2005, 42

Remember the Lord's promise: "I, the Lord, am
bound when ye do what I say" (D&C 82:10). "Isn't it
interesting that the Lord wants us to bind Him in ful-
filling His promises?" said Elder Christoffel Golden
Jr. "We put ourselves in that position simply by doing
what He asks and trusting that He will do what He
has said He will. Perhaps that is one of the most important lessons we can learn in life. . . . God watches
over each of us in a very personal way. It is natural
that He does, because we are His sons and daughters.
We are precious to our Heavenly Father, and often,
prompted by His infinite love, He allows us to have
difficult experiences that help us become more like
Him" (*New Era,* Feb. 2005, 45). Throughout life, we
learn that opposition is needed for us to grow in experience and gratitude, that adversity can make us
stronger and wiser, that beautiful things happen even
on ugly days.

True doctrine, understood, changes attitudes and behavior.
The study of the doctrines of the gospel will improve behavior
quicker than a study of behavior will improve behavior.

BOYD K. PACKER
ENSIGN, NOVEMBER 1986, 17

We must know and understand true doctrine in order to hold back the world and change our attitudes and behaviors. For example, true doctrines of faith, repentance, and forgiveness can help us to find deep peace and feel authentic joy. Elder Boyd K. Packer said, "Secular doctrines have the advantage of convincing, tangible evidence. We seem to do better in gathering data on things that can be counted and measured. Doctrines which originate in the light, on the other hand, are more often supported by intangible impressions upon the spirit. We are left for the most part to rely on *faith.* But, in time, the consequences of following either will become visible enough" (*Ensign,* Nov. 1986, 18). True doctrines are stable and sure, steady and reliable—we can count on them to stand unchanged and bring us peace and joy. Those who learn and apply true doctrines of the gospel will walk in the light of the Lord.

LATTER-DAY SAINT LEADERS QUOTED IN THIS BOOK

Silvia H. Allred—Born October 11, 1944, in San Salvador, El Salvador. She was sustained as first counselor in the Relief Society general presidency on March 31, 2007.

Neil L. Andersen—Born August 9, 1951, in Logan, Utah. He was ordained an apostle in 2009.

Marvin J. Ashton—Born May 16, 1915, in Salt Lake City, Utah. He was ordained an apostle in 1971. He died on February 25, 1994, in Salt Lake City, Utah.

M. Russell Ballard—Born October 8, 1928, in Salt Lake City, Utah. He was ordained an apostle in 1985.

Julie B. Beck—Born September 29, 1954, in Salt Lake City, Utah. She was sustained as Relief Society general president on March 31, 2007.

David A. Bednar—Born June 15, 1952, in Oakland, California. He was ordained an apostle in 2004.

Ezra Taft Benson—Born August 4, 1899, in Whitney, Idaho. He was ordained an apostle in 1943 and became the thirteenth president of the Church on November 10, 1985. He died on May 30, 1994, in Salt Lake City, Utah.

LATTER-DAY SAINT LEADERS QUOTED IN THIS BOOK

Elaine A. Cannon—Born April 9, 1922 in Salt Lake City, Utah. She served as Young Women general president from 1978 to 1984. She died on May 19, 2003, in Salt Lake City, Utah.

George Q. Cannon—Born January 11, 1827, in Liverpool, England. He was ordained an apostle in 1860 and was called to serve in the First Presidency in 1873, serving as a counselor to four presidents of the Church. He died on April 12, 1901, in Monterey, California.

D. Todd Christofferson—Born January 24, 1945, in American Fork, Utah. He was ordained an apostle in 2008.

J. Reuben Clark Jr.—Born September 1, 1871, in Grantsville, Utah. He was called to serve in the First Presidency in 1933 and was ordained an apostle in 1934. He served as a counselor to three presidents of the Church. He died on October 6, 1961, in Salt Lake City, Utah.

Mary N. Cook—Born June 8, 1951, in Salt Lake City, Utah. She was sustained as first counselor in the Young Women general presidency on April 5, 2008.

Quentin L. Cook—Born September 8, 1940, in Logan, Utah. He was ordained an apostle in 2007.

Elaine S. Dalton—Born November 1, 1946, in Ogden, Utah. She was sustained as Young Women general president on April 5, 2008.

Sheri L. Dew—Born November 21, 1953, in Ulysses, Kansas. She served as second counselor in the Relief Society general presidency from 1997 to 2002.

LATTER-DAY SAINT LEADERS QUOTED IN THIS BOOK

Ann M. Dibb—Born June 30, 1954, in Salt Lake City, Utah. She was sustained as second counselor in the Young Women general presidency on April 5, 2008.

Joanne B. Doxey—Born 1932. She served as second counselor in the Relief Society general presidency from 1984 to 1990.

Richard L. Evans—Born March 23, 1906, in Salt Lake City, Utah. He was ordained an apostle in 1953. He died on November 1, 1971, in Salt Lake City, Utah.

Henry B. Eyring—Born May 31, 1933, in Princeton, New Jersey. He was ordained an apostle in 1995 and set apart as second counselor to President Gordon B. Hinckley on October 11, 2007. He was set apart as first counselor to President Thomas S. Monson on February 3, 2008.

James E. Faust—Born July 31, 1920, in Delta, Utah. He was ordained an apostle in 1978 and was set apart as second counselor to President Gordon B. Hinckley on March 12, 1995. He died on August 10, 2007, in Salt Lake City, Utah.

Heber J. Grant—Born November 22, 1856, in Salt Lake City, Utah. He was ordained an apostle in 1882 and became the seventh president of the Church on November 23, 1918. He died on May 14, 1945, in Salt Lake City, Utah.

David B. Haight—Born September 2, 1906, in Oakley, Idaho. He was ordained an apostle in 1976. He died on July 31, 2004, in Salt Lake City, Utah.

Janette C. Hales—Born June 7, 1933 in Springville, Utah. She served as the Young Women general president from 1992 to 1997.

LATTER-DAY SAINT LEADERS QUOTED IN THIS BOOK

Robert D. Hales—Born August 24, 1932, in New York City. He was ordained an apostle in 1994.

Gordon B. Hinckley—Born June 23, 1910, in Salt Lake City, Utah. He was ordained an apostle in 1961 and served as a counselor to three Church presidents. He became the fifteenth president of the Church on March 12, 1995. He died on January 27, 2008, in Salt Lake City, Utah.

Jeffrey R. Holland—Born December 3, 1940, in St. George, Utah. He was ordained an apostle in 1994.

Howard W. Hunter—Born November 14, 1907, in Boise, Idaho. He was ordained an apostle in 1959 and became the fourteenth president of the Church on June 5, 1994. He died on March 3, 1995, in Salt Lake City, Utah.

Elaine L. Jack—Born March 22, 1928, in Cardston, Alberta, Canada. She served as Relief Society general president from 1990 to 1997.

Virginia U. Jensen—Born in 1940 in Salt Lake City, Utah. She served as first counselor in the Relief Society general presidency from 1997 to 2002.

Ardeth G. Kapp—Born March 19, 1931, in Glenwood, Alberta, Canada. She served as the Young Women general president from 1984 to 1992.

Spencer W. Kimball—Born March 28, 1895, in Salt Lake City, Utah. He was ordained an apostle in 1943 and became the twelfth president of the Church on December 30, 1973. He died on November 5, 1985, in Salt Lake City, Utah.

LATTER-DAY SAINT LEADERS QUOTED IN THIS BOOK

Sharon G. Larsen—Born February 6, 1939, in Glenwood, Alberta, Canada. She served as second counselor in the Young Women general presidency from 1997 to 2002.

Harold B. Lee—Born March 28, 1899, in Clifton, Idaho. He was ordained an apostle in 1941 and became the eleventh president of the Church on July 7, 1972. He died on December 26, 1973.

Margaret S. Lifferth—Born March 30, 1947, in Washington, D.C. She served as first counselor in the Primary general presidency from 2005 to 2010.

Neal A. Maxwell—Born July 6, 1926, in Salt Lake City, Utah. He was ordained an apostle in 1981. He died on July 21, 2004, in Salt Lake City, Utah.

Bruce R. McConkie—Born July 29, 1915, in Ann Arbor, Michigan. He was ordained an apostle in 1981. He died on July 21, 2004, in Salt Lake City, Utah.

David O. McKay—Born September 8, 1873, in Huntsville, Utah. He was ordained an apostle in 1906 and became the ninth president of the Church on April 9, 1951. He died on January 18, 1970, in Salt Lake City, Utah.

Coleen K. Menlove—Born July 1, 1943, in Salt Lake City, Utah. She served as Primary general president from 1999 to 2005.

Thomas S. Monson—Born August 21, 1927, in Salt Lake City, Utah. He was ordained an apostle in 1963, was called to serve in the First Presidency in 1985, and served as a counselor to three presidents of the Church. He was set apart as the sixteenth president of the Church on February 3, 2008.

LATTER-DAY SAINT LEADERS QUOTED IN THIS BOOK

Margaret D. Nadauld—Born November 21, 1944, in Manti, Utah. She served as the Young Women general president from 1997 to 2002.

Russell M. Nelson—Born September 9, 1924, in Salt Lake City, Utah. He was ordained an apostle in 1984.

Dallin H. Oaks—Born August 12, 1932, in Provo, Utah. He was ordained an apostle in 1984.

Chieko N. Okazaki—Born October 21, 1926, in Kohala, Hawaii. She served as first counselor in the Relief Society general presidency from 1990 to 1997.

Boyd K. Packer—Born September 10, 1924, in Brigham City, Utah. He was ordained an apostle in 1970 and was set apart as the acting president of the Quorum of the Twelve Apostles on June 5, 1994, and again on March 12, 1995. He was set apart as president of the Quorum of the Twelve on February 3, 2008.

Bonnie D. Parkin—Born August 4, 1940, in Herriman, Utah. She served as Relief Society general president from 2002 to 2007.

L. Tom Perry—Born August 5, 1922, in Logan, Utah. He was ordained an apostle in 1974.

Virginia H. Pearce—Born February 8, 1945, in Salt Lake City, Utah. She served as first counselor in the Young Women general presidency from 1992 to 1997.

Mark E. Petersen—Born November 7, 1900, in Salt Lake City, Utah. He was ordained an apostle in 1944. He died on January 11, 1984, in Salt Lake City, Utah.

LATTER-DAY SAINT LEADERS QUOTED IN THIS BOOK

Patricia P. Pinegar—Born February 3, 1937, in Cedar City, Utah. She served as Primary general president from 1994 to 1999.

LeGrand Richards—Born February 6, 1886, in Farmington, Utah. He was ordained an apostle in 1952. He died on January 11, 1983, in Salt Lake City, Utah.

Marion G. Romney—Born September 19, 1897, in Colonia Juarez, Mexico. He was ordained an apostle in 1951 and was called to serve in the First Presidency in 1972, serving first with President Harold B. Lee and then with President Spencer W. Kimball. He died on May 20, 1988, in Salt Lake City, Utah.

Richard G. Scott—Born November 7, 1928, in Pocatello, Idaho. He was ordained an apostle in 1988.

Barbara B. Smith—Born January 26, 1922, in Salt Lake City, Utah. She served as Relief Society general president from 1974 to 1984.

George Albert Smith—Born April 4, 1870, in Salt Lake City, Utah. He was ordained an apostle in 1903 and became the eighth president of the Church on May 21, 1945. He died on April 4, 1951, in Salt Lake City, Utah.

Joseph Smith—Born December 23, 1805, in Sharon, Vermont. He became the first president of the Church when it was organized in 1830. He was martyred on June 27, 1844, in Carthage, Illinois.

Joseph F. Smith—Born November 13, 1838, in Far West, Missouri. He was ordained an apostle in 1866 and became the sixth president of the Church on October 17, 1901. He died November 19, 1918, in Salt Lake City, Utah.

Joseph Fielding Smith—Born July 19, 1876, in Salt Lake City, Utah. He was ordained an apostle in 1910 and became the tenth president of the Church on January 23, 1970. He died on July 2, 1972, in Salt Lake City, Utah.

Mary Ellen Smoot—Born August 19, 1933, in Ogden, Utah. She served as Relief Society general president from 1997 to 2002.

Lorenzo Snow—Born April 3, 1814, in Mantua, Ohio. He was ordained an apostle in 1849 and became the fifth president of the Church on September 13, 1898. He died on October 10, 1901, in Salt Lake City, Utah.

Delbert L. Stapley—Born December 11, 1896, in Mesa, Arizona. He was ordained an apostle in 1950. He died on August 19, 1978, in Salt Lake City, Utah.

James E. Talmage—Born September 21, 1862, in Hungerford, England. He was ordained an apostle in 1911. He died on July 27, 1933, in Salt Lake City, Utah.

N. Eldon Tanner—Born May 9, 1898, in Salt Lake City, Utah. He was ordained an apostle in 1962 and was called to serve in the First Presidency in 1963. He served as a counselor to four presidents of the Church. He died on November 27, 1982.

Susan W. Tanner—Born January 10, 1953, in Granger, Utah. She served as the Young Women general president from 2002 to 2008.

LATTER-DAY SAINT LEADERS QUOTED IN THIS BOOK

John Taylor—Born November 1, 1808, in Milnthorpe, England. He was ordained an apostle in 1838 and was sustained as president of the Quorum of the Twelve Apostles in 1877. He became the third president of the Church on October 10, 1880. He died on July 25, 1887, in Kaysville, Utah.

Carol B. Thomas—Born May 6, 1942, in Salt Lake City. She served as second counselor in the Young Women general presidency in 1997 and as first counselor from 1997 to 2002.

Barbara Thompson—Born June 13, 1952, in San Luis Obispo, California. She was sustained as second counselor in the Relief Society general presidency on March 31, 2007.

Dieter F. Uchtdorf—Born November 6, 1940, in Osrava, Czechoslovakia. He was ordained an apostle in 2004 and set apart as second counselor to President Thomas S. Monson on February 3, 2008.

Orson F. Whitney—Born July 1, 1855, in Salt Lake City, Utah. He was ordained an apostle in 1906. He died on May 16, 1931, in Salt Lake City, Utah.

Joseph B. Wirthlin—Born June 11, 1917, in Salt Lake City, Utah. He was ordained an apostle in 1986. He died on December 1, 2008.

Wilford Woodruff—Born March 1, 1807, in Avon, Connecticut. He was ordained an apostle in 1839 and became the fourth president of the Church on April 7, 1889. He died on September 2, 1898, in San Francisco, California.

LATTER-DAY SAINT LEADERS QUOTED IN THIS BOOK

Ruth B. Wright—She served as second counselor in the Primary general presidency from 1988 to 1994.

Brigham Young—Born June 1, 1801, in Whitingham, Vermont. He was ordained an apostle in 1835 and become the second president of the Church on December 27, 1847. He died on August 29, 1877, in Salt Lake City, Utah.

Sources

Ballard, M. Russell. *Our Search for Happiness: An Invitation to Understand The Church of Jesus Christ of Latter-day Saints.* Salt Lake City: Deseret Book, 1995.

Brickey, Wayne E. *101 Powerful Promises from Latter-day Prophets.* Salt Lake City: Deseret Book, 2004.

Burton, H. David. "These Are the Times." Address presented at Brigham Young University, Provo, Utah, December 1, 2009. Available online at http://www.ldschurchnews.com/articles/58278/Bishop-H-David-Burton-These-are-the-times.html.

Cannon, George Q. *Gospel Truth: Discourses and Writings of George Q. Cannon.* Selected, arranged, and edited by Jerreld L. Newquist. Salt Lake City: Deseret Book, 1974.

Clark, J. Reuben, Jr., Conference Report, 3 October 1953, 83–84.

Dollahite, David C., ed. *Helping and Healing Our Families: Principles and Practices Inspired by The Family: A Proclamation to the World.* Salt Lake City: Deseret Book, 2005.

———. *Strengthening Our Families: An In-Depth Look at the Proclamation on the Family.* Salt Lake City: Deseret Book, 2008.

Encyclopedia of Latter-day Saint History. Edited by Arnold K.

Garr, Donald Q. Cannon, and Richard O. Cowan. Salt Lake City: Deseret Book, 2000.

Ensign. Salt Lake City: The Church of Jesus Christ of Latter-day Saints, 1971–2010.

Eyring, Henry B. "Child of Promise." In *Brigham Young University 1985–86 Devotional and Fireside Speeches.* Provo, Utah: Brigham Young University, 1986, 122–29.

———. "Always." In *Brigham Young University 1998–99 Speeches.* Provo, Utah: Brigham Young University, 1999, 91–98.

"Family, The: A Proclamation to the World." *Ensign,* November 1995, 102–7.

Grant, Heber J. *Heber J. Grant* [manual]. A volume of *Teachings of Presidents of the Church* series. Salt Lake City: The Church of Jesus Christ of Latter-day Saints, 2002.

Hafen, Bruce C. *The Broken Heart: Applying the Atonement to Life's Experiences.* Salt Lake City: Deseret Book, 1989.

Hinckley, Gordon B. "Messages of inspiration from President Hinckley." *Church News,* 3 Aug. 1996, 2.

———. *Stand a Little Taller.* Salt Lake City: Deseret Book, 1994.

———. *Teachings of Gordon B. Hinckley.* Salt Lake City: Deseret Book, 1997.

Hunter, Howard W. *The Teachings of Howard W. Hunter.* Edited by Clyde J. Williams. Salt Lake City: Deseret Book, 1997.

———. *That We Might Have Joy.* Salt Lake City: Deseret Book, 1994.

Hymns of The Church of Jesus Christ of Latter-day Saints. Salt Lake

City: The Church of Jesus Christ of Latter-day Saints, 1985.

Kimball, Spencer W. *Spencer W. Kimball* [manual]. A volume of *Teachings of Presidents of the Church* series. Salt Lake City: The Church of Jesus Christ of Latter-day Saints, 2006.

——. *The Teachings of Spencer W. Kimball.* Edited by Edward L. Kimball. Salt Lake City: Bookcraft, 1982.

Lee, Harold B. *Harold B. Lee* [manual]. A volume of *Teachings of Presidents of the Church* series. Salt Lake City: The Church of Jesus Christ of Latter-day Saints, 2000.

——. *The Teachings of Harold B. Lee.* Edited by Clyde J. Williams. Salt Lake City: Bookcraft, 1996.

"Living Christ, The: The Testimony of the Apostles." *Ensign,* April 2000, 2–3.

McConkie, Bruce R. *Mormon Doctrine.* 2d ed. Salt Lake City: Bookcraft, 1966.

McConkie, Joseph Fielding, and Robert L. Millet. *Doctrinal Commentary on the Book of Mormon,* vols. 1 and 2. Salt Lake City: Bookcraft, 1987 and 1988.

McKay, David O. Conference Report, Apr. 1964, 3–7.

——. *David O. McKay* [manual]. A volume of *Teachings of Presidents of the Church* series. Salt Lake City: The Church of Jesus Christ of Latter-day Saints, 2003.

——. *Gospel Ideals: Selections from the Discourses of David O. McKay.* Salt Lake City: The Improvement Era, 1953.

Millet, Robert L. *After All We Can Do . . . Grace Works.* Salt Lake City: Deseret Book, 2003.

Nelson, Russell M. "The Family: The Hope for the Future of Nations." Address at the World Congress of Families V in Amsterdam, Netherlands, August 12,

2009, reported in the *Church News*. Available online at http://www.ldschurchnews.com/articles/57741/children-matter-to-families-and-nations-alike.html.

New Era. Salt Lake City: The Church of Jesus Christ of Latter-day Saints, 1971–2010.

Preach My Gospel: A Guide to Missionary Service. Salt Lake City: The Church of Jesus Christ of Latter-day Saints, 2004.

Robinson, Stephen E., and H. Dean Garrett. *A Commentary on the Doctrine and Covenants,* vols. 1 and 2. Salt Lake City: Deseret Book, 2000-2001.

Shakespeare, William. *As You Like It,* in *The Complete Works, Second Edition.* Edited by Stanley Wells and Gary Taylor. Oxford: Clarendon Press, 2005.

Smith, George Albert. Conference Report, Oct. 1949, 4–9; Apr. 1950, 167–70.

Smith, Joseph. *Joseph Smith* [manual]. A volume of *Teachings of Presidents of the Church* series. Salt Lake City: The Church of Jesus Christ of Latter-day Saints, 2007.

——. *History of The Church of Jesus Christ of Latter-day Saints.* 7 vols. Edited by B.H. Roberts. Salt Lake City: The Church of Jesus Christ of Latter-day Saints, 1932–51.

——. *Teachings of the Prophet Joseph Smith.* Selected by Joseph Fielding Smith. Salt Lake City: Deseret Book, 1976.

Smith, Joseph Fielding. *Church History and Modern Revelation.* 2 vols. Salt Lake City: Deseret Book, 1953.

——. *Doctrines of Salvation.* 3 vols. Compiled by Bruce R. McConkie. Salt Lake City: Bookcraft, 1954.

Smith, Joseph F. Conference Report, Oct. 1912, 131–34.

——. *Joseph F. Smith* [manual]. A volume of *Teachings of*

SOURCES

Presidents of the Church series. Salt Lake City: The
Church of Jesus Christ of Latter-day Saints, 1998.

Snow, Lorenzo. Conference Report, Apr. 1899, 1–3.

———. *The Teachings of Lorenzo Snow.* Edited by Clyde J.
Williams. Salt Lake City: Bookcraft, 1996.

Talmage, James E. *Jesus the Christ.* Salt Lake City: Deseret
Book, 1915.

———. *The Articles of Faith.* Salt Lake City: The Church of
Jesus Christ of Latter-day Saints, 1984.

Taylor, John. *John Taylor* [manual]. A volume of *Teachings
of Presidents of the Church* series. Salt Lake City: The
Church of Jesus Christ of Latter-day Saints, 2001.

Uchtdorf, Dieter F. "Can We See the Christ in Christmas?"
First Presidency Christmas Devotional, December 6,
2009. Available online at http://www.lds.org/library/
display/0,4945,8921-1-5016-1,00.html.

Whitney, Orson F. Conference Report, April 1929, 109–
115.

Woodruff, Wilford. *Wilford Woodruff* [manual]. A volume
of *Teachings of Presidents of the Church* series. Salt Lake
City: The Church of Jesus Christ of Latter-day Saints,
2004.

Young, Brigham. *Brigham Young* [manual]. A volume of
Teachings of Presidents of the Church series. Salt Lake City:
The Church of Jesus Christ of Latter-day Saints,
1997.

ABOUT THE AUTHOR

Lloyd D. Newell holds a Ph.D. from Brigham Young University, where he serves on the faculties of Religious Education and the School of Family Life. He has addressed audiences in forty-five states and more than a dozen countries through his seminars and engagements as a keynote speaker and has worked as a television news anchor and news magazine host. He has served as announcer and writer for the Mormon Tabernacle Choir broadcast "Music and the Spoken Word" since 1990. The author of several books, he coauthored, with Robert L. Millet, four previous daily devotional books: *Jesus, the Very Thought of Thee, When Ye Shall Receive These Things, Draw Near unto Me,* and *A Lamp unto My Feet.* Lloyd is the author of the most recent books in that series: *Come, Listen to a Prophet's Voice* and *Let Him Ask of God.* He and his wife, Karmel, are the parents of four children.